GAME

GAME

An Autobiography

GRANT HILL

PENGUIN PRESS

NEW YORK

2022

PENGUIN PRESS
An imprint of Penguin Random House LLC
penguinrandomhouse.com

Pages 373–74 constitute an extension of this copyright page.

LIBRARY OF CONGRESS CATALOGING-IN-PUBLICATION DATA
Names: Hill, Grant, 1972– author.
Title: Game : a memoir / Grant Hill.
Description: New York : Penguin Press, [2022] | Includes index. |
Identifiers: LCCN 2021061033 (print) | LCCN 2021061034 (ebook) |
ISBN 9780593297407 (hardcover) | ISBN 9780593297414 (epub)
Subjects: LCSH: Hill, Grant, 1972– | Basketball players—United States—Biography. |
African American basketball players—United States—Biography. |
Basketball team owners—United States—Biography. |
Atlanta Hawks (Basketball team) | Hill, Grant, 1972—Art collections.
Classification: LCC GV884.H45 A3 2022 (print) | LCC GV884.H45 (ebook) |
DDC 796.323092 [B]—dc23/eng/20220126
LC record available at https://lccn.loc.gov/2021061033
LC ebook record available at https://lccn.loc.gov/2021061034

Printed in the United States of America
1st Printing

Book design by Daniel Lagin

For Mom, forever my hero.

CONTENTS

GAME

I

WE were there for basketball and basketball only. Howard Garfinkel's
Five-Star Basketball Camp was a hoops mecca throughout my teenage
years, a rite of passage for the nation's top prep basketball players to measure ourselves against one another and be seen by college recruiters. The
camps stretched for weeks each summer through different sessions at
Honesdale, the more coveted camp hosted in the Poconos, and Robert
Morris University, near Pittsburgh. In middle school, I had flipped
through a *Sports Illustrated* and first learned about Five-Star, this mystical
camp run by a character named Garf. I attended the first time the summer after my freshman year of high school. Michael Jordan, Patrick
Ewing, and Chris Mullin attended the camp before me. Kevin Durant,
LeBron James, and Chris Paul made the trip after me. Coaches also made
names for themselves as camp instructors. Bob Knight, Jim Valvano, and
Rick Pitino passed through as counselors. John Calipari, then a fresh-
faced assistant at Pitt, was among my coaches at that first camp.

I was headed into my senior year of high school in the summer of
1989 and had become accustomed to the camp's rhythms when I arrived
again in Honesdale. I had attended one of the camps earlier that summer

and impressed enough to earn the MVP of the camp and All-Star Game. Garf was a warden, counselor, and coach all rolled into one, a New Yorker who started the camp far outside the city lights in 1966. He woke us by blasting Frank Sinatra each morning and spent his days motoring from station to station in a golf cart. A cigarette stayed glued to his lips as he talked in bits and spurts.

Everything about the camp was old-school, steeped in tradition. Garf insisted he was running a camp and not a meat market. He bypassed luxuries. We ate breakfast before the drills and rotated every twenty minutes while learning the fine points of various fundamentals. Most of the courts were outside where gnats and flies filled the thick air. A comforting cacophony constantly echoed from the courts lined by birch trees: thudding basketballs, squeaking shoes, shrieking whistles. Lunch usually featured a talk from a big-name coach. We sat in a ring around the court and listened, offering a standing ovation when it ended at Garf's instruction. In order for the afternoon sessions to begin, Garf had to hit his daily shot. We cheered him on, hoping that his attempt found the basket quickly so that we could get on with more instruction and games.

Garf personally identified the best players throughout the country and invited them to attend the camps on scholarships. In return, we served meals and bused tables for the other campers. I viewed the duties as a mark of distinction, proud to earn whatever I received. My parents, Calvin and Janet, had inspired me to work hard and dream big.

You can't teach hungry, my dad always reminded me. Either you are or you aren't.

Players attended to make a name for themselves or enhance their reputation. New York kids populated every camp, and this year's was no different. Those guys swore they invented the sport, but the truth was most of them could ball. I had met Brian Reese at the camp the previous summer and was eager to catch up with him that year. He played forward for a nationally ranked high school in New York and was teammates with a couple other campers, Malik Sealy and Adrian Autry. Brian hailed from the South Bronx, home to one of my favorite rappers, KRS-One.

We were loitering on the outdoor courts, waiting for games to start, when a few campers started a conversation about Lloyd Daniels. Daniels was a New York legend a few years older than us who had bounced around a bit, more of a myth to me than a real player. But some of the New York guys had seen him play and painted him as a much taller version of Kenny Anderson. I was busy imagining a player of that much size oozing that much versatility when Adrian punctured my daydream.

Hey, man, why are you here?

The question caught me off guard.

What do you mean?

You're rich. You live in a mansion. You got money, right? We need this to eat.

Adrian and I were friends, both then and later. He advanced to play at Syracuse and overseas before becoming one of Jim Boeheim's assistants at Syracuse. He hadn't, I don't believe, asked me out of malice, and I doubt he'd even recall this exchange today. But I figured he had somehow learned my backstory, that my dad had attended Yale and played in the NFL, that my mom was a successful businesswoman.

Adrian's question was one of the first times an internal conflict had been projected outward. I grew up aware of my parents' accomplishments. Sometimes, they intimidated. Often, they inspired. We might not have lived as grandly as Adrian or others envisioned, but we were comfortable.

At the same time, I spent most of my childhood wanting to blend into the background. Every article written described me as the son of an ex–NFL player. I'm not necessarily proud of this now, but I used to hate that characterization. I wanted to prove I could stand on my own. Me busing tables showed that I was earning my way at camp. Now it seemed like Adrian was trying to take it away.

Was he implying that I was there only because of my parents? That I needed to travel a specific journey and come from a certain background to be ambitious? Or that I simply was not a good enough player to share the court with him?

I was on the edge of leaving adolescence for adulthood. By that point, basketball had already come to mean much more to me than just a sport. I had spent years advancing to different baskets in my hometown of Reston, Virginia, like they were grades in school at various recreation centers, park playgrounds, and gyms. The local legends clocked in at Twin Branches Court. The court was a blacktop where one rim hung lower than the other, the result of the iron bearing a few too many gravity-defying dunks. The park was a siren call for ballers from all over the Washington metropolitan area, guys a couple years out of school with magic still in their game and ones who went on to make a name for themselves through basketball, like Dennis Scott, who starred for the Orlando Magic, and Billy King, who went on to play at Duke.

That court didn't offer much room to maneuver. With one step over half-court, you'd be at the top of the key. Another and you'd be in the lane. The intimacy forced physicality. It was a man's court. Someone couldn't just walk on and play. You earned your spot. A couple dozen people usually stood near the park's tiny bench. Fights erupted over claims for next. Winners stayed. Lose and you waited another hour or two before setting foot on the blacktop again.

My childhood best friend, Michael Ellison, and I first rode our bikes to watch games at the park at around the age of ten, apprentices watching masters ply their craft. We'd hope for a pause in action when we could lob up a shot before being shouted away. I played for the first time on the court at around the age of twelve, fresh off a recent growth spurt. Honestly, I was probably more nervous to play for the first time at Twin Branches than when I debuted at Cameron Indoor Stadium. As I walked on the court, an old head told me not to mess up, to just rebound and pass.

My opponents were older, stronger. They didn't take it easy on me. They wanted to stay on the court and get their cardio in. I grabbed a rebound. A shove dislodged the ball from my grip. I assumed some knew me as Cal's little son. Maybe they played me more physical for that reason. Maybe not. I just wanted to get the job done. I didn't say much out there. I put my head down, defended, screened, and contributed in any way possible. I fought to not give an inch. A shot went up, the ball careened off the rim, and I grabbed the rebound and laid the ball home.

A purity has always existed in basketball: the game is rooted in democracy. You could be on a team full of strangers with no scoreboard, no coach roaming the sidelines calling plays. Instinct pulls your body in different directions before your brain catches up. The flow of the game dictates when you cut, pass, or shoot. The game exposes you, laying your strengths and weaknesses bare.

Either you can play or you can't. If you can't, you were not going to be picked again. Play the game right and you are rewarded. The ball possesses its own kinetic energy and usually finds whom it's supposed to in the right position at the right moment.

That first time out at Twin Branches, my team traded baskets with the other all the way to game point for each side. I elbowed myself into position. A shot kicked off the rim, into my arms. I looked for an outlet, delivering the ball to a teammate who streaked down the court for the game winner. My team ran the table the rest of the day, playing until our weary legs could no longer run up and down the court and the sun began descending in the sky. I didn't have to wait long the next time I arrived at the park. I was asked to join the team that had next.

The court helped quiet my nerves and jitters during my awkward adolescent years. Basketball had afforded me a purpose and identity.

In the moment, I didn't know how to verbalize all that to Adrian. It was one of those interactions that lingered. Doubting my sincerity about the game was like questioning my existence.

My frustration stayed caged.

I just want to play, I told him, silently vowing to show him why I was there the next time on the court.

I usually tried projecting coolness and fluidity through my play. I dropped the pretenses that next time out against Adrian. I played unte-thered. I drove past everyone and leaped for rebounds against guys whom, a couple years earlier, I had arrived home from camp marveling about to my dad, doubting I could ever rise to their level.

I readied myself for the camp's All-Star Game, the showcase for the soon-to-be college stars and eventual pros. We played the game outdoors on a night cool enough that we wore sweatshirts underneath our jerseys. I hunted down rebounds. I blocked shots. I sliced to the rim for dunks and drew applause and admiration from the coaches, spectators, and other campers. Adrian tried picking me up once on transition defense and be-came another victim.

Camp ended with a ceremony. Garf announced me as the first player to repeat winning the MVP at Five-Star's camp and the All-Star Game twice in the same summer.

That is why I'm here, Adrian, I thought to myself.

For basketball and basketball only. The sport had found me, and I held on to it with a tight grip.

I planned on never letting go.

2

THE bottom floor of our split-level house served as a toy room most of my childhood. As I grew into a narrow-shouldered and slender-legged adolescent, my dad decided to finish the space, adding a Ping-Pong table, a bar, a projection-screen television, and a Betamax—clearly, he bet wrong on that being the technology of the future. But at the time, I was one of the only kids around who could record anything from television. My friend Michael Ellison and I sat on the couch, watching Michael Jackson, the King of Pop, perform his electrifying moonwalk for the *Motown 25* special. We had seen it repeatedly. I had the move down flat, the only sixth grader around who could backslide.

Satisfied, Michael left before my mom returned from work. His presence violated her no guest policy when she wasn't home. I knew she would probably find out I had company without me ever speaking a word. Most people possess five senses. She had six. She worked for the secretary of the army in the Pentagon. At first my friends called her the Sergeant. The ranking isn't high enough, she said. They called her the General and it stuck. My mom was the type of disciplinarian who punished my friends if they misbehaved in front of her. She called their parents herself if they threatened to complain to them first. She never babysat as a child. Then, she was more likely to admire someone else's baby from afar than hold them. She grew up in a segregated pocket of New Orleans. Her parents, Malcolm and Vivian McDonald, crafted dentures from a dental laboratory in the family's basement. In a time when many southern politicians called for separate but equal, her parents taught her that she could be superior. For fun, she and her childhood friends would switch the signs of white-and colored-only water fountains, laughing when a white person drank from a faucet deemed fit only for Blacks. She spent her youth in a thriving Black community. Her first meaningful conversation with a white person did not occur until she departed for Wellesley College. In a foreign world, she didn't bend her self-worth for the sake of conformity. She made the world bend for her. She'd spend her lifetime often as the only woman of color—frequently, the only woman, period—in corporate conference rooms and board meetings. She would often hold the door open behind her, making inroads for others who looked like her to eventually follow.

She based her parenting on intuitiveness while carving that corporate career. She needed to trust me to be alone at times out of necessity when she went to work.

My family had settled in Reston a few years earlier when my dad joined the Washington Football Team. I have only brief flashes remaining of our prior stops. I was born in Dallas just a few months after my dad helped the Cowboys win their first Super Bowl, a drubbing of the Miami Dolphins. He joined the Hawaiians of the World Football League for a short stint afterward, and we relocated to Honolulu.

My dad had recently retired from the NFL but had not left the game behind just yet. Now he worked for the Cleveland Browns, heading a group that helped players combat substance abuse. He also hopscotched from city to city for a variety of speaking arrangements. We were in Reston for the long haul. The town represented a paragon of suburbia, a planned community about twenty-five miles outside Washington, D.C., but the city felt more isolated than that from any big hub. Robert E. Simon, a real estate entrepreneur, concocted Reston with all its man-made lakes, community pools, and forested paths.

Most residents were white, although pockets of diversity existed here and there. A lot of my dad's old teammates lived close by. Joe Theismann waited in the grocery store line like everybody else. Reston accommodated every socioeconomic demographic, from upper-middle-class families to those in subsidized housing. During the crack epidemic, Reston's Stonegate Village Apartments hosted the largest open-air drug-trafficking market outside the District of Columbia. Some of my talented middle school teammates didn't make it to high school after being swept up in the busts.

Simon surely had families like mine in mind when he dreamed up Reston. He envisioned everyone living and working in the community. *That it be possible for anyone to remain in a single neighborhood throughout his life,* he wrote in 1962, *uprooting being neither inevitable nor always desirable.* My parents also rooted in Reston because of the proximity of the schools. About ten elementary schools dotted the community before everyone funneled into the same middle school. I could walk from home to my grade school. A little down the street, the same road hosted my junior high, and without crossing the road, I could also run into my high school.

I was conscious of race as far back as my mind can trace. I was usually one of only two or three Black kids in my elementary school. I played on soccer teams where I was the only Black kid. Safety lies in numbers when you're young. There was comfort in being able to fade into a background whenever convenient.

Some regarded my dad playing in the NFL as a special distinction. He was a person of the people, eternally accommodating when fans approached him while we were out. As a kid, I viewed the interruptions as an intrusion on our time together, especially when he had to devote so much attention to the game during my early childhood. My dad played long before the days of million-dollar contracts. We were not rich. We were not poor either. He drove a Porsche. I hated the car and the attention it drew, wishing that he pulled up in a Ford Escort instead when he was able to pick me up from school.

I found a more diverse crowd at Langston Hughes Intermediate School, but also a disconnect. I wasn't at home with any group. I related in some conversations. I was lost in most. I got into a couple of fights that I didn't dare tell my mom about.

I held my own in one-on-one conversations. I shrank in larger settings. Just the thought of being called upon in class caused an inner panic even when I knew the correct answer. My mind raced in front of my mouth. I stumbled and tripped over words.

One day, my dad asked me if I was gay. There wasn't any homophobia in his question. He was sincerely curious, trying to understand his son, unable to project who or where I would be in the next decade. I never talked about girls, and none called the house asking for me.

No, I replied. I'm not.

I didn't know who I'd be either. If life was a party, I was the kid standing with my back against the wall watching everyone else have fun.

Michael was my key to getting into the social circles I didn't belong in. His mom worked on Capitol Hill for Senator Bill Bradley and often commuted with my mom into the district. He was a year older than me. Separately, our personalities couldn't have been more different. Somehow, together, they meshed. He was the class president, charismatic and smart.

His cousins lived in New York and learned the latest in a burgeoning culture called hip-hop. One day, he introduced me to Melle Mel's "White Lines." Soon, Run-DMC took flight and lifted the art to greater heights. Their music was stripped down, minimalist, the words aggressive, boastful. Run hurled his rhymes with fury as DMC punctuated the couplets.

The culture hypnotized me. The energy and powerfulness drew me in. I dragged my mom to Fresh Fest, where I watched these emerging artists and listened to their booming sounds up close.

After Michael left my house, I would pick up the remote and flip through stations to find a game, any game. I searched for my sport throughout most of my early childhood. My parents told me that "football" was my first word. My dad's quarterback on the Cowboys, Roger Staubach, came up with the name Grant after my parents deliberated for months on the name of the girl they believed they were destined to have. I grew up on football fields, watching my dad play on Sundays in cavernous stadiums, and often imagined myself on the fresh grass, taking handoffs like him, dodging mammoth linemen. But my dad deflatingly barred me from playing until high school, the same time he started playing tackle football. He wanted my body to fill out and was tired of running into youth coaches who imagined themselves as the reincarnation of Vince Lombardi. Devastated, I revolted by never playing the game at all. By high school, I told him I had no interest in football. He'd later say that's the moment he viewed me as smarter than him.

Most mornings, I bypassed cartoons to watch German soccer on television. Soccer was my first legitimate sports love. The open fields provided a freeness, allowing me to run until my lungs emptied. I enjoyed the team aspect of the sport, different personalities and positions unified toward a goal.

My allegiance changed soon after the Betamax arrived. My family gathered in the basement to watch the Final Four. The championship game showcased Carolina and its dynamic freshman, Mike Jordan, against nearby Georgetown and its tower of a freshman, Patrick Ewing. CBS broadcast the college championship for the first time with Gary Bender and Billy Packer on the call from the Louisiana Superdome.

Patrick opened the game with a nice baseline jumper. On defense, he flew everywhere.

James Worthy lofted a shot. Patrick goaltended.

Jordan drove to the basket. Patrick goaltended.

Sam Perkins followed a shot. Patrick goaltended.

His coach, John Thompson, instructed him not to let a shot touch the rim. From the start, he wanted Carolina to know they were outmuscled against Patrick. On the sidelines, Coach Thompson provided a looming presence. He was a big guy, sweating and stalking the court with a towel draped over his shoulder. I'd realize later that his demeanor personified intimidation. One day, I'd be able to tell who was scared on the court before even touching a basketball. Coach Thompson secured points for Georgetown prior to tipoff.

A late Jordan jumper lifted Carolina to a lead. Georgetown still had a chance, until Fred Brown threw a pass straight into Worthy's hands. I saved and savored the tape, watching the film over and over. I studied Jordan's moves, Worthy's motor, Patrick's dominance. I took to always dribbling a basketball and tried to emulate them. I asked for a hoop for our house. My dad declined, thinking that the ball would bump the car in the driveway too often. Another strike against that Porsche.

It was nothing for me to spend hours outside, just my imagination and the ball. One weekend, my dad invited me up to Yale, for a football game. We were joined on the trip by Mr. Cliff Alexander, my mom's business partner, whose daughter, Elizabeth, attended the school long before she became one of the world's greatest poets. We visited her dorm room, and I spotted a basketball hoop in the courtyard below. I'll be down there, I said. They found me a couple hours later, sweat pouring from my body. I didn't have a ball, teammates, or opponents, but in my head I was connecting on game winner after game winner.

At home, I started tuning in to college basketball closely. The Big

East was bubbling. ESPN, then a fledgling cable network, invented the innovative concept of airing sports twenty-four hours a day. That type of commitment required content, and the network partnered with the Big East to broadcast the conference's "Monday Night Game of the Week." I never missed a game. Every contest was a dogfight. Players flew in the air. Elbows crashed into chests. Georgetown boasted Patrick. St. John's showcased Chris Mullin. Syracuse featured Pearl Washington.

I didn't see any other men of color leading a team besides Coach Thompson. He and his team were unequivocally talented and unapologetically Black. It was Georgetown against the world. I took pride in each of their victories.

The Hoyas became my Hoyas.

My devotion became complete when another Michael Jackson—this one played basketball—joined Georgetown.

The choices for recreational activities for Reston teenagers were limited, a coin-flip option between going to the movies or a high school sporting event. My babysitters were sisters who cheered at South Lakes High School. Often, I'd tag along with the family to one of South Lakes' games. At first, I ran through the underbelly of the bleachers at the football games and chased other kids, oblivious to the score or players. Slowly, Michael, a star at South Lakes, piqued my interest at about the same time college basketball took ahold of me. He was the first basketball player I witnessed up close who operated gracefully on the court. My parents noted my infatuation with Michael, who later did an internship under my mom. They invited him to our house for dinner, which felt to me like sharing boiled crabs with God. I felt like an official Hoya myself when Michael committed to Georgetown.

Watching on television was no longer enough. My mom agreed to go in on season tickets with Mr. Alexander. I don't know how she managed everything. She worked all day before returning home. Together, we made the trek around the Capital Beltway from western Virginia to Landover, Maryland, a couple times a week for Georgetown home games at the Cap Centre.

We sat right across from the visiting bench, three rows back. Up close, Patrick was bigger, taller. David Wingate was faster, shiftier. Michael Jackson was still the same. Thompson trusted him from the beginning to play both guard spots. They demolished opponents. I was in the stands, cheering when Patrick dunked all over Virginia's Goliath, Ralph Sampson. As much as I loved them, Georgetown drew disdain on the road. Someone threw an orange at Patrick while he shot a free throw at Syracuse. Fans launched banana peels inside another visiting arena. The cameras only showed it in a flash, but I spotted a picture in the newspaper of fans holding a sign reading EWING IS AN APE.

The wins were not just wins. They symbolized validation. The Hoyas played mean, sometimes blurring the line between fair play and over-aggression. Hoya Paranoia. Coach Thompson wasn't just a coach. He was a patriarch protecting his players and program. Freshmen were not allowed to talk to the media. Interviews with other players were brief. Thompson let their play talk for them.

It was us against them.

———

My dad believed his commitment to the Browns would cause him to be gone only a couple days at a time. The job ended up being more time-consuming. Art Modell, the team's owner, realized that more players were battling substance abuse than he had anticipated. The amount was even stunning to my dad, who had only recently left the locker room. Cocaine was the go-to. The players were in pain, had time on their hands and money to burn through, a recipe for disaster. Some wanted help but were wary that their struggles would be played out on the front page of newspapers. My dad started an in-house program, trying to figure out the best method for them to receive assistance.

A crisis yanked him away for a couple weeks straight. I jumped on a plane to spend the weekend with him. One of the players in the program pulled my dad aside.

You're spending all this time with us, he said. You better spend more time with that little boy, or he's going to end up like us.

The conversation jolted my dad.

When we returned home, he invited me to choose a vacation for just us two, preferably around Easter.

He wanted quality time. I did too.

Fishing? Camping? The beach?

I didn't hesitate. The Final Four.

My dad agreed. He still had connections in the sports world and scored us two tickets.

I prayed that Georgetown would be there to greet me. They rolled through that 1984 season but stumbled out of the tournament prematurely a year earlier. They gained the top seed in the West Regional and drew a first-round bye in the forty-eight-team tournament. My heart stopped and started a few times when Southern Methodist University nearly upset them. The shot clock didn't yet exist. SMU slowed the game down to a glacial pace, and it nearly worked. My Hoyas barely survived an ugly game with a razor-thin 37–36 victory on Patrick's tip-in. Duke wasn't so lucky that day. They were in the same bracket, the third seed, and were upset by Washington in their first tournament appearance under a young coach, Michael Krryzyzawlskil—or something like that. The Hoyas faced a gutted bracket the rest of the regional and made easy work out of Vegas and Dayton.

The field was set. Georgetown against Kentucky, and Virginia against Houston. The plane ride to Seattle was long but worth it. The city sparkled. We were free from the jurisdiction of the General. My dad followed my whims. We woke up when we wanted. Clothes piled on the hotel room floor. We splurged on fast food, the masters of our small domain.

The compromise was that we also had to visit an art gallery each day of the trip. They were brief, half-hour stops, but still the worst thirty minutes of my young life. My dad talked to me about the art, detailing the finer points, his Yale degree in full force. For him, education provided the primary vehicle to transform one's life. His father, Henry Hill, had been a sharecropper in a tiny town called Cross Hill in South Carolina during the depths of the Great Depression. One day, he went to take a drink of water while working. The owner's son tried striking my grandfather with a cord, but my grandfather grabbed it, knocking him off his horse. That night, my grandparents, fearing for their lives, scrambled north under the cloak of darkness. They resettled in Baltimore, where my grandmother Elizabeth Hill eventually taught my grandfather to read. The world opened for him. One of my dad's fondest memories was reading encyclopedias with my grandfather. My dad became the first person from his family to graduate from high school before advancing to Yale; he chose the university more for the promise of its education than with any athletic future in mind. At around the same time, my mom landed far away from her New Orleans home, all the way in Wellesley, Massachusetts, for college. My mom jokes that she called home once while in college, praying that her dad would answer the phone. Had he picked up, she was sure he would have listened to her urgent pleas that she needed to return home. Instead, fate intervened and her mom answered, instructing her to toughen up and telling her that she was as good as anyone at Wellesley. My parents soon met at a transitional, pivotal time for this country, a period of searing events that shaped their worldview. They came of age during the assassinations of Martin Luther King Jr. and Robert F. Kennedy, the Vietnam War, and the fights for civil and women's rights.

The knowledge at the gallery flowed in and out of my young mind. I had no clue that my dad was then planting the seeds that would one day spark my own interest in art. Instead, my primary, pressing concern was whether Patrick could handle Sam Bowie and Mel Turpin.

Torture over, my dad worked some more connections. He gained us passage into parties featuring coaching royalty. I snapped pictures and smiled and posed with Missouri's Norm Stewart and St. John's Lou Carnesecca.

Maybe he'll play for you one day, my dad joked with each coach.

Friday's practices were open to the public. I had been in plenty of football stadiums. My dad played his final NFL game here at the Kingdome. It felt odd, this huge dome repurposed for basketball. The seats stretched as far as my eyes could see. I imagined them filled with fans, cheering for basketball, instead of football, and smiled.

I spotted the enemies up close. Kentucky's Twin Towers, Bowie and Turpin, somehow seemed even taller than Patrick. I walked down the tunnel, trying to get the attention of Michael Jackson. He was too far away to hear me. I screamed the names of some other players. The team was comprised of local players I had watched for a while. Reggie Williams was a Baltimore product. His high school coach, Bob Wade, was my dad's lifelong friend. Michael Graham was from the district and brought another layer of toughness. They heard my shouts, and I'd like to think they knew I was there and that we were in this together.

Another visit to another museum out of the way and game day arrived. Our seats were in the lower bowl. Close, but a decent way away from the court. The cheer squads from each school were already seated by the time we arrived. Hoya Saxa, I chanted along with the Georgetown faithful.

I was nervous. So, apparently, was my team. Georgetown fell behind early, 27–15. Patrick picked up three early fouls and exited the game. Thankfully, Georgetown proceeded to squeeze the life out of Kentucky. Their leader, Dicky Beal, couldn't get the ball inside to Bowie or Turpin. Kentucky missed thirty of their thirty-three second-half shots.

I loved each clank. Meanwhile, we found soft spots in Kentucky's zone, sprinting to the lead and a 53–40 win.

Survive and advance.

The excitement kept me up the next couple nights. Rain kept us in the hotel room until Monday finally arrived. Patrick faced his biggest challenge yet against Houston and Hakeem Olajuwon. Houston had lost in the previous year's championship, just like we did two years earlier. They were just as hungry as us, their wounds even fresher. Patrick asked Coach Thompson how he felt at the morning's practice. Terrible, Thompson replied. Feel better, Patrick said, tonight we're going to be champions. Patrick was true to his word. Olajuwon posed a challenge, but so did Patrick, who forced him into early foul trouble. Olajuwon collected an offensive board inches from the basket. He pump-faked. Patrick stood still, then rose with Olajuwon, disrupting his shot. Was that intimidation I saw? Patrick did enough in the first half to lift us to a lead, and Georgetown switched from a zone to man defense. I called out the schemes to my dad, telling him when and where guys would get the ball on offense. He looked at me, a curious expression on his face. That, I thought later, was the moment he appreciated how completely I was absorbed by the game.

The final twenty minutes ticked away at a painfully slow pace. We held on to the lead, squeezing it, clutching it. The clock wound down.

Ten, nine, eight . . .

This is the greatest feeling in sports, my dad said.

. . . seven, six, five, four . . .

When there's only seconds left and you know your team is going to be on top. It's better than what comes after and what comes before.

It's this. Right now.

Three . . . two . . . one.

Georgetown, 84. Houston, 75.

I was no longer in my seat. I floated, making my way to the lip of the court as the awards ceremony began. This was my celebration too. They cut down the nets. Michael Jackson, a guy from my city, was now a national champion.

I wish I could buy this experience for you, my dad said.

Thompson was guarded even after the win. He was equal parts excited and exhausted. Reporters asked how it felt to be the first Black coach to win a college basketball championship. He was torn. Black players dominated the game.

So, what does it tell you that I'm the first Black coach to win the NCAA? That I'm the first Black coach smart enough? Don't try to sell me that.

He told himself to enjoy the moment, to savor it. He was also conscious of his pessimistic voice.

I'd be able to relate soon enough.

3

COACH Wendell Byrd invited me downstairs to his office within South Lakes High School's gymnasium. I had already spent many hours inside this gym, between cheering Michael Jackson performing on center stage with the bleachers rolled over the adjacent courts and going to summer camps under Coach Byrd's direction throughout middle school. Now I was fourteen, tall, yet gangly enough to fall through a crack in the ground. Basketball tryouts were approaching. I had readied myself, having just spent an hour running with some varsity players, guys whose games I had attended as a fan just a few months earlier. I was still catching my breath, taken aback by their combination of size and speed, when I plopped in front of Coach Byrd.

I've been watching you, he said. I really like what you're showing out there. I want you to try out for varsity.

In Coach Byrd's mind, of course, he was bestowing an opportunity. But I instinctively cringed, thinking only of the impending ostracism. I had an October birthday, which meant that I was always the youngest kid in my grade. High school was already overwhelming enough. Kids throughout Reston—preppies, athletes, cheerleaders, doughboys, those from subsidized housing, and ones who lived in mansions at water's edge—all poured into South Lakes. It was a world of older, confident teenagers, and I was still an observer. I was more at ease with adults than with my peers, having grown up in a household with just my parents. Sometimes, they hosted dinner parties with their friends where someone toasted how far they'd all come. Growing up, I recognized that part of the Black experience was identifying with the overcoming of a struggle. It could be dizzying to celebrate a communal triumph having bypassed the unifying hardships of my parents' generation. I didn't spend much time wondering if I had missed out on anything with kids my own age. I was content filling my days watching television, playing sports, or tagging along with my parents on errands.

At school, I was a square in any social circle. I could play ball, yet I never thought of myself as the most talented player on the court. I was in a couple so-called gifted classes, although I never mistook myself for the smartest kid in the room. Michael Ellison again carved inroads for me. He had already been in high school a year and had adapted as needed to the social hierarchy. He had played on the freshman basketball team, along with Rob Robinson, another friend who I never even knew could play until he surprised everyone by trying out and becoming one of the better players. South Lakes athletes wore ties to school on game days. In middle school, I had joined them in solidarity, the only eighth grader at Langston Hughes decked out in a tie. I'd hurry to catch their games once my school day ended and even offered them water during breaks in the action.

Michael and Rob were set to play on junior varsity. The thought of leapfrogging them in the basketball pecking order, of transforming from a glorified water boy to playing varsity ball in a couple of months, was, in my opinion, asinine. Most of those guys were driving cars. They had girlfriends and facial hair. I looked up to them. Varsity? I didn't even want to play junior varsity. I had hoped to play on the freshman team with the same group I had teamed with the past couple of years. That way, basketball wouldn't impede on the soccer season.

I don't recall what, if anything, I said in response to Coach Byrd. He was an African American man approaching his forties who projected a constant steadiness and didn't make time for drama. In response, I probably stuttered. In fact, I'm sure I did, because I stuttered whenever nerves struck, which was every time someone asked me to speak. Coach Byrd encouraged me to discuss the offer with my dad. I agreed. He's someone who would listen to reason.

That night, I waited for dinner before retracing the conversation with Coach Byrd, punctuating it with a *can you believe that?*

My dad didn't miss a beat. You should, he said. You can play with those guys.

I offered a couple mumbles and stumbles, anything to stop the momentum stacking against me.

You're doing this, Grant.

He said it in a tone of affirmation, telling me that I could do it, trying to ease my anxiety about playing against kids who were older and, in my opinion, better. I wasn't buying it: I retreated to my room, closed the door, and muffled my cries with a pillow. This, I thought, was a form of child abuse.

My self-perception was like looking into a fun-house mirror, a disconnect that went on for years. I couldn't see myself, my play, from the same vantage as others. Instead, that nagging, persistent doubt of whether I was good enough settled in and took up occupancy in the back of my mind. Others had already ascertained qualities in me that it took years for me to recognize and accept. I shunned the spotlight at every turn. A few months earlier, administrators had asked my dad to address my school's student body during an assembly. He was still working with the Browns, running their drug treatment program at the height of the

Reagan administration's War on Drugs, when "Just Say No" slogans proliferated on every campus with a teenager on it. They hoped that he could scare some kids straight. The thought of my dad at school scared me straight into the nurse's office. Even today, I'm not proud that I feigned sickness just to skip the assembly. But the thought of my dad at school and the unwanted attention it would bring left me mortified. I heard my name called over the intercom as his speech wound down, someone requesting that I come onstage to take a picture with my dad. Paralyzed, I didn't budge.

As awkward as I was socially, sports provided community. I was tall and could handle a basketball, and my teams typically won. I credit my dad for the fact that I always felt comfortable with the basketball in my hands. This was hardly an era when tall players handled the rock with any regularity. Most bigs played with their backs to the basket, taking a plodding dribble or two before lumbering into a premeditated move. I had played on a pretty bad youth team at the age of eight when, as the tallest kid on the court, I was instructed by the coach to go inside and grab rebounds. I dutifully performed the task, only the ball seldom found me once I passed it out. The next season, my dad suggested that I just bring the ball up myself after collecting a rebound. I followed his advice, learning that my height allowed me to look over the defenses and gain passing angles. I could guard taller players inside and developed a fluidity in maneuvering past most defenders. Smaller guards couldn't knock me off course. Post players couldn't stay in front of me.

The versatility helped that summer before freshman year when I played Amateur Athletic Union basketball for the first time. Our team, the Northern Virginia Hawks, won the Potomac Valley before prevailing at the state level and qualifying for the nationals all the way in St. Louis. My dad arrived early to scope out the competition and watched as our first opponents took the court in shiny jumpsuits. Placing a booming stereo on the court for their warm-ups, their players performed dunk after dunk. This was my introduction to the Detroit Superfriends, an adolescent version of the Harlem Globetrotters. They were headed by Chris Webber, who looked too tall to run so fast, and Jalen Rose, a smooth lefty who was seemingly capable of dropping the ball into the bucket on command. Next, my dad turned his head to look at my team, a collection of suburban, mostly white kids with bad haircuts, outfitted in plain white T-shirts and shorts. He started mentally readying a comforting speech to follow our inevitable blowout: no one had expected us to reach this far; we had tried our best; we'd be better the next year; and so on. Instead, we won decisively. Our coach, Jim Warren, had prepared us for the moment. We conducted his motion offense to perfection, dissecting their defense. Our press forced them into mistake after mistake. My dad ended up delivering the consolation speech to a devastated Chris.

We advanced to beat a team from Kansas in the semifinals and an Indianapolis team for the championship. I thought I had played well enough to earn the MVP and told my dad as much. (That may sound off after detailing my confidence issues, but I was playing among kids my own age, most of whom were a grade below me. When you're that young, a level playing field makes all the difference in the world.) The honor instead went to my friend Jamie, Coach Warren's son, who converted a late layup in the clincher. The tournament featured other players I would become familiar with over the years, future pros like Howard Eisley, Alan Henderson, Voshon Lenard, and Jamal Mashburn. The result boosted my confidence in believing that I could hold my own against players from my age-group. But the thought of playing varsity, as well as the sensory overload that was the first few weeks of high school, was overwhelming.

I headed to the gym as soon as the final school bell buzzed on game days, sitting on these familiar bleachers, watching as the freshman team steamrolled their way to an undefeated season, wishing I shared the court with them. I could usually squeeze in the first three quarters of the junior varsity game, where Michael and Rob held their own, before the varsity team assembled for our night game. My teammates were all seniors except Jerome Scott, a junior and our star player. I had watched and admired Jerome like I once had Michael Jackson. I would go home and mimic his crossover dribble, trying to incorporate it into my own game.

As a child, I never dreamed of one day playing for the Los Angeles Lakers or Washington Bullets. I didn't even think it'd be possible for me to play at Georgetown. Those destinations seemed too outlandish for my small imagination. Instead, I fantasized about one day playing for South Lakes. That reality happened sooner than I ever anticipated. Having tried out and made varsity, I started alongside Jerome, gaining confidence and comfort with each practice and game. Coach Byrd ensured that we were always the best-conditioned team on the floor. He was as tough as a given situation necessitated and served as a father figure to a lot of my teammates, some raised without a male voice in their households.

My teammates alternated calling me Fetus because of my age and Bambi because I was 70 percent legs. They were mostly kind and tolerated me despite our age difference. John Lewis, a senior point guard who lived a couple doors down from me, took me under his wing. John had a little brother younger than me. Throughout my childhood, I had spent more time with him than with John, who seemed decades older with his deep love of sports and his boom box that always blasted early hip-hop music. John offered me rides home from practice. After road games, our team often gathered at his house, where his parents assembled a collection of cold cut sandwiches. I would prepare myself a roast beef sandwich before I walked back home, while the rest of the guys readied themselves for a Friday night party.

In games, I was again stationed in the post, playing power forward. Most of my buckets originated near the basket, courtesy of drop-offs from John and Jerome. I played off instinct and hustle. Often, I could use my length to find the ball before other players. I opened everyone's eyes except, possibly, my own. Soon, my first recruitment letter arrived from Denny Crum, the coach at Louisville. *Dear Grant, we're keeping our eyes on you and are excited to watch you progress.* Maybe playing college ball wasn't so unrealistic. In my head, I was already wearing the red and black. Our team, the Seahawks, won the Great Falls District before losing to West Springfield in the first round of the state tournament, a squad headed by Coach Warren.

That summer, I rejoined Coach Warren's AAU team. We qualified for the fourteen-and-under championship tournament in Bellevue, Washington, stirring warm memories of my first Final Four experience. Chris Webber and his Superfriends also landed in the tournament, and to me they looked even bigger and better. Chris had lost any trace of adolescence in the year since we first met. He simply overpowered opponents. I was already dreading having to defend him when the Superfriends lost a close contest in the semifinals to Alan Henderson's Indiana team. Alan's team also nipped us in the finals by a bucket. But I had played with the confidence that came from competing against older players. Throughout the tournament, I'd routinely collect a rebound, bring the ball all the way downcourt, and dunk in transition. I accepted the MVP trophy in defeat. Life, it was already clear, was a mixed bag of numbing self-doubt and moments of powerful affirmation that provided the fuel for subsequent steps.

———

Through the years, my dad and I had continued our pilgrimage each spring to the Final Four. I had sulked at Kentucky's Rupp Arena in 1985 when Villanova somehow topped Georgetown in the championship game. The next year, in Dallas, we bypassed a hotel room and stayed at the house of Mark Washington, one of my dad's former Cowboys teammates. His daughter was a serious gymnast, enough so that their home featured a balance beam in the living room. I was more impressed when we stopped by Roger Staubach's home so my dad could catch up with his quarterback. Roger's home showcased a full basketball court with fiberglass backboards. I laced up my new Air Jordan shoes and killed a couple hours on the court, imagining that I shook free from defenders to hit game winners.

The only real problem with the weekend was that for the first time we were at the Final Four without Georgetown as a participant. Michigan State, behind an otherworldly performance by Scott Skiles, had ousted the Hoyas earlier in the tournament. Kansas, Duke's opponent, piqued my curiosity. I had caught them a couple times on television: they were led by a tall, versatile sophomore forward, Danny Manning, who was graceful for his size, a player I hoped to emulate on the court. I also looked forward to watching some local Duke players, Johnny Dawkins and Tommy Amaker.

Johnny's commitment to Duke was the spark for much of what the program evolved into over the next few decades. A few years earlier, I had attended the McDonald's Capital Classic Game, eager to watch Michael Jackson measure himself against top high school competition. A couple other players caught my attention that night with their electrifying performances: Johnny and Len Bias. Johnny was freakishly athletic, a small standing out among a forest of trees. I flipped through my program. *Johnny Dawkins. Mackin Catholic High School. Committed to Duke University.* Johnny was a special player. The same thing happened the next year. I was in the crowd, at the game, watching another guard dominate. That time it was Tommy, a guard from just down the road in Fairfax, Virginia, who had decided on Duke.

I started placing Duke on my list of teams to pay attention to. They were terrible Johnny's freshman season. Slowly, I witnessed the formation of a foundation, piece by piece. Guys like Danny Ferry, Mark Alarie, and David Henderson joined with Johnny and Tommy. Suddenly Duke wasn't an afterthought. They competed with Georgetown. They became Carolina's rival. They suffocated the opposition with a smothering defense.

That was exactly how they reduced Manning's impact in Dallas: their swarming players nullified his gifts. I was on the edge of my seat as the game teetered back and forth. Johnny Dawkins desperately tipped a ball to Danny Ferry for a layup that broke a late tie. Tommy Amaker secured the final points of the game with a couple of free throws, lifting Duke into the championship game against Louisville. They lost that title game—a theme for a few years—overwhelmed by a sensational performance by a freshman, Pervis Ellison. Even so, they were impressive. Duke played hard but still looked like they were having fun under that coach with the funny name. Three years earlier, this team, this program, did not exist on anyone's radar. Suddenly they had entered the NCAA tournament as the top-ranked team and played for a championship.

But I'll be honest as to where my head was at the time. The championship game had just ended. My dad and I enjoyed the ceremony as fans filtered out of Reunion Arena. Some, I noticed, were removing large decals that hung on the arena's wall and commemorated each participating university. I desperately wanted the Georgetown placard. My dad looked at me as though I were crazy. It was massive, probably ten by twelve feet. I would have had nowhere to put it even if we somehow managed to wrestle it down.

Duke departed Dallas without a championship. I left without my Georgetown decal but with my Hoya fandom still pure and intact.

The summer of momentum after my freshman season propelled me throughout the rest of high school. As a high school sophomore, I still attended Georgetown games as a fan. Only now Coach John Thompson started frequenting the South Lakes gym as well. He wasn't the only prominent college coach. Most, I figured, were dropping by to recruit Jerome, who was still uncommitted at that point. Looking back, Jerome deserves a lot of credit. He could have regarded my quick ascension as a threat. Instead, he facilitated my development and viewed me as an asset to the team. He remained the focal point, yet I learned how to pick my spots to be impactful, averaging twenty-two points a game that year. We played Washington-Lee, a powerhouse school from Arlington, Virginia, in the district finals. We had beaten them a couple of times already, but they always posed a challenge and flexed Crawford Palmer, a McDonald's All-American, who later became my teammate for a short time at Duke. I had never played in front of such a lively crowd, an atmosphere I'd soon become accustomed to on a regular basis. Fans spilled out of the seats and crowded the baselines. We trailed by a bucket with just a few seconds left when I stole a pass out of our press and dunked the ball home. Following a defensive stop, Jerome found me on an alley-oop that ended the game. Roy Williams later told me it had been the most entertaining finish to a high school game he had ever witnessed. I didn't even know he had been inside the gym.

That summer of 1988, my AAU team added a lithe guard named Randolph Childress. We destroyed teams on our way to the fifteen-and-under championship game at Arkansas State University, where we again faced Indiana. My mom invited one of her classmates, Hillary Clinton, and her family to the game. Hillary, Bill Clinton, the state's governor, and their young daughter, Chelsea, sat in the bleachers with my parents as I earned another MVP. Our families headed to a fast-food joint afterward before we spent the rest of the day at a water park, joined by Chris Webber. By then, my parents had formed a friendship with his family, and my mom planned to drop us off the next day at Nike Camp, hosted on the campus of Princeton University.

Governor Clinton, he's going to be president of the United States one day, my mom said on the drive to Princeton's leafy campus. I had never heard of the guy before the previous day.

Yeah, sure, I thought, realizing later what my mom had proven for years: it's never wise to doubt her.

In the fall, I no longer needed my parents to chauffeur me around. My mom took me to obtain my driver's license on my sixteenth birthday. My parents gifted me the 1972 Mercedes-Benz 280SE that my dad had purchased for my mom when she was pregnant with me. The thought of driving a Mercedes was as unsettling then as being picked up in the Porsche when I was younger. But the car provided independence. No one ever wanted me in their car when the team grabbed burgers after a practice or game, because I'd always have to be driven home early to meet the General's curfew.

I was still somewhat awkward, even with my growing popularity, facilitated by my basketball development. I had attended school with most of the same classmates for years. Now more started noticing me. They initiated conversations, and, somewhat surprisingly, I often found myself able to engage with them. The ease didn't translate to my first television interview, which took place around this time. I stumbled through a series of answers so nonsensical that my dad joked I had better start practicing or else it would be a blotch on the family name.

We were a supportive, balanced team my junior season, the top-ranked squad in the Washington metropolitan area. After a year of seeing me operate in transition, Coach Byrd trusted me to initiate our offense. College coaches were a constant presence in the gym. This time, I knew they were here for me, with Jerome now off to the University of Miami. Word got around during the school day, so by the time I entered the gym, I knew whether Coach Thompson or Coach Dean Smith was in attendance. A season of promise, though, ended on a disappointing note. We won districts and regionals but dropped the state semifinal matchup to a Hampton High team full of football players who outmuscled us.

———

Coach Byrd, I was certain, had to be tired of having his mailbox jammed with my recruiting letters. Thankfully, by around the time of my interaction with Adrian Autry at Five-Star, I had heard from every college I was interested in and had imagined myself in different jerseys, on different campuses throughout the country.

I narrowed my interest to four schools: Georgetown, Carolina, Duke, and Michigan—the Wolverines fresh off a championship in 1989.

My parents agreed that I should scope out the schools by taking unofficial visits to the campuses. My mom accompanied me to Michigan. I found the Ann Arbor campus beautiful but frigid. I met Loy Vaught and Rumeal Robinson and made a point to tell them how much I admired their games.

Trips to North Carolina State, Carolina, and Duke could be knocked out in one weekend—a visit to the Tobacco Road coaching legends of Jim Valvano, Dean Smith, and Coach K, the least accomplished, at that point, among the triumvirate. The State stopover was out of respect for Valvano and his program. I couldn't consider the school seriously. Pending punishments over NCAA infractions had turned recruits, including me, cautious about committing.

The Carolina visit had me the most excited. My dad drove me to Chapel Hill, where we were escorted to Granville Towers, home to the school's freshman and sophomore basketball players. My bedroom wall featured a picture of Michael Jordan, cut out from a magazine, shot in those very dorms. This was the same hallowed place, I thought to myself, where Jordan and James Worthy walked around. Two sophomores, Rick

Fox and King Rice, met us. Hubert Davis, a freshman from near home, dropped by to say hello. The rapper Slick Rick's voice wafted from a nearby boom box. *Knock 'em out the box, Rick, knock 'em out, Rick.* Soon, we were walking around campus, where the players showed off the glistening Dean E. Smith Center and I envisioned myself on the court, decked out in Carolina blue and white.

Birds sang as the sun shone through the window the next morning when I woke up at the Carolina Inn. A perfect morning, capping a perfect trip. My decision was made.

There's no reason to even visit Duke, I told my dad.

We made a commitment, he said. They're expecting us. We need to at least check it out.

My mind was still at Carolina during the short ride to Durham, where we stopped outside a neat, bookish building. This was Cameron Indoor Stadium? It looked more like a library than a basketball arena. Tommy Amaker greeted us and escorted us inside. The interior was more impressive. I felt like we had walked into a scene from *Hoosiers.* The sparkling arena was cozy, intimate. We dropped by Coach K's office, where we exchanged quick hellos. I had had a couple conversations with Coach by that point, nothing of too much substance, although I had already ascertained that he was a person of integrity. Soon, Billy King joined Tommy to take my dad and me on a campus tour.

Both were as polished as the basketball arena as they reflected on their families, their journey to Durham, and their time at the school as we admired the Gothic architecture and towering cathedrals on campus. They peppered my dad with questions about his background, about being one of the few Blacks on Yale's campus in the 1960s. In Tommy and Billy, I saw a confident pair, secure in themselves. I was mostly quiet throughout the walk, absorbing their presence. My dad more than held our side of the conversation. I was sure he would be just fine if I decided on Duke and matured into someone like those guys. The visit nearly over, we stopped at the dorms to greet some of the freshmen on the team whom I knew a little bit: Brian Davis and Crawford Palmer, both Washington-metro-area guys, and Christian Laettner, whom I had met briefly at Five-Star a couple years earlier.

A few weeks later, Duke invited me to a dinner commemorating their season and celebrating their seniors. They were sending off members who helped put the program on the map, guys like Danny Ferry and Quin Snyder. My dad and I took our seats in the back of the banquet hall. Snyder took the lectern, offering a heartfelt, endearing speech as he addressed Coach K.

Coach, in this case, language is insufficient, he said. Words fall way short when I try to describe the emotion I feel for you. Last night, I began to remember some of the words you used to help us win games. But winning games was really secondary. They were words that you said to instill values in us that we carry forever. I'd like to repeat some of those words: "commitment," "integrity," "toughness," "honesty," "collective responsibility," "pride," and "love." After each word, you feel a different emotion. And to me, those words and those emotions are Duke basketball. But there's one word I save for last, because that is the word that meant more to me than all the rest. In a hotel room in Seattle, you used the word "friend." It's that word that I'll remember and cherish.

This, I thought, was a family that would be great to join.

As the summer wound down, Carolina and Duke had separated themselves. I still planned on taking official trips to the others, but for the most part it was a two-horse race.

Originally, Virginia had been included among my top schools, but their coach, Terry Holland, announced that summer that he would be leaving the university. I had recently helped Michael Ellison move into his dorm to start his freshman year in Charlottesville. Somehow, word had trickled to Holland that I was on campus, and he asked to meet with me. I lay low. The university still hadn't named his replacement, and I couldn't commit to a program without a coach.

———

At this point, you would be right to wonder about what had happened to my Georgetown devotion.

It was the program of my childhood and still one of the best teams in the country under the steady stewardship of Coach John Thompson. From Michael Jackson, I learned that the players viewed Georgetown's academic coordinator as demanding, borderline difficult. Daily, Michael said, freshman players were required to meet with the coordinator, reporting to her the topics of their classes and the status of their homework. In retrospect, she was just doing her job and likely a good one at that. Some college coaches vomited empty, obligatory platitudes concerning the academic well-being of their players. At Georgetown, Thompson ensured that his players graduated.

School, if I'm honest, wasn't my primary consideration. I was also a teenager with that strict curfew throughout adolescence. That summer, for example, Brian Reese and Chris Webber, a year behind me in school, had spent a weekend at our house while visiting colleges.

On a Friday night, we piled into the Mercedes to catch a party. I caught up with a couple friends, introducing Brian and Chris. We couldn't find Chris when it was time to go. As my mom had told me repeatedly, my curfew was midnight, not 12:01.

Finally, we located Chris.

I'm staying. I'll get a ride back.

Dang.

I didn't want to look weak in front of Chris.

I also didn't dare break curfew and found the only compromise that seemed plausible. I left Chris at the party and drove back to my house with Brian.

My mom walked downstairs as we entered the door.

One teenager. Two teenagers.

Where's Chris?

Someone from the party is going to bring him home.

Oh no, no, no, no, no. Chris is staying here, so Chris is under my care. Go get Chris right now.

We were all under the command of the General. She had walked to the kitchen and started prepping coffee, a bad sign.

Don't make me go to this party and bring Chris back myself.

I was embarrassed, but I'd rather be embarrassed than in trouble. We headed back to the party. At that point, I'd have carried Chris out myself. Luckily, he probably spotted the urgency in my eyes and agreed to leave.

So, the thought of attending Georgetown, a school so close to home, had lost some appeal. I wanted a bit of freedom. I realized how fully my mom was ingrained into my life later when my high school allowed the senior class to decide our commencement speaker. The choices included a local television personality and professionals in medicine and educators. My class voted for my mom above them all.

She was known and appreciated by the entire student body. She volunteered for everything and was always president of the Parent-Teacher Association. When our class wanted to do something different for prom, she suggested for it to be hosted at the atrium area of the Galleria at Tysons II, an upscale mall. I didn't get in trouble much, but if I ever did, she knew about it before I left school.

I appreciated her dedication then and even more in retrospect. However, part of being an adolescent was preparing myself for independence. As high school continued, what had been weeks-long visits to my grandparents in New Orleans and Baltimore during summers became weekend visits. I didn't attend a lot of parties, partly because of my mother's rules but mostly because basketball was now all consuming. I recognized that it would be the conduit that would allow me to experience the world outside Reston. If I attended college in North Carolina, my parents, I figured, would be close enough to arrive quickly in case of an emergency, yet far enough away not to drop by unannounced.

———

Home visits provided the first opportunity for college coaches to meet with recruits outside campus. It was a chance for coaches to charm families, discuss their program, and fortify the promise that they could be trusted to chaperone their son from adolescence into adulthood.

Coach K, during his trip to our house, talked about his humble beginnings growing up in Chicago and how basketball provided a place in this world for him through his playing days at Army to his coaching days at Duke. He popped a cassette into the player. Video of Duke practices sprang to life as he narrated his coaching philosophy. He addressed me and dissected my game in detail. He told me that I had the chance to be special, that I was versatile enough to play point guard and defend a center. At some point during the discussion, I no longer felt as though Coach K were recruiting me. He was already coaching me.

You don't have a position, he said. You're a basketball player, a special one. Now, you're going to have to work hard. I don't believe in giving anybody anything. I don't make promises about starting or minutes, but I see greatness in you. You can do things that I can't teach, and it's important for me to put you in the right environment and atmosphere so you can do those things.

Our conversation revolved around basketball. My parents also participated in the dialogue and interjected with questions every so often.

Coach K inevitably steered the conversation back toward me, soliciting my feedback, measuring my responses.

I could sense the hunger in his voice and viewed the sincerity in his eyes. He would do everything possible to facilitate my development. In turn, he believed I could help him break through the final barrier. He had been to the Final Four. He wanted a championship. He saw the potential peaks we could reach. I had proven myself on the high school level, but the thought of competing against college players unnerved me. The funhouse mirror was never far away.

The visit was brief. I don't even remember if he stayed for dinner.

We picked up our conversation a few days later when I made my official visit to Duke and sat inside his office.

While you're here, try envisioning playing here, being part of this program, attending classes, ingraining yourself in the community, he advised.

He guided me to the Oak Room, a dining hall restaurant on West Campus. A handful of players were already seated around a circular table, including Laettner and Brian, my student hosts for the weekend. The players, I noticed, were at ease around Coach. They smiled and cracked jokes with him, a distant cry from the typical authoritarian relationship a coach had with his players. The meal was about to end when Coach offered another piece of guidance.

If you know what you want to do, make that decision. Don't waste everyone's time and don't waste your own. Don't have the weight of that decision hovering. If you know, you know.

If Coach K finessed the message, Laettner and Brian hammered it home.

They threw a party for me that night. Hip-hop music blasted as we entered a house a couple blocks away from campus. Everyone seemingly knew one another. The athletes seemed to blend seamlessly with the rest of the student body.

If you come here, we're going to win the championship, Brian said. Just get the pen. He wants to come. Call Coach. Let's get the pen.

I laughed in the moment. But the rhythm of the entire weekend, from picturing myself on campus to meeting Coach K and his wife, Mickie, or Mrs. K, as the players called her, to attending a women's soccer game, just felt right.

Coach Dean Smith was scheduled for a house visit soon. My official Michigan visit was approaching. My dad was hyped that the trip coincided with a weekend that the Wolverines hosted Notre Dame for a football game. Michigan's coach, Bo Schembechler, had already invited us to watch from the sidelines.

Maybe I'm just drinking the Kool-Aid. But if I know what I want to do, then why waste my time?

I'm going to commit to Duke, I told my parents on my arrival back home.

They talked me down, insisting that I at least honor our appointment with Coach Smith. Meeting with Coach Smith, they said, could validate my feelings toward Duke if they were as strong as I said they were. Also, my mom reminded me, I had been wearing a Carolina T-shirt around the house only a month earlier. My parents allowed me my autonomy in sorting through my options, but they wanted me to think them through carefully. My dad was methodical about any choice; if he was going to purchase a new car, he was the type of person who would do months of research and test-drive many candidates before he made a firm decision.

I was open-minded the day Coach Smith arrived, joined by one of his assistants, Phil Ford. Coach Smith was a legend, a dynamic talker who quickly drew my dad into a deep conversation. Both Coach Smith and my dad had fascinating careers in sports. My dad had recently left the Browns and joined the Baltimore Orioles as their vice president for personnel. They talked about the integration of the Atlantic Coast

Conference, politics, baseball, football. My head swiveled back and forth as though I were watching a tennis match. The conversation was engrossing, just not one I was an active participant in. The topic that I was most interested in exploring, of how I'd fit in at Chapel Hill, was broached lightly, but not substantively.

It was getting late. I had some homework left to do. I thanked Coach Smith and Coach Ford for visiting and politely excused myself from the table. I didn't intend any offense by leaving. I really had schoolwork, but Coach Smith later said that he knew he had lost me when I left the dining room.

The next morning, I woke up with clear-eyed conviction.

I'm committing to Duke, I told my parents.

I'm certain.

My mom knew that it had to take a lot to sway her son, whom she had taken to Georgetown games for years and who had idolized the players at Carolina.

My dad asked me to postpone the decision a week. He still wanted to see Michigan play Notre Dame. We canceled the visit. He may still hold it against me. We missed a classic game that featured Rocket Ismail returning two kickoffs for touchdowns.

But when you know, you know.

———

My closest high school friends, Michael and Rob, had graduated by my senior year of high school. We were not as deep as my previous South Lakes teams. My high school career ended with another loss to Hampton in the state semifinals. Duke, that spring, tore through the NCAA tournament and arrived at the title game against the powerful Vegas Runnin' Rebels. I rooted for my future school, although a slice of me had hoped to be part of Duke's first championship team. I watched the game knowing that possibility was intact when Vegas subjected Duke to a merciless thrashing.

A few months later, I was invited to play at the Junior World Championship Qualifying Tournament in Montevideo, Uruguay. It provided another opportunity to measure myself against talented players from around the country and, this time, the world. Our team consisted of mostly rising sophomores, guys like Darrick Martin and Calbert Cheaney, who already had the benefit of a college season and were destined for the NBA. I started as we ripped through the games, playing mostly positionless basketball. That Montevideo gym was the coldest arena I had ever played in. The entire inside resembled a giant slab of cement, and dust particles swirled in the air as we accepted our gold medals, topping Argentina in the gold medal contest.

I had just played with players who had already made collegiate imprints, yet my nerves kicked in that fall as freshman orientation approached. I know it may sound crazy, but it is consistent with where my head was at that time. It was a gargantuan step for a shy, slightly insecure guy whose confidence wavered. How could I make the impact that Coach K predicted from me? How could I compete in Duke's classroom, let alone the court? Panicking, I called Tommy Amaker, who had just become an assistant under Coach K. Maybe it wasn't too late for me to enroll at a safer, smaller school, just around the corner.

I don't think I can do it, I told him. I should just go to George Mason.

Boy, you better get your ass over here, were the words that came to his mind during the call, Tommy later told me. But instead of saying that, he listened to my complaints and patiently talked me down.

At that age, my mindset simply didn't allow me to appreciate how good I was or how good I could be. It was a constant struggle. I could perform in a setting like Uruguay, yet still be fearful of the next step.

I needed to be pushed. I needed someone who believed in me more than I believed in myself. I found that person in Durham.

4

OUR goal is to win the championship, Coach K said once he gathered our team inside the locker room following the first day of classes. He approached the whiteboard. *1991 National Champions*, he scrawled for emphasis. He had whispered a symphony of sweet nothings to me throughout the entire recruiting process. Rumors swirled that July that he was debating leaving Duke to take over the Boston Celtics. I had committed to Duke, but mostly I had committed to Coach.

Coach was a letter writer. To this day, I anticipate his handwritten notes every birthday. He sent me a note then, a couple weeks after the speculation, writing that he had decided to stay, that he loved Duke and he remained excited about the opportunity to coach this young team.

I had spent the previous couple of weeks falling into a routine. My parents made the drive with me to Durham. I had spoken with my new roommate, Tony Lang, a couple times on the phone by the time of move-in day. He was from down south in Mobile, Alabama. A gifted athlete, he was also smart, the valedictorian of his class. That day, we made our way to our dorm in Hastings, walking up to the fourth floor and crossing a hallway.

Our parents were in instant harmony. Tony's dad introduced himself as Onion. Why? Because my basketball game's so cold that when they watched me, people cried. Someone else's father with a hilarious sense of humor? I knew he'd get along just fine with my dad.

We told our parents goodbye and joined the entire freshman class at Sarah P. Duke Gardens, acres upon acres of flowers that burst in a rainbow of colors, hilly slopes, and calming ponds. Students, my classmates, approached us, asking to pose for pictures and scribble signatures on scraps of paper. Some recited my high school statistics. In Reston, I had attended school with the same group for years. No one looked at me much differently as my skills evolved and talent developed.

The fact that I was not just a basketball player but a basketball player at Duke, on a team with great expectations, was starting to sink in. I flashed back to when I was four, leaving RFK Stadium with my dad. Fans, corralled in a chain-link fence, screamed and clamored for his attention.

All right, I told myself. This is like my dad walking at RFK. This is where we are right now. This will probably be the new normal.

Soon, I laced my shoes inside Card Gym for an open run. The air inside loomed sticky, heavy. The entire building felt like a relic from the past. A running track was suspended above, looping around the court. Below, a couple of recent graduates, Johnny Dawkins and Danny Ferry, lofted shots up on one of the tiny courts as students played volleyball in an adjacent area. Those guys had left their imprint here, part of the tradition of current pros who gathered for games every fall before fanning out across the country to resume their NBA journeys. As distinguished as they were, they had not been able to pull Duke across the finish line.

A championship. This team? This year?

Our locker room was small, intimate, cage-like. Stools rested in front of our stalls. Student managers draped laundry nets inside the lockers that included our practice jerseys and socks. We had taken pictures in our Duke jerseys, and those portraits were displayed above them. After Coach's declaration, I glanced at my teammates. We were young. A couple D.C. kids, Christian Ast and Kenny Blakeney, and Marty Clark, a guard from Chicago, were part of the freshman class with Tony and me. Three sophomores, including our point guard, Bobby Hurley, and five upperclassmen made up the rest of our roster. Christian Laettner was the only junior or senior who had really gotten some burn in Coach's rotation the previous season.

Coach continued, punctuating his sentences with expletives in place of exclamation marks. He didn't curse every other word, but spliced them carefully, almost artfully. The f-word, he later testified, was such a versatile word that it could be used as a verb, noun, or adjective.

Whoa. This was intense. This was the same mild-mannered guy in my parents' home?

I know now that Coach K began each season with that goal, no matter the composition of his team or how difficult the season ahead. I'd come to appreciate that every pep talk, practice drill, and space between games prepared us for that destination.

Back then, I had to wonder if either he or I had knocked our heads.

He remembered that team in Vegas, right? The Runnin' Rebels ran this Duke squad off the court a few months earlier in the championship game. That core would have raced off to the NBA following that steamrolling had they come of age just a few years later. Instead, they returned all their main pieces—Larry Johnson, Stacey Augmon, Greg Anthony, and friends. People were already speculating whether they could beat NBA teams. Meanwhile, we had lost quality, valuable seniors like Alaa Abdelnaby and Phil Henderson.

I stole another look at my teammates. No chance. Nada. Zip.

I would have placed money that no one else really believed we'd be playing deep into the tournament either. Yet Coach was still going on and on about how we were going to win it all, peppering his points with an expletive here and there.

The meeting broke. His words loomed in the air, just staying there, not really hitting home yet. The season still felt far away; I was caught up in the rhythm of attending classes, lifting weights, and playing pickup. Thomas Hill, a sophomore, advised me that the atmosphere would get more intense at the approaching Blue-White intra-squad scrimmage.

Just wait, he predicted.

The game was open to the public, marking my debut in front of the Cameron Crazies, our devoted student section that often camped for days outside Cameron just to secure a place inside the building. I wore my new jersey number, 33. When it came time to choose, my first couple options were off the table. I had displayed 32 throughout most of high school, a tribute to my two MJs, Michael Jackson from Reston and Georgetown and Magic Johnson of the Lakers. Here, that was Laettner's number. I would have proudly chosen my dad's jersey number, but Danny Ferry's career ensured no Duke player would bear 35 again. I'd have even gone for 34, but Crawford Palmer already had it. I could live with 33, though. Patrick Ewing had worn it proudly at Georgetown.

Thomas didn't lie, I thought to myself. I didn't play well during the scrimmage that pitted freshmen and seniors against sophomores and juniors. It honestly took a couple of times to adapt to that environment with every fan seemingly courtside, deeply invested in each possession, even during a scrimmage.

I liked our team now that I had witnessed us a few times in action. We were built from the inside out by Coach. He secured the foundation in Laettner, as well as Crawford, two McDonald's All-American post players. His next class featured guards like Bobby, Thomas, and Billy McCaffrey. Last, he imported swingmen like me and Tony, Swiss Army knife players who could mix and match, defend multiple positions.

Bobby, I quickly realized, was more athletic than I had thought. His game was full of energy. He was the son of not just a coach but one of the premier high school coaches in New Jersey. It was like Bobby had memorized all the rules just to learn how and when to break them. Most coaches wanted structure, especially from their point guard. With Bobby, that would've been like trying to place a hummingbird in a plastic bag. He played fearlessly, probing and attacking. It was a quality I believed Coach admired in Bobby. He encouraged Bobby to rely on his instincts, accepting the inevitable turnovers, trusting that Bobby's overall play would outweigh all else. The fact that he was trying, attacking, was important.

I played with Bobby on the first team, and with each practice I was seeing the further carving of a team identity. As much as Coach instructed us to be united and disciplined on defense, he gave us a share of offensive freedoms.

Against zones, college offenses typically turned timid, tossing the ball around the perimeter. Defenses shifted and the ball often stayed outside the paint. Dribble penetration was stifled. Coach implored us to attack the gaps in zones off the dribble. He wanted us into the teeth of a defense in the hopes that two defenders would collapse onto one ball handler. If the defense stopped the penetrator, he could kick the ball out for an open shot. If not, the ball handler could find his own shot. We tried to spread the court and strain a defense before going one-on-one. It was basketball in its purest, prettiest form.

Our roster featured a few seniors, Greg Koubek and Clay Buckley. They were technically the captains. It didn't take long to discern, though, that Laettner and Brian Davis were the alpha males, the big personalities that either united or divided a team. Their collective confidence bordered on arrogance.

We all know a Laettner. First of all, he was cool, full of personality and a magnet for attention.

He was annoyingly good at seemingly everything.

Ping-Pong?

He demolished all takers.

Piano? He taught me how to play Force MDs' "Tender Love" on the keyboard.

He also knew that he was good at everything and told everyone about it. He was the team's big brother. Socially, he showed ease with the brothers, enough so that I could've sworn he grew up in a Black neighborhood instead of just outside Buffalo. Laettner loved hip-hop. I mean, he was deep into hip-hop. Anyone could recite a couple Digital Underground lines from that era. He knew Chubb Rock's lyrics. He recited the Jungle Brothers. It didn't appear he devoted as much time or energy toward our white teammates. He was in his element, though, when we hung out at North Carolina Central University, the state's historically Black college down the road, or on campus at the Black bench.

The bench was a spot in the middle of the quad where a lot of African American students congregated between classes.

It was dedicated to the class of 1948, an era when Blacks were not even allowed on campus. Somehow, slowly through the years, Black students took it over. The bench became a nexus for deep discussions, fraternization, and gossip among the school's Black student body. The joke was that if you stayed long enough, every Black student who had ever attended Duke would eventually stop by.

Much of the conversation at the Black bench and the rest of campus that fall circulated around North Carolina's senatorial race between the Republican incumbent, Jesse Helms, and his Democratic challenger, Harvey Gantt.

Helms employed David Duke–level divisive politics, appealing to barely veiled racist fears against Gantt, who had served as Charlotte's first Black mayor. Helms had once derided the historic 1964 Civil Rights

Act as the single most dangerous piece of legislation ever introduced in Congress.

You needed that job and you were the best qualified, but they had to give it to a minority because of a racial quota, warned one of his ominous advertisements. *Is that really fair? Harvey Gantt says it is. Gantt supports Ted Kennedy's racial quota law that makes the color of your skin more important than your qualifications.*

There was no Google. *SportsCenter* made up most of my television viewing. I learned about Helms and his disgusting politics from enlightened fellow students. For the first time in my life, I really homed in on the stakes of an election. I had taken a civics class in high school. We engaged in current events and local politics, the troubles of D.C.'s mayor, Marion Barry, the teachings and speeches of Malcolm X and Martin Luther King Jr. Those conversations were superficial compared with the ones that surrounded this senatorial contest.

That race impacted us all. Duke's student body was intimate, compared with other universities. At times, I felt like I was at a slightly larger high school. For weeks, we seldom talked about the approaching basketball season, movies, or music. We engaged in deep discussions on serious issues that affected North Carolina politically, from a policy standpoint, and reputationally, from a national perspective. The interactions proved my instincts right about Duke, beyond just basketball: I was stepping into an ecosystem where an expectation existed, not just to be successful on the court, but that students were there to develop their intellect at all times, and not only inside the classroom.

One of the things I enjoyed most my freshman year was that the athletes lived in regular dorms, sprinkled in with the rest of the student body. The setup allowed me to foster a wider set of relationships, to feel a part of the larger university. I met Christina Murphy, a senior, who became like the big sister I never had. We lost touch after she graduated, but in those early days she provided a sounding board where I could project my anxieties about competing on the court and in the classroom at Duke. She also gave me advice, like which girls I should stay away from. Our relationship was purely platonic, and I was always grateful for her during that period of my life.

The conversations with Christina and others were both enlightening and intimidating. You think our basketball team was talented? I formed bonds with students who advanced to become groundbreaking doctors, influential lawyers, powerful politicians. Everyone I met seemed opinionated and passionate, whereas I had spent a childhood without much of a social life beyond sports, and I occasionally still hyperventilated words when I got overly excited.

Students erected booths campaigning for Gantt at the Bryan Center, our student union in the heart of West Campus. Every day, our student newspaper, *The Chronicle*, featured a front-page update on the race. For many, this provided our first glimpse at divisive political tactics. Helms had firmly planted his roots on the side of segregation, racism, and homophobia. The hope of uprooting him galvanized students of all colors on campus. We were embarrassed that he represented our state. A significant number of Duke students hailed from the New York metropolitan area, and some of my out-of-state friends were inspired enough to change their registration to vote in the midterm election.

Gantt admirably refused to be pulled into the mud. Students were surprised that Michael Jordan, probably the state's most well-known son and certainly its most famous Black man, did not throw his support behind Gantt. Later it came out that Jordan had joked on a bus with his Bulls teammates that Republicans bought sneakers too. I wonder if Jordan's endorsement could have tilted the race. Gantt lost by about a hundred thousand votes.

Unbeknownst to me at the time, Dean Smith had asked my dad during my recruitment to publicly blame Jesse Helms and his politics if I decided to commit to a school outside the state. The request just showed where Coach Smith's heart had been for decades.

———

Laettner's occasional obnoxiousness aside, we were a fairly close-knit group. Coach K insisted that freshmen rely on upperclassman teammates to foster camaraderie. For example, he prohibited freshmen from bringing cars to campus. Tony and I called Brian Davis whenever we needed to go to a party off campus or attend a movie. Even now, I can hear his voice, insisting that he'll be arriving outside in his Volkswagen Jetta in just a few minutes.

Brian grew up in Prince George's Capitol Heights. He was a good high school basketball player, not a great one. No disrespect. I just definitely scratched my head when I read that he signed to Duke. Years later, Mike Brey, an assistant coach, filled in the gaps by telling me that Duke didn't so much recruit Brian as Brian recruited Duke. Brian was one of those guys who would use basketball as part of his journey, not the end goal. He always played the long game, chess when the rest were playing checkers. He interned at increasingly impressive businesses every summer and was the first person I ever saw wearing brands like Armani and Hugo Boss. He was fun to be around, but he could also be a blowhard.

Alone, he was the life of the party. Together with Laettner, they formed quite a pair, propping each other up on and off the court. Laettner was peak Laettner with his buddy at his side. I'll never forget the time someone showed me one of Laettner's magazine interviews.

My three areas of focus, he said in the story, are school, basketball, and Brian.

An on-campus rivalry existed with some of the school's football players. They talked trash to Laettner and Brian, teasing them about their friendship.

You know who keeps the lights on on this campus? Brian would declare. It ain't y'all. Y'all want new uniforms next year? Y'all need to shut up.

Together, inside Brian's Jetta, we caravanned to a Chapel Hill party for one of our first group outings. Enemy territory. I spotted Brian Reese, my friend from Five-Star who was now a Tar Heel. We didn't even acknowledge each other. The rivalry between the schools was deep, even though we had yet to play each other.

Later, Laettner called, instructing Tony and me to hurry up. He had purchased a new car, a Honda Accord, and wanted to take us for a spin. Tony hopped in shotgun. I jumped into the backseat. He drove to a hospital with a massive new parking lot still slick from a recent storm.

I had no idea what he was doing. Laettner floored it in the parking lot, pulled the clutch, and performed donuts. I gripped my seat, hoping, praying that I would survive the evening. He finally stopped, returning us to our place.

What? Why? How? I was simply confused. This dude was the player of the year, and now he was out here acting like Evel Knievel.

Laettner was cool with us, but a tension existed between him and Bobby. Laettner was always on Bobby, incessantly poking and needling, needling and poking. It was constant, to the point where even as a bystander I felt fatigued by the interactions. On the bus, he dissed Bobby's suit. On the training table, he made fun of how Bobby stretched. Occasionally, Laettner would just pick up a random shoe in the locker room and toss it at Bobby. Personally, I didn't get it. I wanted to keep my point guard happy. He was the guy feeding me the ball, getting me buckets.

Bobby was a tough, proud kid. His dad could probably whup us all. One day soon, Tony and I agreed, Bobby was just going to have to swing on Laettner no matter the repercussions.

At one early practice, Bobby dribbled the ball while Laettner yapped. Bobby entered the paint, stopped, and launched the ball right into Laettner's face, not even trying to make a play. Bobby immediately took off with Laettner a few steps behind him. Thankfully, the one thing Bobby had on Laettner physically was speed.

Maybe Laettner was like that a little with all of us, gauging to see how we reacted to different situations. He made fun of my ears, and I brushed him off. He just took it too far with Bobby, to the point of often being a jerk. He could very easily have broken his spirit. Laettner was one of a kind, a personality I had never witnessed before or after (except for a brief time together as professionals). He kept things on edge, ingesting tension for fuel.

———

Those early days moved fast, so fast that today I can hardly recall my college debut.

I started my first game. It was a privilege to start as a freshman at Duke, and I didn't take it lightly. We beat Marquette in the Preseason NIT. If I had to stretch my mind, I probably scored about a dozen points, most from our motion offense and layups. I certainly was not asking for the ball.

We followed with another win, inside Cameron, over Boston College. Next, we hit the road, traveling to New York and the Garden, where we faced Arkansas. A year earlier, the Razorbacks fell in the Final Four against Duke. They had a player, Todd Day, whom I enjoyed watching. I'm still a sucker for big guys who can shoot and operate on the perimeter.

Arkansas wiped the floor with us. Really, it was not even close.

Coach, again, you sure about that prediction?

Soon, we were set for a showdown against Georgetown, my Georgetown, in the arena where I fell in love with basketball, the Cap Centre.

It ended up being the worst day of my life.

I had a ten-page paper due the same day for a writing course that I procrastinated starting until the last possible minute. I scrambled to borrow a computer and hammered it out the night before.

Sometime after midnight, I finally finished. I planned to ease it under my professor's door on my way to the bus and the airport. We were flying the day of the game, a fluke that didn't happen again during my four years in Durham.

Instead, my fingers slipped, managing to fumble upon some fatal combination of keys. The entire thing was deleted, vanishing off my screen. I spent the night frantically rewriting the paper. I even woke up Kenny Blakeney and his roommate, Steve Spurrier Jr., just to figure out how to print the thing.

I turned in the paper and sprinted back to my dorm with barely enough time to shower, dress, and meet our bus at Cameron.

We were a somewhat undersized team. Most teams were against Georgetown, with their twin Goliaths, Alonzo Mourning and Dikembe Mutombo. Before I knew it, I was jostling Mutombo in the post, giving up several inches and no doubt hours of sleep to him. I barely possessed the wherewithal to register that I was playing in a televised game against a school I rooted for, in front of John Thompson, a coach I grew up adoring, inside an arena where I had watched dozens of games with my mom.

My legs dragged. Each change of possession required a conscious, deliberate choice to run up the court. Honestly, if I scored, I don't even remember it. They ran up a lead. We crept back in once Mutombo collapsed with leg cramps. He was like a giant oak going down to the ground, and I can recall, as we were huddled in a time-out afterward, that I could have literally fallen asleep that moment. That was probably the only game of my Duke career, maybe my entire life, when I ever felt so out of it. We just were not ready for the game. I was not ready. Georgetown maintained their edge for a narrow victory.

What a homecoming.

As time went on, I learned how to better manage my time during the season. Having a lot on my plate forced me to be structured and focused. I learned to juggle schoolwork, practice, travel, games, and my social life. But not necessarily in that order.

I frequented the university's library more often to avoid the distraction of people popping in at my dorm. But people often hung out at the library as well, and I often lost myself in conversation before realizing I had been there for a couple hours without getting any work accomplished. I decided to venture farther into the library where fewer people congregated in the stacks. But that storage area was narrow, dark, and quiet, and I'd find myself dozing off there before I'd gotten much of anything done.

I mostly crammed my way through my freshman year, stiff-arming reading or homework until the last possible moment. I didn't get consistent sleep or retain much information, but I managed my way through. My next three years at Duke involved acclimating myself to the school workload, just like I had to do on the basketball court. I learned to do a portion of assignments each day instead of waiting until the last minute and creating unnecessary stress. As a result, I earned better grades and was able to better comprehend the material. Both were wins.

Over the next few games, I was awake—for one—and adjusting, trying to mute the anxiety that arrived with performing at this level, that part of me that had made that call over the summer to Tommy Amaker. There were players, some my contemporaries, who desired a stage and spotlight early in their college careers. They did Jedi mind tricks, constructing a confidence that outpaced their skill, which then allowed their play to outpace their abilities on the court.

Those guys and their will amazed me. I was comfortable sliding in, filling a role, and sought consistency for our team and myself. We found a little of that following the Georgetown loss by stringing wins over a pre–Fab Five Michigan team, Harvard, Oklahoma, Lehigh, and Boston University.

Oklahoma and their terrific guard, Brent Price, were a key test for us, and my first legitimate road game just before Christmas. CBS aired the game with Jim Nantz and Billy Packer on the call.

The Sooners pressed, trying to force the tempo. We scrambled, limiting their three-point shooting in the second half as I contributed nineteen points. Thomas Hill locked down Price, and we handed Oklahoma their first home loss in fifty-one games.

After the Arkansas and Georgetown losses, a win like that offered comfort. On the flight home, I started believing, hoping, that maybe I could impact games on this level like the rest of my teammates.

No matter if our team was up or down, Laettner continued impressing. His fundamentals and footwork were textbook. With a feathery touch, he was our best free-throw shooter. Yes, there was that edge to him. It was a quality that made you antsy until you were in the foxhole with him.

Bobby, while tough, could be impacted by exterior forces like an opponent or the officials. One day, Coach played us a montage of Bobby reacting to various calls by throwing his hands up or being dismayed over the officiating. One by one, Coach asked us how the video made us feel. He showed another clip, one of a stoic Bobby on the court, collected and determined. Coach posed the same question.

It makes me feel like we're going to win, I said.

Coach liked switching up arrangements when we traveled, allowing various teammates to know one another better. Tony roomed with Laettner when we traveled for an early Atlantic Coast Conference game against Virginia.

It was late and I was restless, so I went to see what was going on in their room. Not long thereafter, six or seven of us were acting like the college kids we were, slap boxing and wrestling. At one point, the hotel's manager knocked, asking us to quiet down. We were silent for a couple minutes before revving back up again.

The next day, Virginia blitzed us in an afternoon game in front of a large contingent of my friends and family. Laettner was our only consistent scorer. The rest of us didn't even belong on the court.

Afterward, no one spoke during the long bus ride from Charlottesville to Durham. When we parked, Coach K instructed us to get dressed and taped. He wanted us on the court in fifteen minutes.

We had just played in a game. We were about to practice?

I turned to Brian. Is this normal?

It's going to be one of those types of practices, he said.

I had seen Coach passionate, intense, thoughtful, measured.

Following the losses to Georgetown and Arkansas, he voiced his dissatisfaction. After this day, I could say that I had seen him livid, embarrassed over our effort.

We scrambled to get ready for practice, still exhausted from the game, and began with taking charge drills by forming two lines. A person from one line ran full speed at a person in the other, who absorbed the contact and fell backward.

Next, we assembled at the baseline. Coach rolled the ball out as two players dove, fighting for possession. Soon, we were onto five-on-five scenarios. The defense had to run whenever the offense scored.

During one of these drills, Tony rose for a dunk, and when I tried blocking his attempt from the weak side, his elbow connected with my face. Blood gushed from my nose. Immediately, I knew it was broken.

Practice stopped as I was attended to by our medical staff. You're welcome for the breather, guys. The staff guided me to a hospital where the bleeding finally stopped. I caught a glimpse of myself in the mirror, horrified at the reflection. I looked like I had just gone a round or two with Mike Tyson. A doctor said he would have to manually realign the bones and cartilage. First, he inserted a nasal spray that constricted the blood vessels, maneuvering what felt like a crowbar deep up my nose.

The discomfort was otherworldly. I couldn't help but cry. The staff offered some pain relievers and sent me on my way. The freshman dorms were still closed because we were on a winter holiday recess, so I retreated to the Durham Hilton. My head hit the pillow, ending one of the longest days of my life.

In the morning, a throbbing headache woke me up. I showed up at practice, where I was met with concern. Everyone agreed that I should be monitored. Coach K volunteered his house.

He drove us over after practice. His place was a step or two above the Hilton. The real Krzyzewskiville. Mrs. K offered me the room of their daughter Debbie, who was also a Duke student currently living in an apartment off campus. That first night, my brain felt as though it were trying to rattle outside my forehead. Unable to sleep, I ventured into the kitchen, amazed at the array of Häagen-Dazs pints to choose from.

From a nearby room, I noticed the glare of a monitor and peeked my head around a corner. It was two in the morning. Coach K was watching reel-to-reel tape from one of our practices on a projector, taking notes.

He glanced up, noticing me, and motioned for me to join him for a few minutes. Prior to that interaction, I was oblivious to the amount of dedication and hours he poured into his craft. I attended practice, worked hard, left, and continued with the rest of my life. It hadn't really registered that his job extended beyond the moments we were together. I had a deeper appreciation for his commitment.

There are inevitably turning points every season when a team can either splinter or unite. Greg Koubek called a meeting at his place after the Virginia loss, pleading for us to play together. Brian singled out Bobby's play as our problem, and the Jersey in Bobby erupted. Thomas Hill spoke in his defense. Bobby and Billy McCaffrey eventually stormed out.

I played on teams where I had been sucker punched or drawn into fighting, but I had never seen anything quite like that. I still wondered why Brian and Laettner seemed to pick on Bobby so often. To me, he offered everything he had each game. Years later, I found out that the strains predated my arrival. Laettner had to slowly earn his starting spot, scrapping for minutes when he came to Duke. In his mind, Coach gifted Bobby the keys the moment he stepped on campus. Bobby might have had Coach's trust. He still had to work for Laettner's.

Once the pain subsided, I was outfitted with a face mask that reminded me of Jason's from those slasher movies. I hated wearing it, but it was the price of being medically cleared to play.

Coach, we were fully aware after the practice from hell, was challenging us. We responded by nearly doubling up a Georgia Tech team featuring a talented Kenny Anderson and won comfortably over Maryland, Wake Forest, and the Citadel.

We were practicing with Carolina looming next at Cameron. It was a routine session. No one lagged, beyond a missed defensive assignment or a sloppy play or two, normal of any practice.

After one such mundane miscue, Coach's whistle shrieked. He was upset, disappointed in our mindsets, and ordered us out of the gym.

As I retreated to the locker room, the practice cycling through my head, I wondered where and what we did wrong. The older players, having been kicked out of a practice or two in their time, instructed us to wait a couple minutes. Then we returned to the court.

Word filtered to the assistant coaches. Coach K came back. Practice resumed.

In hindsight, I wondered if Coach planned all along to kick us out to send us a message. I was glad that the older players showed resolve in sending a signal back to him that yes, we were ready for the moment.

After practice, conversation revolved around the Carolina game. There's nothing like it, my teammates explained.

To that point, we had played good, quality teams, deep squads like Arkansas, Oklahoma, and Georgetown. I sensed the energy ratchet up even more as we entered conference play, partly due to the familiarity between the programs, the teams, and their coaches. There was a shared history you were entering, even if you were just stepping in for a couple pages of a chapter.

Could the magnitude ramp up even more?

The anticipation for the Carolina game on campus was palpable. Students cycled through matchups between classes. The lines that the Crazies formed to secure tickets began earlier than ever, snaking longer than the eye could see.

Duke, between the university and the hospital, was the largest employer in Durham. We were only seven miles apart from that campus in Chapel Hill. Inevitably inside a cafeteria, bookstore, or café, a Carolina fan worked behind enemy lines and would slyly sneak in a word or two of trash talk. I don't know if other rivals like Michigan and Ohio State or Florida and Florida State also had such a tangled, intimate relationship.

To be fair, Carolina's fandom was not just understandable but relatable. They were successful, historic, a state school—actually, the state's school. From Frank McGuire to Dean Smith, Carolina boasted a tradition of cutting down nets and winning championships.

Meanwhile, we were the upstart private university with students from all over the country who just couldn't cross that ultimate finish line.

The noise was earsplitting when we took the court the evening of the game. Rick Fox quickly spurred a Carolina run. We forced them into a few turnovers. The game was mostly even when we witnessed a leap in Bobby's maturation and our team's unity.

A year earlier, as a freshman, Bobby lost focus against Carolina's King Rice, who psyched him out of his game. Carolina's defense had featured a lot of traps, designed to pester a ball handler outside his comfort zone. Back then, Bobby reacted, got flustered, and committed ten turnovers to his single assist. The team didn't have many penetrating guards beyond him. When he couldn't navigate a path, the entire offense collapsed.

Now we were more resourceful. Billy McCaffrey and I could handle the rock, relieving some of Bobby's burden. Bobby was also older, better. At one point, he and Rice dove on the floor for a loose ball.

Coach prioritized toughness, both mental and physical. Diving for loose balls was a requisite to play for him. He often told us stories of growing up the son of first-generation Polish Americans in Chicago's West Side. A mugger once tried robbing his mother. "Tried" was the operative word. She refused to release her grip until the frightened robber fled. When asked why she had not given up her purse, she answered with a question of her own: Why would she? It was her purse.

We should, Coach would say, scrap for every ball that touches the hardwood with the same mindset. There are no fifty-fifty balls. Every ball has Duke on it.

He valued the same mindset for taking charges. It was so ingrained in me by the time I got to the NBA that without thinking twice, I took the brunt of Karl Malone barreling toward me with a full head of steam. It required sacrifice and selflessness to put your body on the line for the team's sake.

If a player wasn't willing to dive on the floor and take charges, he didn't last long in that program.

All of us were primed for a fight. Coach included. One of my favorite moments of each game was watching Coach K walk out onto the court. He entered like he was anticipating a street fight. Poised, collected, but at the ready. In later years, I occasionally tried sneaking into his office to catch him off guard. I never did. You remember those Dave Chappelle sketches with Charlie Murphy? The ones where Rick James radiated his aura with that glow? It sounds weird, but that's Coach. Confidence and leadership radiated from him.

That was the mentality he expected of his players.

Bobby knew that. He fought for the ball, refusing to react when Rice approached him after the two had become entangled.

Laettner, from nowhere, stepped between the two, shoving Rice.

A true big bro. He picked on his teammates for his own amusement. He was just not going to let anyone else mess with us.

The sequence was pivotal and not just in the moment. It carried over the next couple of seasons in cementing their relationship: they would guard each other's backs and value winning above all else. The two ran hot and cold away from the court. One would never know that from watching their synchronicity during a game. A lot of Bobby's threes were the product of Laettner collecting a rebound and kicking the ball out to him. A lot of Laettner's buckets originated from Bobby penetrating into a defense and finding him.

We surged in the second half, coasting to a healthy win in my first taste of the Carolina rivalry.

We were elated. Coach cautioned us to accept the high but not to let our emotions overwhelm us. We played North Carolina State in a couple of days at their place, and it would be another charged atmosphere. It's a quick turnaround, Coach said, this is exactly how it'll be during the tournament.

Of course, we were a no-show at State, lacking in purpose and effort. As great a game as we played against Carolina, we were the opposite at State. Our short bus ride home from Raleigh felt like it dragged on for hours. Coach broke the silence on our arrival. With the exception of the Virginia game, we typically went our separate ways once back at Cameron. Instead, he gathered us in the locker room. Once inside, Coach voiced his disappointment that we couldn't handle the success of winning a big game and be emotionally prepared for the subsequent one.

By the next day, he was still fuming. We found a cleared locker room. The portraits, the nets, they were all gone. Our laundry piled up in the middle of the room for us to sort out ourselves. It was all part of his psychology—forcing us to learn, to grow, to be upset and demand more from ourselves.

I'm sure our uneven play frustrated Coach. It was disheartening for all of us that we stumbled on cue each moment we appeared primed to become a dominant, reliable team.

That aim for consistency was on our minds as we bounced back with wins over Clemson, Georgia Tech, Notre Dame, and a revenge victory over Virginia, no extra practice or broken nose needed.

———

Chris Webber and I stayed as close as we could. He dominated his high school competition, a man among boys, as the best Michigan product since Magic Johnson. He asked me about my experience at Duke. I told him that it was fulfilling. Coach K demanded a lot. He also got the best from players.

I wasn't surprised Duke survived the cut when Chris whittled down his choice of colleges.

I hosted Chris for his recruiting visit. He arrived just as Louisiana State came to town, and that night we caught a glimpse of some of the NBA's All-Star weekend. Shawn Kemp amazed everyone in the room during the dunk contest by leaping and bringing the ball to his knees before windmilling it home with ferocity. Everyone except Chris. I can do that, he said casually. No one doubted him.

Chris sat behind our bench while we took down Shaquille O'Neal and the Tigers at Cameron. Laettner shut down Shaq in the game, limiting him to four points after halftime.

We organized a quick party for Chris at a house Laettner and Brian

Davis rented. We were aiming for a quiet atmosphere, a setting where we could chop it up about playing together at Duke. But word traveled fast. Everyone wanted to see the nation's top recruit. I arrived a little late. I had bumped my hip diving for a loose ball during the game and spent some extra time with the medical staff. When I got there, people already spilled out the door. I wiggled my way past them, spotting people I recognized from North Carolina Central University and North Carolina A&T.

Chris, I'm sure, viewed Duke as a preppy, private school. Coach K ran a tight ship. Laettner and Bobby were the offensive fulcrums. I hoped Chris could see the truth beyond that. Anyone could find their place here, just like I did. Coach K's skill was in melding individuals into one team.

I greeted Chris and sensed that he was pleasantly surprised. He sat down, held court, absorbing it all. People approached him, asking about his decision. He played it coy, not offering a commitment one way or the other.

Would he fit here? Coach K asked the next day. Would you want to play with him?

Yeah, I told Coach. He'd fit right in.

I could already imagine how dominant we'd be with Chris. We'd be Vegas. The Runnin' Rebels were always out there on the periphery. I saw their clips on highlight shows. They were demolishing competition, slicing through opponents.

A few weeks later, Chris announced his commitment to Michigan. The decision surprised me because, from the conversations we had after the party, I thought he was leaning toward Michigan State to follow in Magic's footsteps. I don't know if we ever had a legitimate shot at Chris. Recruits typically didn't leave when their home states featured blue-chip programs. I had played at the McDonald's All-American Game in Indianapolis a year earlier when Eric Montross had just spurned Indiana for North Carolina. I felt the tension, and really the disdain, that people had for Montross over his decision. Webber had even more potential. I thought he was too big of a recruit for the state to lose.

We were peaking, playing our best basketball at the right time of the season. Even our infrequent losses provided moments of affirmation. We traveled to Arizona to play a Wildcat team whose entire roster was seemingly seven feet. We clawed to force the game into one overtime and then another. The game was so tense, the air so dry, that the gum I grinded on dissolved into paste by the time the second overtime opened. We dropped the game, knowing that we could and should have beaten them. It was a different emotion from what had accompanied the losses to Georgetown and Arkansas, when I departed wondering if we belonged on the court at all.

We took care of Carolina at their place and played them again a week later at Charlotte in the championship of the ACC Tournament. Coach explained the difficulty in defeating a team three times in one season: they were familiar with us, hungry for revenge. I didn't think we were complacent or overlooked them. They were just sensational in the game and hammered us. No one liked losing or being embarrassed. In retrospect, the loss was humbling, offering a reset and confirmation that we were not good enough to simply show up and win.

After the loss, we met in a restaurant to watch the NCAA's tournament selection show: we were seeded third in the Midwest Regionals. I watched Coach closely, curious to witness his reaction. I had seen him seethe over losses, instilling a collective hatred for losing. He had cleaned out our locker room the last time we didn't compete in a game. This time, he chalked it up as just a bad evening. With the regular season and ACC Tournament behind us, we now faced a six-game season in front of us.

For years, I had watched the tournament, first from my basement, then attending Final Fours in person. It was the place of origin stories for basketball superheroes. To participate in it, to feel a sense of optimism about my team, didn't seem real. It was difficult focusing on anything else in the days leading up to the tournament. I was locked in at practices. Any class I attended was a blur.

As we traveled to Minneapolis, Coach broke down the larger journey into smaller steps, advising us to focus on the bracket's three other teams and to win the weekend's four-game tournament.

We were prepared and raced past Louisiana Monroe in the opener.

Iowa, in our second-round matchup, tried the Oklahoma gambit of pressing us. We turned their strengths against them by situating Bobby at the free-throw line, while Thomas Hill, Brian Davis, and I hovered around mid-court. Laettner often bypassed Bobby to inbound the ball to one of us. From there, we were off to the races.

We were sprinters. We joked that if one of us was in front of the other, we might have yanked him back just to dart in front of him. In earlier games, we'd have so many fast breaks that I swear Laettner occasionally grabbed a rebound and plodded up court with the ball before handing it off to Bobby, almost as if to insist that he touched the ball that possession.

We were up and down the entire Iowa game. Teams that liked to press, Coach said, do not like to be pressed themselves. We flew on defense, harassing Iowa out of its comfort zone, denying their wings, applying pressure, attacking, and dictating. We transformed the game into a dunking field day and coasted to an easy win. "Skywalkers," I believe, was how we were described in the next day's paper.

Our next grouping, we were aware, would be more challenging. We flew home for a brief respite before departing for Michigan. A team out for revenge was dangerous, Coach admonished us. Connecticut, our Sweet 16 opponent, possessed a year's worth of pent-up motivation. Laettner's dramatic jumper as time expired in overtime upset the top-seeded Huskies in the previous season's Elite Eight. I picked up a couple early fouls in the game, taking a seat on the bench. Fortunately, the rest of the team played in sync. Laettner and Greg Koubek paced our offense. With just under six minutes left, Laettner and Connecticut's Rod Sellers scrambled for a loose ball. Sellers landed on top of Laettner, elbowing him in the face and using his forearm to crash Laettner's head into the floor.

Look, I think all of Laettner's teammates wanted to do that to him at some point. But we knew a team was unraveling when they lost their composure. We didn't need Laettner's late heroics that game. We never trailed and advanced for a comfortable victory.

A step away from the Final Four, St. John's blocked the path. They were talented, tall, and deep, led by Malik Sealy, a versatile scorer. Thomas and occasionally Brian would be looked upon to limit Sealy. Thomas had come to Duke as the least-recruited classmate, trailing Bobby and Billy McCaffrey, and didn't play much as a freshman. He had gained momentum throughout this season, displaying toughness and defensive resolve, to the point where Coach would have been remiss had he kept him off the court.

On defense, we were united against St. John's, tethered to a string, convinced that we were the better team. Their big man, Robert Werdann, aggravated an ankle injury. He was their pressure release, which meant we could squeeze them tighter. Fouls limited their top guard, Jason Buchanan. Thomas and Brian did their jobs in funneling Sealy to help. We were too deep, too focused, too much for St. John's in the win.

I waited for the moment to wash over me, still slightly shocked at how we had matured over the last couple of months. We were going to the Final Four in Indianapolis. For Coach K, it would be his fifth trip in six seasons. For me, it was the destination I wanted to go above anywhere else as a kid, the place where my fascination with basketball had blossomed into a passion for sport.

Vegas awaited. They were undefeated, unblemished, and really unbothered in their last forty-five games.

I'm giving you the day off, Coach said on our return from Detroit to Durham. Get some rest. Don't do anything crazy like shaving your heads bald all of a sudden.

———

Some teams are happy making the tournament, grateful for the opportunity to partake in the grand show. Some universities are satisfied for decades by making a Final Four. In Michigan, we bypassed cutting down the nets. Qualifying for the Final Four, Coach said, wasn't our goal.

Been there, done that. Times five.

Vegas, he continued, is a great team. As great as they've been, they haven't been in a close game all year. We've been in countless nail-biters. We've won some, lost some. They've forced us to grow.

My mind traced back to some of our practices. We cycled through countless end-of-game situations where, for example, the starters took the ball out down five with a minute left and we played it out from there. Coach sometimes recorded the sessions or took notes. Meeting with us afterward, he queried us on our decision-making, all to prepare us for a game's tense moments.

We can't get knocked out in the first few minutes, Coach said. We have to attack early. We're going to keep it close. We're going to handle their pressure. At the end, we are the ones who have been in tight games, who know how to close it out.

He was not just telling us that we were going to win. He explained how.

Vegas, we knew, was probably gazing past us to the championship game. The fashion in which they dismissed Duke a year earlier was still probably fresh in their minds. It was also still in the forefront of the minds of guys like Laettner, Bobby, and others who experienced the humiliating blowout. In practices, the starters played against seven defenders as we readied for their speed, pressure, and athleticism.

For the Final Four, I, of course, wanted to look as fresh as possible. All the Black players on the team frequented the same barber, this older African American gentleman whom Phil Henderson introduced me to while he was back on campus during the fall. His barber's chair rested in the corner of the bustling shop along with his German shepherd. The barber was a character, witty and wry, who often smoked and sipped on a little something as he cut hair.

Typically, he kept my flattop nice, high, and tight. Tony Lang and I visited him the evening before flying to Indianapolis. The barber sat Tony in his chair. He was on one that night. I clocked the empties on the counter, and he went through a couple more cans while tending to Tony's hair.

Next.

He beckoned me to sit down and started in on my hair. He had me turned away from the mirror, facing Tony. Soon, Tony was frantically motioning at me. His eyes were big, yet I was not quite catching the drift of whatever he tried passing along.

The barber finished, passing me a handheld mirror to inspect his work.

Somehow, I audibly cringed. My hair was jacked. I didn't know if his alcohol had started kicking in midway or what. There was no fade, no blend. Even the lineup was jagged, crooked like it wanted to go one way and ended up in a foreign destination. I fumed, arguing with the barber.

Tony shrugged and laughed, saying that he tried warning me.

This was the Final Four, the stage of stages. I debated shaving my head. Coach's warning echoed in my head, his reminder to not do anything crazy. I kept the cut, donning a hat for the plane ride to Indianapolis. That's how embarrassed I was.

Vegas on my mind and a crooked cut on my head, we checked in to a hotel crammed with Duke folks near the airport. A few of us visited a mall the night before the game. On a whim, we ducked inside a karaoke joint.

Tony, Brian Davis, and I, as well as one of our student managers, a friend, Mark Williams, danced and sang, or tried to dance and sing, to popular songs like "My Girl" by the Temptations. Someone taped it. Afterward, we watched the performance inside the hotel room of Tony's dad.

We laughed at our lack of vocal abilities. The parents? Their mouths were as agape as mine was at the barbershop. They were stunned, undoubtedly thinking we were oblivious kids, fledgling lambs blissfully unready for the next day's slaughter.

Luckily, we were at the RCA Dome. We had played in domes throughout the tournament—the Metrodome and the Pontiac Silverdome. Plopping a basketball court in the middle of a football field rattled depth perceptions. By then, we were used to it.

Coach's voice rattled through on the jump ball. Attack from the beginning. I anticipated the tip, stealing the possession, and streaked downcourt to lay the ball in. The sequence settled any lingering jitters.

Larry Johnson started on me defensively. I doubted he was accustomed to defending someone on the outside, a player capable of handling the ball and making plays. On defense, I matched against Stacey Augmon, a talented All-American. I always admired how he moved on defense, gliding, using his length. Laettner guarded their big, George Ackles, sagging off enough to help Greg Koubek against Johnson. Essentially, we dared Ackles to beat us.

We limited Johnson. Anderson Hunt, their off guard, picked up the slack and erupted for a scoring binge. We countered each punch, almost paranoid about allowing them to get too far in front. We were present, in the moment, fighting, picking up on their small tells of agitation.

The half ended with us down a bucket. I thought we all believed that we could compete with Vegas coming into the game, despite the concern of our parents. The first half provided the evidence, an exhale that we could not just compete but, like Coach K had preached, win.

Neither team gained much separation in a tense second half. With every stop in play, Coach offered confirmation, telling us we were exactly where we needed to be. Like Coach predicted, the experience of partaking in so many close games and practicing end-of-game situations took over like muscle memory.

Collectively, we did our jobs. Brian Davis stepped in the path of Greg Anthony, their steady point guard, and drew his fifth and final foul of the game. But Hunt was still having himself a day. With their amount of talent, someone was bound to break free. We were still bottling Johnson as I strangled Augmon into one of his worst college games.

Just three minutes remained. Brian and Koubek missed a couple of bunnies in the lane. Ackles tipped in a ball, providing Vegas with a 76–71 lead. We kicked the ball around, knowing that if we didn't answer and they came down and scored again, the deficit might be insurmountable.

The ball found Bobby a couple feet beyond the three-point line. He had played miserably in the previous season's championship and earlier this game took a shove from Johnson. With no hesitation, Bobby raised and shot. I looked at his body, the fluidity in his motion, the confidence in his face—all the things Coach harped on with Bobby—and I knew the shot was pure long before it splashed home.

Coach referenced that shot for years. At that point, we were a team incapable of winning the big one. That bucket from a player who struggled in the same matchup a year earlier at a juncture when the game could have gone either way offered us renewal.

Brian converted a three-point play with about a minute left, and Johnson's free throw knotted the game, 77–77.

Laettner collected my miss and was fouled on his putback attempt with about ten seconds left.

Time-out. Coach instructed us how to defend the final seconds.

When Christian makes these free throws, this is what we want to do, he started.

Coach didn't offer directives on what we would do if Laettner missed. He believed Laettner would sink both. I was confident in him too. Misfiring, I was certain, didn't even cross Laettner's mind.

Calmly, Laettner dropped in both free throws. Vegas called time-out as we prepared for a final defensive stand. When they came out, Johnson looked at the basket, hesitated, and passed to Hunt. When Hunt's desperation three ricocheted off the backboard, I tracked down Bobby.

Typically, we were consciously subdued after a game, win or lose. We had played Georgia Tech earlier in the season with Kenny Anderson offering us all we could handle. Thomas Hill won the game on a late layup. We were told not just by Coach but also by the older players to save the hollering for the locker room. We did not celebrate on the court unless we were commemorating a championship.

In that moment, we couldn't help it. Bobby leaped into my arms. The moment was the greatest feeling on a basketball court I experienced during my four years at Duke.

It was a sensation of pure joy, a sense of accomplishment deeper and even more rewarding than winning our first championship over Kansas a couple days later or repeating the following season. I recalled the excitement in Michael's voice as I explained to him over the phone Coach's belief that we would beat Vegas shortly before we flew to Indianapolis. He heard my conviction and, unbeknownst to me at the time, immediately placed a couple tiny wagers with fraternity brothers on Duke, probably the only person in the country who made a couple dollars from the game. No one, outside ourselves, thought we could win. This put us on par with the upsets I had watched growing up, teams persevering despite the odds. North Carolina State over Houston. Villanova topping my Hoyas. There was a blanketing pride in being the David who downed Goliath. It was like we were erasing an ending already preordained, authoring our own. There was, I'd learn, a collective exhalation and weariness in reversing roles, being the Goliath who defeated David.

I caught Coach in my periphery. Already, he was trying to calm us down, knowing it would all be for nothing if we didn't handle this high better than we did the Carolina win.

———

Growing up, sometimes during a break in action at Twin Branches, I would grab a ball and try over and over to dunk it.

This ritual took place for months during my middle school days. Each fraction of a centimeter closer provided the inspiration to continue.

Then, one day, it happened.

The ball barely crept over the rim. I might have even drawn some iron. But I had dunked.

I did it again the next day and again the day after. From then on, I didn't have to try to dunk anymore. I had it figured out. I just did it.

That's what I equated with the Vegas win. All season long, we had resiliency and grit in trying to show we were consistent and championship worthy. The Final Four victory proved it, propelling us in the championship game against Kansas and even into the next season.

Speaking of dunks, I streaked out early in the championship. Those first couple of steps in transition from defense to offense were crucial, the birth to many a successful fast break.

Bobby had the ball. He took a couple dribbles, looked up, and lofted the ball toward me. Instinctively, I jumped probably higher than I've ever leaped before and slammed the pass home. The game continued. Only later, as we were accepting trophies, did I even recall the dunk when "One Shining Moment" played and they looped the game's highlights. That was crazy, Brian Davis told me. He had his own highlight in the game, a dunk when he caught their defense sleeping and finished off an alley-oop with a devilish grin aimed right at the camera.

Only BD would know exactly where to find the lens in that moment.

We were locked in that game, living inside every moment. Kansas had upended Carolina earlier in the tournament, denying us an in-state championship game. I did my job in bottling Alonzo Jamison, who had just earned the MVP of his region. We played with purpose and determination, and the outcome never felt in doubt.

We had reached our peak and, at that point, began traveling downhill.

Soon after, I witnessed the benefits of being a national champion. Or, more accurately, the perks of rolling with Brian Davis, the national champion. Brian, Laettner, Tony, and Thomas all visited my house once school was out.

Dad, as a birthday present, had bought me a Toyota Land Cruiser. Michael invited us to a formal at the University of Virginia. Laettner, of course, was the only white dude in attendance. He was in his element, as always, comfortable as ever. It was actually admirable.

We drove back to Durham that weekend. Somehow, Brian was now connected with Bell Biv DeVoe's tour manager. They were coming up to Carolina for their next concert and sought a pickup game.

We obliged, telling them to meet us at Chapel Hill High School. We bet, and if they lost, they had to bring us onstage at the concert. Bobby ran circles around them. It was hard not to laugh. Really, Michael Bivins was probably the only member of the group who maybe, possibly, had dribbled a basketball before.

That night, we attended their concert at the Dean Dome. We were excited, watching Keith Sweat and Johnny Gill perform from close range. Then Bell Biv DeVoe came out. They motioned for us to join them. Laettner, Tony, Brian, and I walked onstage. They were the biggest R&B group around at the time. Their dancers crowded us, getting into the groove. I wondered if this moment could possibly get any better.

I gazed at the audience, attempting to take the moment all in.

In the first couple of rows, right in the center of the crowd, I spotted Carolina's Rick Fox. The look of utter disgust on his face was palpable.

I honestly could've left college with no other experiences. That moment, right there, would've been enough.

5

WHAT we have, we won, Coach K said, nobody is going to take your title. We have the banner. We have the trophy. We have the championship rings. We went to the White House.

We're not defending anything.

He was at the whiteboard again. *1992 National Champions*, he wrote.

A coach could strategize in myriad ways. He could do all the prep work beforehand, watch film until his eyes hurt, scribble the perfect play. If he didn't have players truly ready to buy in, to hang on every word he preached as the gospel truth, then he had a problem.

Part of coaching, at least a commonality in the good ones, is the ability to cultivate and nourish that unyielding faith. It was one of Coach K's innate characteristics, the skill to nudge and push his players to trust in him, themselves, the team.

He chose his words intentionally, paced deliberately. We were not defending or protecting anything that was already rightfully ours. We were not going to be protective or timid, waiting to absorb an opponent's punch.

No. We were continually chasing. We were the aggressors. We were hungry in pursuit of a championship.

The reframing worked. I had never looked at our title defense from that lens. Flip it, and the burden eased. We were to play offense instead of defense. Attack instead of react.

I had spent the summer slowly acclimating, accepting an infant popularity. I was a national champion, the Duke starter with the crazy haircut. I became conscious of stares. People noticed me and approached either with compliments or to jokingly talk trash. I had started to feel more comfortable in social settings. I took a public speaking course as a freshman. So much of life, I was learning, relied on being able to communicate, sell, project, present. The course was learning through interacting, reciting speeches, maintaining eye contact, critiquing one another.

One day, a radio show back home requested a joint interview with my parents. By then, I had moved into an on-campus apartment with Tony Lang. People were always dropping by, blasting music, blaring the television. I ducked into the bathroom for the spot, answering a couple of questions. My responses were thoughtful, reflective, relatively mature. The words didn't spill clumsily from my mouth. My parents called me after the interview and complimented me, no doubt wondering what had happened to their reserved son. I told them that I thought it stemmed from the success and the profile of playing at Duke. It forced you, whether in interacting with the media or being noticed around campus and town, to become comfortable with being uncomfortable.

Now, our team's destination made clear, Coach K focused on Brian Davis, jotting his name on the whiteboard.

Below Brian's name, Coach K wrote *student.* Below that, *athlete.* Below that, *community organizer.* Below that, *entrepreneur.* He added several more titles before circling the first two. This, he said, is what we need you to focus on. We stifled laughs. I'll give it up to Brian and Christian Laettner, who would again be our emotional leaders. Coach could get on them, but they never rolled their eyes or dissed him when we were alone. They took the digs, and the rest of us, the underclassmen, followed their lead. The message was obvious. It was time to refocus and align our priorities.

Laettner was back. So was Bobby Hurley. They were still somewhat distant. Laettner was Laettner after all. But it was nothing like the year before. Winning had a way of thawing relationships. We returned nearly every major contributor from last season. We were the new Vegas, the assumed preseason favorite, the proven commodity, the team that opponents were going to circle on their schedule long before they were even on our radar. Cherokee Parks was our significant addition. He was a laid-back California kid, regarded as one of the best bigs in a talented class. Cherokee was looked on as Laettner's successor in the lineage of Duke bigs. Laettner had taken over for Danny Ferry, and I always got the impression that Danny had not exactly extended the welcome mat for Laettner. Laettner could be hard on most of the team, but he immediately took Cherokee under his wing. Cherokee could shoot, possessed lively legs, and protected the rim.

Curious students had occasionally filed into Card Gym to watch our open runs a year earlier. This season, the crowd doubled and tripled in size. We put on a show. After losing a couple of guys who transferred, Coach K opted to fill out the team with a walk-on and held tryouts among the student body. Ron Burt, the roommate of Mark Williams, earned the spot. We had all balled with him before and knew that he was an athlete. He was a likable, energetic guy who ended up becoming our sacrificial lamb. Our first unit featured me, Laettner, Bobby, Brian, and Thomas Hill. Ron was often point guard of the second unit, alongside Cherokee, Tony, Marty Clark, and Christian Ast. Often, we claimed a steal and sprinted out on a fast break with a lonely, helpless Ron back on defense. RON BURT! we would yell as either Brian or I rose and finished an alley-oop from Bobby over his head.

Those were the moments I fondly recall from those early practices, how in sync we were from the beginning. We'd sometimes run a half-court drill where possessions were supposed to alternate with every defensive stop. Only, the starters usually scored again and again, and we typically never switched until Coach K called for one. We'd laugh afterward, arriving in the locker room and spotting Ron Burt sitting on the floor, exhausted, defeated.

Coach K tweaked his approach each of my four years at Duke. He altered his methods as needed, applying pressure here and easing it there. He recognized that an inherent pressure existed, even if it was unspoken, in vying for back-to-back championships. The feat hadn't been replicated since those great UCLA dynasties. He had dragged us to the finish line last season. My sophomore year, he carefully paced us to ensure that we stayed sharp and fresh. Our practices were not as long or physical. The occasional moments he did choose to light into us carried greater heft.

We opened with an exhibition game at Cameron against the USSR. Leading up to it, all I could think about was watching them beat the 1988 U.S. Olympic team from the basement of my parents' house. They downed a talented squad guided by John Thompson that featured Danny Manning and David Robinson. It was not the same team that we were going up against, but it was close. NBC was here with Al McGuire on the call. I was jittery but didn't play like it. A mild injury sidelined Laettner, but the game still became a dunkfest. On one play, I took flight from just inside the free-throw line and crashed the ball through the rim. My teammates, those who ran with me in the scrimmages, believed I had taken that next step. Now everyone else hopefully saw it as well. Coach K had prodded me to be a leader that season, to not show deference to Laettner or Bobby. The exhibition provided a large step in that direction and we won easily.

In those days, Coach K often scheduled a game for a senior in his hometown, a gift to us for leaving home and trusting in him. For Laettner, we ventured to upstate New York to play Canisius at Buffalo Memorial Auditorium. We exited the plane and were immediately met by a horde of people, including the mayor, who gifted Laettner the key to the city.

People were starting to show up wherever we traveled, trailing us from the gate to baggage claim. Laettner was the focus of most of the adulation, whether in his hometown or elsewhere.

People had packed the duplex arena by the time we tipped off the next day. We had our way with Canisius, and the game turned into one of those open runs at Card Gym. Everyone secured their own highlight. Everyone but Laettner. Coach K pulled him aside at halftime, telling Laettner that this game was for him and he was not even being aggressive on offense.

I'm good, Laettner said. I want my hometown to see how good my teammates are.

That, in a lot of ways, was the beauty of Laettner. He was again in the conversation for national player of the year, a focal point for the top-ranked team in the country, playing in front of his friends and family. He wasn't interested in showing off for them. Instead, he wanted to show off his teammates. Laettner was often my biggest cheerleader. I would finish a dunk or make a steal, and there he was, clapping his hands, pumping me up. I know that doesn't necessarily fit neatly into the narrative of Laettner that developed since our years at Duke. But when we needed him, Laettner nearly always responded.

I don't know if a college player experienced the scrutiny that Laettner faced until Zion Williamson arrived at Cameron decades later. I always found it interesting that whenever, wherever we went, Laettner and Bobby received the bulk of the ire from the mostly white student bodies and certainly all the most vicious taunts.

Me, Brian Davis, Thomas Hill, we might have been booed, disdained for wearing the opponent's insignia, but I don't recall ever hearing anything personal or racial from fans in college.

It surprised me when Laettner conceded years later the difficulty he found in those moments, especially when fans attacked his sexuality.

For years, I had thought this man was made of Teflon. It seemed like nothing ever rattled him. He seemed to embrace it all, inhaling it like a wrestling villain and shielding us from a lot of vitriol that would've otherwise been directed at the rest of us.

———

Michigan nearly caught us slipping.

We arrived at the Crisler Arena to play the Wolverines, still relishing a pivotal victory over St. John's in the ACC/Big East Challenge.

Michigan had yet to arrive on our radar. We weren't looking past them. We just weren't really looking at them either. They were ranked eighteenth overall, and we had demolished them last season at Cameron. Chris Webber and Jalen Rose, I knew, were over there making some buzz as freshmen. But they hadn't played anyone yet, just local tune-ups like Detroit and Eastern Michigan. They weren't even the Fab Five yet. Jimmy King and Ray Jackson came off their bench.

I hoped to make early work of them before returning to Durham to focus on a test. They looked at the game as their national debut in the spotlight. Laettner keyed a first-half run, and we cruised early, up by seventeen points. Exams, here I come.

We were used to teams bending to our will, especially when our defense choked the life from a team early. They instead showed some backbone and resolve. Jimmy King nailed a couple of three-point shots. Chris was everywhere. They reeled off fourteen straight points, talking trash, mostly to Laettner. It wasn't really a conversation, nothing in depth or personal. Laettner, of course, loved it and yapped back.

We were tied at 63, 65, and 67. At one point, I was up tight on Chris, in his face, with the shot clock running down, yet he rose over me, drilling home a three.

Crap.

Laettner misfired a three, and the ball looped high in the air. Coach always said that if we secured an offensive rebound and a putback wasn't immediately available, kick the ball out as fast as possible to a shooter. The defense was usually unraveled, and the shooter would likely be open with time to lock in. Successfully executed, it was a demoralizing sequence for an opponent to force a defensive stop, only to allow a three-pointer the same possession. For us, Hurley was often that open player, hovering around the line.

Me, Laettner, Brian, Thomas—we always crashed the boards.

I was able to tip the ball to Bobby. He caught it, attempting a three, while being fouled by Chris. At the line, Bobby knocked in the three free throws.

Jalen's bucket opened the extra session. We saw the fight leave them when Chris fouled out, and we did not let the opportunity escape us. We were money from the charity stripe. I sank two. Laettner added a pair, and Bobby iced the game with a couple more. We escaped, barely, with an 88–85 win.

They probably should have beaten us. I knew then that they would never get that close. They would never catch us sleeping again. We were better coached. We had been in tighter moments, played in more close games.

We didn't scare.

———

Conference play opened after a lengthy holiday layoff. Coach K gave us the respite to pace us over the long season. Every conference game, we figured, would be dragged out, contested. The Michigan game was evidence that we were everyone's target. Most of the ACC schools featured a future pro player or two or three. Their programs were proven, their star players college fixtures for the last three or four years. Even Florida State, conference newcomers, flexed soon-to-be NBA mainstays like Sam Cassell, Bobby Sura, Doug Edwards, and Charlie Ward.

It didn't matter.

We rolled, stacking up win after win.

I was handling the ball more often, running in transition, often guarding the opposing team's best offensive player. We were so confident that we sought competitiveness wherever we could find it. Minutes for college players were precious, right? You didn't pace yourself when you were that young. Every one of us wanted to play forty minutes a game. We were on our way to blowing out Boston University when Coach K placed our second unit into the game. Boston slowly chipped away at the lead, causing enough of a dent that Coach subbed the starters back in and we reclaimed control. Once we got back home, Coach ripped into the second unit inside our locker room.

All this success right now, it's the starters, he said. They're the ones out here getting it done.

I knew he was trying to get them going. Cherokee, for instance, was mired in a funk. We thought that he would make us deeper, stronger up front, especially with how he had played early against St. John's. We needed him. But an ankle injury impeded his progress. Then Laettner started getting on him. I wasn't sure if he believed Cherokee didn't work hard enough or if he just wasn't seeing the desire he thought he had spotted early. The warmness had dissolved.

I'm not going to give you guys minutes, Coach told the second group. You have to earn them. I'll play the starters forty minutes if I have to.

Those words were motivation . . . for the starters.

They're going to come for us, Thomas said while the starting five huddled in practice the next day. Guys, I want to play forty minutes. Let's get after them.

We held nothing back during the scrimmage.

RON BURT!

Coach K had tried challenging the subs by pitting them against us. He had attacked their pride. They responded by being smacked in practice. We were too good, especially when dangled motivation, even against our own teammates.

The memory of what it felt like to lose was slowly drifting away. It had been a good ten months since our last loss, that no-show against Carolina at the ACC Tournament.

––––––

We were finally starting to feel like the standard-bearers in our own state. All the Duke Final Four appearances hadn't stood up to Carolina's championship pedigree. Now we had one too and were the top team in the nation, having reeled off seventeen straight wins when we went down Route 15-501 to face the Tar Heels.

It marked my first visit to the Dean Dome since the concert. They still possessed a deep, talented roster despite Rick Fox's ascension to the NBA.

We were tasked with taking a gym bag containing toiletries for the postgame shower, along with our shoes, for the nearby road games when we took a bus. Student managers laid our jerseys, socks, and warm-ups in front of our lockers.

Our shoes, really, were our sole responsibility as far as our playing gear.

I exited the bus, entered the locker room, and sifted through the bag to start getting dressed.

Nothing.

I didn't feel my Adidas. I dumped out the bag.

Crap. I had forgotten them back at Cameron.

I asked Mark Williams if he had an extra pair. No luck. Could the bus go back to get them? Not a chance. My mind started scrambling, thinking to all the times I had lost my house keys. Mark said he had no choice but to tell Coach K.

Coach walked over, and I thought of all the ways he was going to rip into me. Instead, he strolled past me and approached an unassuming Christian Ast, who sat three seats away.

Christian, what size shoes do you wear?

Fifteen.

Give Grant your shoes. You're not dressing.

He walked away. That was the entire conversation. Cold. Ice cold.

Ast slid his shoes off and handed them to me. I felt bad. Honestly, I did. Ast, if you're reading this, I apologize, even though we both know your Adidas saw more action that night with them on my feet.

In that moment, I was also relieved, but carried the added burden of knowing we needed to win or that fallout would land on me for not arriving mentally prepared.

We played a mixture of boxing and basketball in a seesaw game. Something happened with Bobby in the first half. He was in and out of the game with the trainers working on him on the bench. I stole a couple glances over, but the game consumed me. With Bobby out, I tried to keep us righted. Each team made their own stand. We were down two points with less than a minute left. Carolina's Eric Montross was tight on Laettner, causing him to miss on a drive.

That was Montross's overdue payback. Over the summer, Laettner, Thomas Hill, and I had played together in Cuba for the Pan American Games. They made the mistake of rooming Laettner with Montross. Laettner took the rivalry between our schools so seriously that he didn't say a word to him. Instead, he dragged his mattress out of the room each night and slept in the kitchen area.

With twelve seconds left, Carolina had possession and seemingly the game, only Brian Reese missed a layup. We went to Laettner again. He bypassed a three, took a couple steps in, and saw his runner kick out.

Game over. We had lost, 75–73. Their students stormed the court.

We retreated to a somber locker room. Bobby elevated his legs, soaking his foot in ice.

My dad visited our apartment the next day between classes and practice. Somehow, he had found out before me that Bobby was out indefinitely with a broken bone in his foot. He was tough, I thought. He had not played like his usual self for most of the game but had still gritted it out.

Coach K hadn't lit into me about the shoes, but now I thought he was sure to make an example of me at practice, with our dream of a perfect season shattered.

When Tony and I headed over, Mark Williams stopped us, saying that Coach wanted everybody dressed and in the locker room.

We're meeting in the locker room? Not the court?

It was going to be one of those kinds of meetings.

We were in there, waiting, when Mark and the other managers informed us to head over to the football stadium. Man, I thought, we're about to be running all afternoon.

To our collective surprise, a dessert station awaited to serve us.

The sun shone down. We sat on the grass, devouring sundaes.

You hear stories about the mental tricks a coach like Phil Jackson employed. I never really regarded Coach K as someone like that. In Coach, I saw someone who read his team and adjusted like an offense would to a defense. He knew when to push to gain as much as possible from us, but just as important, he was cognizant of when we needed to replenish ourselves. A day earlier, we had lost our first game in months and our point guard. We were teenagers, dealing with the constant pressure of trying to chase the magic of a season earlier. We needed a reset. I don't even think we practiced that day or dwelled on the burial of a flawless season.

The goal was to win a championship. If we had learned anything from the year before, it was to make sure that we were playing our best basketball at the right time. We had beaten a Vegas team that had entered the Final Four undefeated.

With Bobby out, Coach shifted me to point, vaulting Tony into the starting five. He was hyped for our next game, a trip to Louisiana State and another matchup against Shaquille O'Neal. Tony nearly chose to go to school there to stay closer to home, but I guess Coach K had also gotten to him first. I was happy for him. He had started a couple games our freshman year but hadn't really found a groove.

We planned to slow the game down, control its tempo. I was a different ball handler from Bobby, who was always pushing, pushing, pushing. I viewed myself as a caretaker, entrusted to initiate our offensive sets.

Shaq and Laettner both played at the top of their games. The titans almost canceled each other out. But Shaq was a one-man show. We came in waves, crashing and harassing Shaq whenever he was in the paint, doubling and tripling him. On offense, Laettner took Shaq outside his comfort zone, to the perimeter. Laettner had shot threes sporadically as a junior. As a senior, he had developed into one of the best marksmen in the country. We beat them, a team with a generational specimen, pretty easily. We were better, taking comfort in knowing that the Carolina game could now be retroactively regarded as a blip rather than the beginning of any trend. Even better, Tony had played assertively, and Cherokee was starting to get healthy.

We reeled off a couple more wins before traveling to play Wake Forest, where our focus, unfortunately, didn't accompany us. We performed sloppily, making mistakes we didn't normally make, while they played great. Somehow, we were in it late, down three with a couple seconds left and forced to go the length of the court. Coach K drew up a play to try to get Laettner a shot. I took the ball out from the far end. Trelonnie

Owens, all nearly seven feet of him, did jumping jacks, trying to obscure my sight line.

Laettner started at the free-throw line extended from our bench and darted the court's width, almost like a wide receiver. He was supposed to catch the ball, turn, and then have the whole side of the court to try to score. I cocked the ball back, looping it far and high in the air. I watched as its trajectory curved more than I had intended. Laettner grabbed the ball, but his momentum carried him just out of bounds. Turnover. Another loss. Another team's fans stormed the court.

What happened with the pass? Laettner asked in the locker room.

I thought back on some advice from Jim Warren, my AAU coach. He always told us that when we inbounded, never grab the ball from the official before our team was set in place. He also said that the defender was always supposed to be a few steps from the line, but the inbounder didn't have to be on the line. He could take a couple steps back.

If I'm ever in that situation again, I thought, I'm just going to step back a bit.

My bad, I told Laettner. Won't happen next time.

No one expected ice cream that time. Coach K was pissed. It was one of the few times that season when he was legitimately upset, disappointed in our performance and focus.

Our bus stayed quiet the hour or so it took to get back to Cameron from Wake.

I want everybody taped and dressed in fifteen minutes, Coach said.

I tried to be in the present. There was not a lot of time for reflection throughout the season while juggling school and team obligations. As I got taped, my mind drifted to a little over a year earlier to our practice after the Virginia loss. We had come a long way in a short time, maintaining the pressure of being the top team all year. We had suffered a couple of hiccups, yes. But Bobby would be back soon. I had noticed him on the bike, working out, getting closer. I was also tired, pulling nearly forty minutes every game. I guess the fantasy of all those minutes was better than the reality. I was in the starting lineup. Yet I also backed up Bobby at point, and there wasn't a backup for me.

We didn't practice, thankfully. Coach K laid into us, lashing into Laettner the hardest. He called Laettner a prima donna, telling him that he would've been better off declaring for the NBA instead of returning to Duke. Man, he's getting into him, I thought. Laettner, in my opinion, hadn't even played poorly against Wake. We were all off. In confronting him, Coach challenged all of us.

For a coach, it was genius to send a message to a team by getting after its best player. Wins could gloss over a lot of mistakes, masking issues that needed addressing. The real chances for growth, the time for sincere introspection, arrived after losses. That was the time when individuals collectively looked into the mirror. I didn't know if Laettner really needed to be singularly pushed.

We, as a team, though, needed that jolt.

———

Bobby practiced. We neared full strength.

Our health didn't last long.

My back was turned when Laettner and Cherokee Parks got into it at practice. Laettner shoved Cherokee, causing him to awkwardly spill over and into my leg. I mostly got out of the way, although my ankle was sprained.

I didn't dress against Virginia our next game, and the moment offered me a chance to take in Laettner's jersey-retirement ceremony before the contest. The irony of Laettner being in the doghouse, yet here everyone was celebrating his time at Duke, was not lost on us. I wasn't sure if Bobby was fully healthy yet, but he gave it a go in my absence. We secured the win, and Laettner played like his normal self, performing without a care.

Winning was a cure-all, except for my sprain.

The staff told me to stay behind, to rest and rehabilitate while the team flew to Los Angeles for a huge game against UCLA. The decision didn't sit well. It was a matchup I had looked forward to, the opportunity to play at a historic venue like Pauley Pavilion. Now I couldn't even enjoy the atmosphere? Bobby had traveled to road games while injured. Maybe our medical staff worried my ankle would swell during a long plane ride. I decided not to force the issue. Instead, I watched the game at Coach K's home with his family as we handled a quality opponent.

From the first day of that season, our chemistry and talent showed. Injuries forced us to adapt. We were now more methodical and deliberate. Tony remained a starter, and our defensive length disrupted offenses. I was out again with Bobby still playing himself into shape when we played one of our final conference games against Clemson. Before we knew it, we were down twenty.

Coach K pulled all the starters except for Brian.

Now, Brian was a senior co-captain with Laettner, and I write this affectionately: his confidence in himself often far exceeded his actual playing abilities. Often, his confidence was contagious, spreading to his teammates like a pathogen. In that way, his voice proved invaluable. He had us at times thinking we could dominate Michael Jordan's Bulls.

Against Clemson, Brian was as hot as I had ever seen him, nailing jumpers, getting to the charity stripe. Without him, they would have blown us out, but he and Laettner clawed us back into the game. Thomas connected on a couple late free throws, and we escaped with a one-point win.

It was one thing to steamroll teams. It showed character and grit when you were knocked back on your heels, not playing well, and still forged a path.

The bus met us just outside the locker room at Littlejohn Coliseum. We were able to avoid a cluster of fans trying to get a peek at us. We were a traveling rock show at times. You would have thought that Laettner was a lost member of New Kids on the Block. It could sometimes be overwhelming.

On the bus, Brian pulled out a box score from the game. He read off his statistics.

All you so-called All-Americans, huh? Y'all ain't too good for me to save you.

Only BD.

———

Tony Lang continued playing steady, consistent minutes. It was freeing for a player to know that his coach wouldn't automatically yank him for any minor transgression. As a starter, he found his footing.

At practice, I tested my ankle with a couple dunks. Yep, the bounce was back. I knew I could get out there again, when Coach K pulled me aside.

I don't want to mess up Tony's momentum, he informed me. I'm going to bring you off the bench and keep Tony in the starting lineup.

What about my momentum? I had worked hard, pushing myself to be healthy for our season's end. I wasn't sure if Coach intended to bring me off the bench for just a game or the rest of my time at Duke or whether I would be on the court at the end of games during closing time. I didn't ask. I still was not comfortable openly challenging Coach. I internalized it as a demotion, through no fault of my own. Any player who tells you he doesn't want to start is lying to your face.

Still, I was happy for Tony's stability. He came to Duke highly recruited. He supported me while I played even as he sometimes struggled.

It didn't affect our dynamic as teammates or roommates, though I'm sure it had to be difficult for him.

Coming off the bench provided a different rhythm, and I was looking to make an impact in my first game back at Cameron as we sought to avenge the loss to Carolina. Laettner, on the block, located me as I cut across the baseline. I dunked all over Eric Montross, wrapping my legs around his torso while hanging from the rim. We ended up with a decisive win.

Our regular season was over. We had maintained the top ranking all the way through.

On the bus down to Charlotte for the ACC Tournament, Coach K relayed his plan to keep me on the bench.

I staged a silent protest before the opener against Maryland. It was tradition for bench players to stand at the start of the game until the starters secured our first bucket.

The ball went up. Everyone stood. I stayed glued to my seat.

Tommy Amaker gave me some side eye. Now, Amaker always had a steady demeanor. There is little surprise that he became Harvard's men's basketball coach. Back then, he was only a couple years removed from wrapping up his own playing career. We all had varying relationships with the assistant coaches. They offered different perspectives from Coach K. Sometimes, they held us accountable. Other times, they whispered words of encouragement. Amaker was like a cool uncle. Tony and I often hung out in his office before practice, sifting through fan mail, shooting the breeze, talking music, hoops, and life.

You're not going to stand? Amaker asked me.

No, I ain't no bench player.

He smiled.

In Charlotte, we dominated the three games, blitzing past Maryland, Georgia Tech, and Carolina. We were clicking, probably for the first time since early February. Everybody was healthy and, not to minimize the regular season, conscious that these games were starting to matter, even as my own miniature act of defiance continued.

———

And then we nearly blew it early in the tournament.

Throughout my Duke career, Iowa was annually, stubbornly on our schedule. They were annoying and athletic, eternally seeking to stifle our rhythm with their full-court press. The previous year, we were able to turn their aggressiveness against them. We hoped for a repeat when we met Iowa again in the second round after easily disposing of Campbell in the tournament's opener.

Thankfully, we were playing at Greensboro Coliseum, close enough to home that we might as well have played the game at Cameron.

We coasted early and were up double digits in the first half. With their season on the line, they played like a team possessed. Iowa sliced into our lead with the help of some ill-timed turnovers, cutting the deficit to eight in the second half.

On a break, Bobby passed to a streaking Thomas Hill. He missed the layup but was fouled.

Before free throws, we always huddled together. Coach K harped on us to constantly talk, talk, talk, that the free flow of communication was an unselfish act. It was nothing for Coach K to kick a player out of practice if he wasn't overtly chatty. By talking, a player projected outward instead of running circles inside his own head. Talking on the court kept one present. Typically, the huddles were quick opportunities for us to discuss adjustments or relay what we were individually witnessing from a defense.

On this occasion, we gathered near our bench. Bobby and Thomas started in on each other. Thomas believed the pass should've arrived earlier. Bobby countered that he should've converted the bucket anyway.

We were within earshot of Coach K, who beckoned for a time-out.

We've got a chance to win a championship, and you guys are just messing around, he said. Come on, really?

He stood, walking toward the end of the bench. I thought he just needed some water, but he kept going. Was he so disappointed that he planned on walking out of the arena? The argument among us continued.

Coach might have used some more colorful language, but his message when he finally returned boiled down to this: if you guys don't straighten up, we're going to lose this game.

Laettner rose, looking Coach in the eye.

We're not losing, he said, before strolling over to the scorer's table. We were still in the time-out. Presumably, Coach wasn't done addressing us. He let Laettner continue on his way. A lot of coaches, especially in the heat of the moment, would have been insecure and internalized the interaction as an act of insubordination. Coach appreciated that passion. Years later, I was reminded of the moment while watching Coach K discuss Laettner during an ESPN documentary.

You have to think about Christian like fire, he said, and you are the superintendent of a building. If you handle him the right way, he can heat up every apartment in the building. But if you don't approach him the right way, he'll burn the building down.

That game, Laettner heated up. We regained our composure, got control of the game, and sent Iowa home again, advancing to another Sweet 16.

6

THERE was little time to prepare for opponents during the tournament. After a while, the venues, games, and opponents cascaded, one after the other, the only tying thread being the primal need to win in order to survive.

We were in Philadelphia after recently discarding Seton Hall in the Sweet 16. It was an emotional game for Bobby Hurley. He had played against his younger brother, Danny. The Hurleys were a tight-knit family. Some big brothers breathed to torment their siblings. At times, I was certain Laettner believed all of us were his younger brothers. And then there were brothers like Bobby. I always gathered that he was protective of Danny, eager to carve a path for him to follow. Bobby won the matchup and we won the game, advancing to play Kentucky.

They were a program rebuilding a ruined dynasty in the wake of NCAA violations. Only a few years earlier, Rick Pitino had been a guest speaker during my Five-Star camps. He had advanced to become Kentucky's young coach, fresh off a short stint in the NBA with the Knicks. His team featured Jamal Mashburn, someone I had known since our days on the AAU circuit. The guy had to have hit his growth spurt in the womb. Even back then, he had towered above the rest of us.

That was about the extent of my Kentucky knowledge.

With a few decades of hindsight, we should have been more prepared for Kentucky. They were in the Regional Finals for a reason.

Coach K summoned us for a quick film tutorial on their offense.

What are they doing? I wondered throughout the session.

Most teams conducted conventional, familiar offenses. Defensively, our objective was to disrupt that rhythm. Kentucky was one of the first teams that unabashedly embraced shooting three-pointers, resembling pseudo precursors to the Phoenix Suns team I played on years later with Steve Nash and Mike D'Antoni. They were also small. Mashburn played power forward. Gimel Martinez, who masqueraded as their big, often situated himself at the top of the key rather than the post. Their offense was built on space and trust, full of disciplined movement and crafty cuts. Doze for a second and they embarrassed a defense on a backdoor slip for an easy layup.

My protest over, I entered the game. We were in control, yet not gaining much separation. They, like Iowa, tried pressuring us the length of the court. We responded calmly, causing Kentucky to switch from a man defense to zone. They were reacting to us, absorbing our tempo. As the aggressors, we were chasing, constantly chasing, and carved a double-digit lead.

Desperate, they scrambled and ramped up the defensive pressure. The mother-in-law, I heard Pitino describe his defense in later years, because of its constant, persistent harassment. Coach K had prepped us, telling us to absorb their expected run.

They were conditioned, probably the most in-shape team we faced all year. Their defense attempted to wear out Bobby, and his natural reflex was to try to take them all himself.

Mashburn found a hot hand, lifting Kentucky back into it. We clung to a small lead when Aminu Timberlake, a Kentucky forward, stumbled after challenging Laettner's shot. Laettner stepped on his chest, drawing a technical. We are eternally fortunate that he was not kicked out of the game. In this era, he would have been ejected. No question.

Maybe we were overconfident. Maybe we took our foot off the pedal. Maybe they were just that good.

Sports is all about momentum, and it now resided squarely on Kentucky's side.

I wasn't considering the stakes of it all, the chance to continue on a path toward history. I was doing all I could, helping to alleviate some of Bobby's ball-handling burden, crashing the boards, and trying and often failing to contain Mashburn. Thomas Hill was coming up big. Laettner wasn't missing. Yet they were still right there with us, too close for comfort.

The mother-in-law indeed.

The entire game was one loose ball bouncing on the hard court, teasingly there for the taking. All of us dove and scrambled, trying to claim it as ours.

———

Bobby had a chance to win it. His legs were shot, his shot just off, and the game traveled to overtime, where Laettner kept us in it.

Good, bad. Fire that warmed the building or the accelerant that burned it all down.

We tied the game when I corralled Hurley's missed three and kicked the ball right back to him. This time, the shot was true.

Everything, all of it, seemed lost a little later when Kentucky's guard Sean Woods shook free from Hurley and slipped in a prayer of a running bank shot over Laettner that put Kentucky ahead by a point with about two seconds remaining.

Kentucky celebrated. So did their fans. We motioned for a time-out.

It's over, I thought. The season is over. Guess I'll be at Myrtle Beach next week instead of the Final Four.

Chaos erupted all around us. Coach projected calmness inside the huddle.

We're going to win this game, he said.

I don't know if this is true, but I heard Coach K requested that student managers film him during games on the sidelines. He reviewed the footage later, ensuring that he continually modeled a steady demeanor.

He bypassed a Knute Rockne–type speech, training his eyes on me.

We have to throw the ball the length of the court, he said.

Grant, can you make the pass?

In practice, we performed two-man drills, alternating with a teammate, taking shots, and rebounding down the court. The length of the passes built, culminating with a baseball pass the length of the court. I threw strikes in the drills. It was in the genes, I joked. I should've been a quarterback. There was some truth in the jest. My dad had played quarterback before shifting to running back at Yale and in the NFL. He had the abilities to quarterback a team. The rest of the world just hadn't caught up yet.

The beach was gone. I was back in Philadelphia, in the present, inside the Spectrum.

I noted that Coach K didn't tell me to make the pass. He asked. The question empowered me with ownership.

Yes, I said.

Coach K turned to Laettner. He was not leaving that huddle early.

Can you make the shot?

If Grant makes the pass, I'll make the shot.

Cocky. Confident.

The buzzer sounded. The refs called us back onto the court. In my gut, despite the odds, I trusted we were going to win. I would do my part, and Laettner would find a way.

I took my place at the baseline, finding to my delight that no one was guarding me and the ball. Kentucky had instead decided to double Laettner. I had a clear line of sight. Briefly, I thought of my pass at the end of the loss at Wake Forest.

This was the next time I had promised to Laettner.

We had some other action going on. Teammates cut here and there. It was all window dressing to distract that the ball was going to Laettner.

The defenders were at his back. I only saw Laettner. The pass exited crisp and felt on target as it beelined to him.

He caught it and dribbled.

No, no, no.

Only two precious seconds remained. Was he going to be able to get the shot off? He found his rhythm and released the ball.

It felt like the ball took more time to leave his hands and locate the basket than the full-court pass had. Watching the shot felt like that scene from *The Natural* when Roy Hobbs hit his home run. Time passed in slow motion.

Often, a player knows a shot is good the moment it flicks from his hands. Muscle memory forms through repetition. This time, I could see his shot would fall the instant the ball released from his fingers—just like with Bobby's shot the previous year.

Splash.

Pandemonium. It was like everyone had been shot out of a cannon. Our bench exploded. Our cheering section detonated. Christian streaked away like a sprinter. We were celebrating in the locker room. I didn't even remember making my way back there.

Now it was Brian Davis's turn at the whiteboard, payback for how Coach K began the season with his message toward him.

Brian Davis, first African American in four Final Fours, he wrote.

Only BD.

———

It's telling that one of the NCAA tournament's most memorable sequences did not happen in a championship game or even at the Final Four. It endures because of when it happened, at a time when basketball was spreading globally and the tournament was gaining popularity through the rise of cable television and blue-chip programs like Vegas, Duke, and Kentucky running the same unit of players back from year to year.

To this day, I can't watch that entire game. It's one of the few times we played overconfidently. I feel responsibility in allowing Mashburn to get hot and for Kentucky to get that close. It was the most scared I felt that entire season, including the couple games we did lose. But I'll always keep that pass and shot close in my mind.

Anything can happen during the tournament. That sequence is timeless proof.

———

By the time we played Indiana in the Final Four, it was almost as though Laettner had emptied out everything he had against Kentucky. He was not looking for his shot in Minneapolis. Luckily, Bobby was again Bobby, catching fire early on.

In the game, I tweaked my knee diving for a loose ball. As Dr. Frank Bassett, our head physician, inspected my leg on our bench, I thought to a lower-extremities anatomy course I had taken that semester.

I had discovered the class by accident. Laettner had taken it as a junior and occasionally discussed it with us in between tormenting all of us. My interest in it had ranged from zero to zilch, until a premed student I was casually dating the first semester recommended it, saying that she'd help me out as needed.

I took a flier on it, knowing I could drop the class if it ended up being uninteresting.

We broke for winter recess. The girl and I broke up for good.

Of course, we ended up side by side, dissecting the same cadaver in the class, with Mark Williams and Kenny Blakeney as the parties to our awkward group. She didn't say two words to me the entire semester, speaking over me to Mark or Kenny whenever she felt the need for conversation.

To my surprise, the class fascinated me. Mark, Kenny, and I were probably the only students who were not in premed. We usually grabbed lunch right before the class started. On days when we needed to identify the parts of the femoral triangle—the vastus medialis, the vastus lateralis, sartorius, the gracilis (I might be bragging, but I can still rattle off the names)—I couldn't help but think that the mass of muscles in front of me resembled the meal I had just eaten for lunch.

It was one thing to read about the body's anatomy in a high school science book. It was quite another leap to break down an actual leg, starting at the top of the hip and working our way down, gripping the fascia's connective tissue, exploring the maze of muscles, studying their origin, examining where they inserted into the body. The class met twice weekly. Mark and I had only a small window once it ended to prep for practice. I would rush to wash the strong pickle-like odor of formaldehyde out of my pores before changing into my gear.

Dr. Bassett didn't teach the course, but he oversaw the program.

Doc, I think it's my medial epicondyle, I told him through clenched teeth.

Dr. Bassett looked up, glowing with pride.

Son, I'm so proud of you, he said in his country baritone. You're right on.

I could've been wrong. I was not certain if it was my medial epicondyle that hurt. Just the fact that I threw that out there made him momentarily beam. Little did I know that that anatomy class would come in handy down the road and I would end up knowing far more than I ever could have imagined—or wanted to have imagined—about leg muscles.

In the second half, I gave it a go. We escaped with a narrow win and were again championship bound.

The buildup to the game had centered on Coach K against Bobby Knight, more so than Duke against Indiana. Knight, of course, had coached him at West Point, and Coach K served on his Indiana staff for a stint.

Typically, there was a rhythm to a game's end. Coach usually addressed us immediately after a loss. After a win, he typically convened with the assistants for a little while as we unraveled from tape and iced up before he spoke to us.

We were waiting for Coach after the Indiana game, and he ended up taking awhile. I didn't think much of it at the time. A lot of fanfare and distractions circulated around the Final Four.

I did notice his eyes when he first arrived before us. They were bloodshot. You could tell he had just shed a couple of tears.

I don't know all the details of what happened between the two, whether Knight had stiffed him for a postgame handshake or not. It isn't my relationship to detail. I just know that I had never seen Coach K shaken in such a way immediately after a game during my time at Duke.

Michigan awaited us in the championship game.

I was blissfully oblivious to the developing perception of Duke as a program loathed outside Durham. We were mostly sequestered during the season, encouraged to ignore the media, which mainly consisted of local papers and national magazines.

People showed us love whenever we ventured out. Durham hosted a rich African American past. Freed slaves had developed the neighborhood of Hayti along the city's southern tip, following the Civil War. They transformed the area into an economic hub, founding hundreds of flourishing Black-owned businesses that dotted Fayetteville, Pettigrew, and Pine streets, including the North Carolina Mutual Life Insurance Company. W. E. B. Du Bois and Booker T. Washington canvassed the area, labeling the district a model for other Black communities to emulate.

Urban renewal forced a lot of Hayti's economic decay, but it still hosted North Carolina Central University. I attended as many social gatherings there as I did at Duke.

A supportive Black community existed in Durham, one that loved Duke basketball.

Now, was that Black community going to be front and center, camping out for days and nights in hopes of scoring tickets like the rest of the Cameron Crazies?

Nah.

Players received only three tickets to divvy up among family and friends for games. So many times, I packed as many people as possible, usually Black friends, elbow to elbow in the Land Cruiser before driving over to Cameron before a game. I parked and we all exited. One turn led to the locker room, the other into the arena. They were on their own once we reached that fork.

I understand the appeal of the Fab Five. I always have. They were the evolution of why I fell for the Georgetown Hoyas as a child. They were young, Black, athletic, aggressive. They were the program—not the coach, not the athletic director, not any booster. They succeeded with their own style and swagger, flexing autonomy and personality when most of college basketball was trained to follow and respect tradition. They did not ask for approval. They aimed to take respect. The Fab Five was hip-hop come to life during an era when Public Enemy's urgency captured everyone's consciousness.

Scrape a layer or two beyond the surface. Being a Black man isn't a monolithic experience. Duke and Michigan wasn't a matchup centered on white versus Black. Of anyone, I was the Dukie who sort of fit the preppy caricature, having grown up in the suburbs as the product of two parents with distinguished careers. Most of my Duke teammates were the products of blue-collar backgrounds. Laettner's dad was a printer for *The Buffalo News*. Bobby's dad coached high school ball. Coach K's father worked as an elevator operator, and his mother cleaned homes.

I sometimes wonder, if things had flipped, if we had been at Carolina or a state school with our same team and style of play, would people harbor the same ingrained feelings about us and the success we experienced?

I do know that we didn't feel privileged or owed at Duke.

What we had, we won. Nobody was going to take it away.

It was time to earn another championship.

We're not concentrating on shocking the world anymore, Chris Webber told the media. Our strength is that we don't respect anyone.

Got them.

The scare Michigan provided earlier in the season was still fresh in our minds. We respected their capabilities on the court. We knew entering the game, perhaps for the first time during the season, that we would lose if we didn't come to play.

We were locked in, even when our teams gathered before the game. A long tunnel separated us inside the Metrodome. Their guys chirped, mostly, I assumed, at Laettner.

The back-and-forth didn't bother me. It was all background noise. I was inside my own head, trying to stay focused.

I was starting again, replacing Brian, who was on crutches after sustaining an injury against Indiana. There would be no silent protest this game. I needed to be at my best from the jump ball. I was also motivated. A day earlier, I had ventured to our hotel's gift shop to grab a newspaper featuring a Final Four pullout section for a keepsake. It was a habit I picked up from my dad, who collected every newspaper clipping and magazine that mentioned me. I opened the paper to a story that dissected each of the championship game's matchups, delivering one side an advantage. In the description of Grant Hill against Ray Jackson, the writer gave the edge to Michigan, because *Hill's a bench player.*

I hadn't read a newspaper the entire tournament, maybe the whole year, and this is what I got when I did? I was a Duke starter. I had worked hard to earn that spot, inhaling it as part of my identity, using it for stability. For a while and for the team, I had sacrificed my spot, my role, part of myself.

I was not giving it up so easy again. All right, I thought, I'll show them a bench player.

We were ready, but so was Michigan. Chris went coast-to-coast and delivered a behind-the-back pass to Rob Pelinka. They doubled Laettner every time he caught the ball, and despite all of his accolades it was not a look we were accustomed to seeing in college. Laettner struggled in the traffic and turned the ball over. Coach K reminded us that it was a long game. We've taken their best punch. We're still standing. Let's give them ours.

It was Bobby who lit into Laettner at halftime, the one time he completely let Laettner have it, a complete reversal from the previous season. He challenged Laettner in that moment, telling him that freshmen were kicking his butt in his final college game.

It worked. Laettner ignited in the second half. Bobby bounced the ball on a string. I exploited holes in their defense, navigating driving lanes to facilitate shots for Laettner or get to the basket myself.

They dropped their heads after foul calls and bickered with one another and the referees. They had seen this before.

We had too.

They knew they couldn't beat us. We scored every possession down the stretch, closing the game for another championship.

In the craziness afterward, I spotted David Webber, Chris's little brother. He was bawling his eyes out. His brother's team had lost, but I had heard he was a fan of mine. I took off my jersey and handed it to him.

A couple decades later, Chris brought up the exchange. I'm sure, at the time, it was a little awkward that he had just lost a championship game to us and came home to see his younger brother toting my Duke jersey.

Why'd you do that? he asked.

I'm not sure, I told him. I guess I just wanted to comfort him.

But I sure wish I could have that jersey back.

———

There was a feeling of euphoria and accomplishment in winning a championship. Even in a blowout, those final five, four, three minutes were filled with bubbling anticipation and excitement, just like when my dad described to me his own joy at winning the Super Bowl.

A year earlier, following the win over Kansas, I didn't want the night to end. In the locker room, we danced to ear-rattling music, shell-shocked that we were the last team standing.

I was exhausted after beating Michigan. We were back-to-back champions with a cemented legacy.

I was sure we all had the same thought.

That was hard.

I'm not sure if we ever acknowledged the weight of being the top-ranked team throughout the entire season. As we pursued the second title, we were always pushing for the next win, trying not to allow doubt or fear to creep into our minds.

I drummed up enough energy to party and celebrate for a while before finally getting back to my hotel room.

Man, I'm glad that's over, was the last thought I remember before drifting off to sleep.

7

THAT summer, I was one of a handful of college players invited to La Jolla to help prepare the Dream Team for Olympic competition.

Sunny San Diego skies and the chance to learn up close from Michael Jordan and Magic Johnson? I couldn't say yes fast enough. I hoped that the practices would provide a nice interruption from the humdrum pace of training and summer school sessions.

Most of the Dream Team existed to me only in highlights. Everyone except Patrick Ewing. He was Georgetown family and tolerated me hanging around occasionally during his late Hoya days. I still remember the time he asked me to spot him for a pizza at his place when he had emptied his pockets, only to find lint. Maybe he would finally pay me back.

I had familiarity with most of the other college players who joined me. Bobby Hurley was playing. The rest of us were a collection of talented players sprinkled across the country—guys like Chris Webber, Jamal Mashburn, Eric Montross, Rodney Rogers, Penny Hardaway, and Allan Houston.

I was friendly with most of them. I never regarded Michigan and Chris as true adversaries like, for example, Carolina and Montross.

Michigan had to beat us at least once in order for the matchup to evolve into an actual rivalry. Individually, I was cool with the Fab Five. A couple weeks into the summer, Juwan Howard and I had teamed as co-counselors at Nike Camp. We spent most of the time laughing and enjoying ourselves, with little mention of the championship game. Chris and I also stayed on solid terms. I was under the impression that his time in college was dwindling anyway; the NBA beckoned. It would be good to catch up with him in San Diego.

I arrived a couple days early with some time to kill. Allan, Jamal, and I chilled in the lobby of some fancy hotel that I would never see on the road with Duke. Allan and I had roomed together years earlier at a high school camp, and he caught me up on his college life at Tennessee.

A couple of older guys recognized us, striking up a conversation. They were cordial, describing themselves as college basketball fans, and inquired why we were in town.

We're just here to be sacrificial lambs for the Dream Team, I joked. There was a reason no NBA players had agreed to be test dummies against these guys.

The middle-aged men raved about a new beach, just down the road, and asked if we wanted to get our toes wet.

The sun beamed in a cloudless sky. The crisp wind blew through the air. We were some nineteen-year-olds with nowhere else to be.

Sure, why not?

We hopped in a car with these strangers, parking on a bluff a few minutes later. I could already hear laughter. We descended down to the beach after making our way through a trail of shrubbery.

Everyone, as far as my eyes could see, was getting sun in all the places where the sun shouldn't be shining.

Stunned, I didn't say much. No offense. I just didn't know these guys like that. Before our new friends started sliding their trunks off, Allan, I believe, stammered that we needed to get back to the hotel in time for practice. They thankfully didn't think much of it and drove us back to the hotel, where we saw Penny checking in.

I'm not sure whether he noticed our flushed faces as we made our way past him.

———

The following day, we lambs made our practice debut.

Roy Williams supervised our group. He was a Tar Heel before and after, but I didn't hold it against him. He instructed us to race up and down the court against the Dream Team and utilize our speed against the seasoned players. He wanted Bobby to dribble-penetrate before kicking the ball out to the shooters like Jamal and Allan. Meanwhile, Penny and I were asked to continually attack, while Chris and Montross battled in the post. Play like the Europeans, Williams advised.

Larry Bird walked into the elevator when we returned to the hotel. The legends must have been arriving. Bird surprised me. In person, he was just as tall as Chris. He offered me my first taste of NBA trash talk.

You boys better be ready tomorrow, Bird said in a midwestern twang. Can't wait till you guys get to the NBA either, so I can bust your asses.

His words danced in my mind as we overlooked the Dream Team practice inside UC San Diego's gym the day of the scrimmage. Just then, Charles Barkley finished a seismic dunk over Karl Malone. My eyes ping-ponged from one All-Star to the next.

I walked onto the court, taking a seat. Jordan. Magic. Bird. Barkley. Malone. Yep, they were all here. Even Christian Laettner was out there, a true outlier as the only rising NBA rookie chosen for the team.

It could have been butterflies or false confidence, maybe a mix of the two. The college guys started hyping one another up, telling each other to get after them. They dribbled the same basketball as us. We were in college, yes. Yet each of us was accomplished in his own right.

Grant, you've got MJ, Williams said.

Crap, was my first thought. A more serious expletive might've been my second.

Michael Jordan was no longer Mike Jordan, the Carolina sophomore who hit the game winner at Carolina that I watched on the basement Betamax. He was an NBA champion, at arguably the height of his abilities, well on his way to forging a career as one of the greatest ever to play the game.

I can't let that matchup consume me, I thought, as Magic sauntered onto the court.

When I was growing up, my bedroom featured a life-sized Magic poster on the back of the door. I had lived for those Sunday games on CBS that showcased the Lakers against the Celtics, Magic against Bird. He was a ball handler with size, and I envied his vision and wizardry.

Magic, his game and charisma, was synonymous with the NBA's growth in expanding the game's reach into America's mainstream, and now the world's.

I gazed at him, recalling the devastating news of only a few months earlier. We'd regularly file into the basement of Trent Hall for a meal after Duke practices. We used the time to bond, talk trash, joke. It was those small moments, on the bus, flying to a game, sharing a meal, that added up over a season in building a team's cohesion.

That time, ESPN was cycling in the background. Magic walked to a lectern, and the banter ceased when he disclosed that he had tested positive for HIV. The rest of the press conference was a blur. Tears welled in my eyes. I buried my head. When I looked up, most of my teammates seemed shocked as we all felt a universal sense of imminent loss. We feared Magic had just delivered his own death sentence.

Then, right around the time we bounced back from the Carolina loss with the win at LSU, Magic surprised everyone by playing in the All-Star Game. Some players showed initial apprehension in sharing the court with him. Yet the league had allowed him to play, and those initial concerns disappeared once Magic played like Magic, showcasing an unrivaled enthusiasm for the game, nailing three after three. He earned MVP honors and collected high fives from both teams.

His Olympic participation served as his official comeback to competitive hooping. We collegians were overjoyed to compete with him, regarding our sharing the court with him as an honor.

I picked up Magic on a switch early in the scrimmage. I watched him as a youngster and always wondered why sly, smaller guards didn't just reach around Magic, pick his pocket, and steal the ball. He could no doubt handle the rock. But I didn't really consider him one of those innately crafty ball handlers. He played quick, not fast. He covered a lot of space in a short amount of time, yet his game didn't reflect explosiveness. An alluring eternity elapsed from when he dribbled the ball against the court and when it returned to his hand.

As he barreled toward me, I reached out for the ball and was promptly disciplined with a forearm shiver that knocked me on my heels. He was strong as an ox. Lesson learned. Guess there was a good reason why he rarely committed a turnover.

Thankfully, a shove wasn't the only tutorial Magic offered during the scrimmage.

Despite Coach K's insistence on it, talking on the court still didn't come naturally for me. I adjusted as best and as quickly as possible, because talking at Duke was a prerequisite for playing at Duke. Coach mostly built our defense around the pressuring of ball handlers. Bobby became the focal point of that attack, while we denied the wings. We were taught to defend aggressively, and that involved communicating and trusting that if you overplayed, an alert teammate would have your back if an opponent tried to cut behind you.

The Dream Team constantly talked to one another on the court. I saw that they valued communication as much as Coach. Magic's voice rose above everyone else's. He held different conversations at once, directing traffic with one hand, bouncing the ball with the other.

Still, we gained momentum and, to our collective surprise, were outplaying the Dream Team. Bobby created fits for Magic, dashing and darting past the taller guard. The rest of their defense collapsed. Allan wasn't missing from deep. I didn't see Jordan in front of me. Just the rim. Chris played fantastic in transition.

Even Laettner caught some of the whupping.

We didn't dare talk trash to them. With one another, we were vocal, encouraging, pushing, believing.

The Dream Team is the greatest collection of basketball players ever assembled. It was possible, even probable, that they did not view us as a serious challenge. They were still in the beginning of harmonizing, becoming familiar with one another's traits and habits as they prepared to advance to the Olympics.

Meanwhile, we were college kids, too ignorant to know any better, out for blood. We dominated them pretty badly. We scoffed when the trainers scurried to erase the scoreboard before allowing the gaggle of media inside the gym. Allan and I returned to our hotel room, giddy over not just being in the presence of all that collective greatness—I had taken a picture with David Robinson after the scrimmage like any fan would—but actually beating them.

Coach K served as an assistant to the Dream Team coach, Chuck Daly. I'm sure he was proud to see me and Bobby hold our own against the pros. In later years, he insisted that Daly substituted Jordan out at key times. He wanted to ensure that the Dream Team would lose in order to deflate their sense of infallibility. Possibly. Maybe. But I doubt it. Coach may be partly trying to protect the Dream Team's legacy. Take Jordan out and who replaced him? Clyde Drexler, another perennial All-Star.

Regardless, winning provided us collegians with one heckuva bragging right. We already knew that no one would believe us if we told them.

That scrimmage was probably the highlight of my basketball career to that point, even more than the championships. Those were impressive, but this was the Dream Team.

Let the record show that we were the only squad to ever beat them.

Of course, it was somewhat fool's gold.

They destroyed us over the next few scrimmages. Jordan and Scottie Pippen alternated guarding Bobby. They used their length and quickness to choke him out of the driving lanes. Allan's shot wasn't as true. I turned the ball over. All of a sudden it's like we couldn't dribble and walk at the same time.

Basketball consisted of just a slice of the trip. The Dream Team, especially Scottie, accepted us. Just a glimpse of how they operated away from the court was eye-opening.

Scottie pulled up in a red Corvette and invited me on my first golf outing. Penny and Allan, who practically grew up on the golf course, joined us. Allan and Scottie were the only ones dressed for the sport. I might've noticed a snicker or two when I showed up in some Karl Kani shorts and Jordans.

I didn't know what I was doing and played terribly. Thankfully, I improved over the years—more than I can say for Charles Barkley.

Another afternoon, just the college players ventured onto the course—me, Bobby, Chris, Rodney, and Allan. We tore up the green in the carts, racing up the hills trying to perform stunts. I bet we're all still banned from playing there.

That night, we relaxed in Magic's suite while several members of the Dream Team played cards. We collegians were strictly spectators. I don't think all of our collective bank accounts could hit the minimum to sit at the table. Magic won big and collected about twenty thousand dollars. I still don't know if I've ever seen that much cash piled in front of one person.

Only a couple of years earlier, I had questioned whether I could play at a program like Duke. All the college players who traveled to La Jolla were on the verge of the NBA. Some of us would evolve into All-Stars. I think those scrimmages—at least the first one—provided us all with a shot of confidence.

It did for me. I left fully confident that I could one day compete in the NBA. I had competed against players who had advanced to make some noise in the league. I had held my own against Larry Johnson in the NCAA tournament, and he had collected rookie of the year honors. Doubt, though, had still lingered until the scrimmage.

Meanwhile, the NBA was gaining in popularity after an impressive run in the 1980s. Jordan was the dynamic, marketable star who checked all the boxes of athleticism, grace, and charm. Phil Knight at Nike possessed the foresight and savviness to develop a brand around an individual player like Jordan. Throw in David Stern, a keen observer who skillfully wielded the power of television and publicity, and you had a recipe for a sport on the precipice of gaining a world audience with the Dream Team serving as global basketball ambassadors.

Most of us who played in La Jolla benefited financially from the inroads made by the greats we scrimmaged against.

Rodney and I caught a flight back to North Carolina together. We were already reminiscing while at baggage claim, knowing that those few days would forever link us.

How did a person return to finish summer school after that?

Thoughts of the NBA were nudged aside as I started imagining our team absent the personality and play of Laettner and Brian Davis. How could we fill that vacuum?

Guess I'll have to be even more communicative, I thought, as I watched the Dream Team stampede through the Olympics, thankful that we played a minor role in fine-tuning that machine.

My summer finished with an internship at my mom's consulting firm. I use the term "internship" loosely. My mom joked that I would fetch everyone's lunch most of the morning, then spend all afternoon grabbing my own food.

Often, I performed some light administrative task and spent the rest of the day mining the mind of Mr. Cliff Alexander, her business partner, for his perspective on historical figures like Malcolm X, Stokely Carmichael, and Lyndon B. Johnson. He knew them all, having participated in so many pivotal junctures in our nation's history, from playing a role in the passage of the 1964 Civil Rights Act, to serving as the chairman of the U.S. Equal Employment Opportunity Commission under Johnson and becoming the first African American secretary of the army.

Around that time, I read *The Autobiography of Malcolm X*. Our history was often glossed over in most textbooks. People like Harriet Tubman, Martin Luther King Jr., and George Washington Carver might have received a couple of passages. Malcolm X maybe received a few obligatory sentences. I really didn't learn much in school about the contributions of Blacks and people of color who were instrumental in building this country. My education was rounded out elsewhere. The knowledge provided by Public Enemy and KRS-One whetted an appetite for knowledge, and I sometimes flipped through an encyclopedia or headed over to the Know, a Durham Black-owned bookstore, thirsting for more.

Mr. Alexander provided it firsthand. He spoke deeply, elegantly, and personally about Malcolm and Martin, the struggle for civil rights, and the March on Washington, the moments my parents had witnessed and talked to me about. The conversations were enlightening, expanding my worldview and widening my appreciation for the generation before me, people like Mr. Alexander and my parents.

As Mr. Alexander spoke, my eyes were often drawn to a piece of art that hung on his office wall. It was a beautiful, vibrant painting, somewhat abstract.

I was not the same kid who once had to be dragged by my dad to art galleries. My parents had expanded their eclectic art collection throughout my childhood. My dad collected art from all corners of the globe: historic African American art, delicate sculptures from Japan and China, artifacts from just about everywhere.

It's a Romare Bearden, Mr. Alexander told me. I recognized the name from my dad. Bearden was widely considered the godfather of African American art. Bearden himself had gifted Mr. Alexander the piece.

I promised myself to keep learning more about Bearden, his life, his work.

As my dad often reminded me, to be ignorant of your past is to remain a boy.

8

W H Y poke a bear? Why jab at one that has already trampled your hopes, demolished your dreams, stepped on your fantasies, lessened your legacy?

In some ways, we were punch-drunk from consecutive championships. All I had known was spring celebrations at Duke. There was not just a belief that we would continue the good times but an expectation. Coach K snapped us from our reverie, gathering us inside an area where we rarely assembled, the old players' lounge, deep inside Cameron's belly. To get there, we walked through the locker room and entered a hallway where we encountered a fork that led either to the coaches' bathrooms or to our current lounge and walked up a narrow staircase. Coach beckoned us to sit on a couch that could host most of us.

He wanted a change of scenery. We all sensed he was readying an important message. Now an upperclassman, I could anticipate some of Coach K's moves. He had already requested that I assume more responsibility in leading the team, which included new faces like Chris Collins, a guard from Illinois.

Coach played a video. In it, Michigan's guard Jimmy King dismissed

Bobby Hurley as just an average guard, and Chris Webber anointed Jalen Rose a better player than Bobby.

I had just watched Bobby take it to Magic Johnson. So did Chris.

All good. Michigan was on our schedule again, a championship rematch at Cameron, our second game of the season after playing Canisius in our opener.

I knew Chris was just trying to hype Jalen. The ploy backfired. Cameron rocked that game. Hurley played like a man possessed. On the court, he usually talked only to his teammates. That game, he was animated, adamant, yelling to everybody that no one on the court could check him after draining a three-pointer. The outcome was never really in doubt. It was one of those rare regular-season wins where our emotion was on display as we hugged and congratulated Bobby.

Come after one of us and you come after all of us.

For those keeping score, that would be wins over Michigan at their house, at ours, on a neutral court, with Christian Laettner, and without him.

Still, we were a different team early that season. Our fire, that blaze that could burn it all down, but more often fed us fuel, was missing. Laettner was a mirage in the fall. He had trained at Duke when we returned to campus, playing pickup, regaling us with stories of Michael Jordan and Charles Barkley and his Dream Team experience.

The season started and he left, embarking on his NBA career as the third overall selection for the Minnesota Timberwolves. Brian Davis was also gone. I had no doubt that he was preparing himself for a number of promising business ventures. A void existed and not just from the departure of their production. We would miss their internal competitiveness, their ability to constantly rise to the occasion and be held accountable in the moment.

I had moved to an off-campus apartment with Thomas Hill and Tony Lang. They were both more confident now, more comfortable on the court. Cherokee Parks was primed to come out from Laettner's shadow, and we were counting on him to break out and assert himself as an inside presence. Bobby, whatever the outside chatter, was the nation's best point guard.

The goal was the same as always, to be the last team standing. There was no pressure, Coach K said, because we were a different team. He was back from his own Dream Team experience and putting a greater emphasis on weight lifting. He had noticed that the pros had focused on their strength in their preparation for the Olympics; the old adage that lifting weights messed with your shot was dissolving. He encouraged us to be bigger, stronger.

Quickly, we realized that our defense had taken another step forward. Bobby was a tireless ball hawk. Thomas remained a stopper. Tony was long and could guard anyone. Cherokee was quick, especially around the rim.

I started taking pride in being not just a cog in our defense but the gear that got us going, trying to shut my man down and help my teammates disrupt offenses and instigate chaos.

A team identity was forming as we zigged and zagged over the United States and Pacific Ocean, with pit stops in Dallas, Los Angeles, and O'ahu on the long journey to the Maui Invitational. We were behind schedule by the time we touched down and headed straight to a practice at the Lahaina Civic Center before even checking in to the Marriott Marquis.

The tournament's games were all slated to be televised during evening prime time back home, which meant that we would tip off early in the afternoon. We trudged to the arena as our parents congregated, laughed, and soaked in the sun at a hotel pool overlooking the ocean's many shades of blue. The games were daily, so we didn't have time at night to go out.

We had traveled halfway across the world to Maui and didn't even have time to dip our toes in the sand.

The civic center was intimate. My high school gym probably held more than the couple of thousand people these stands could bear. I glanced around, recognizing the different insignias and faces beneath the basket, along the baseline. Lakers polo? That was Jerry West. In the Pistons T? Yep, Jack McCloskey.

NBA personnel were also dropping by our practices more often. I hadn't noticed them as much the previous two years. Maybe, Laettner was such an elite player that the pros didn't bother scouting him in person or I was just an underclassman, oblivious to my surroundings. I took mental notes now when I spotted scouts at practice and games, the same way that I used to sense the presence of John Thompson, Dean Smith, or Coach K at one of my high school practices.

I was pumped to perform in front of them. I was not one to hunt for numbers. Scoring wasn't my end all. It was just not my personality, even though I knew Coach, especially this season, was adamant that I look for my shot more often.

Occasionally, my athleticism towered over other skill sets. Observers could spot my leaping ability. I was satisfied playing to the game's rhythm, happy to impact the outcome in the flow, whether it was scoring, facilitating, or defense.

More Magic than Michael.

And, if I'm honest, maybe I just was not that player yet, the one who wanted the ball in his hands as time wound down. Focusing on my team instead of myself dimmed the spotlight. This was Bobby and Thomas Hill's team. They were the seniors. Yet I was also trying to lean into leading more, filling that void, standing out instead of fitting in.

It helped that we were still winning. The Michigan win allowed us to regain the top overall ranking. We swept through Maui, topping De-Paul, LSU, and BYU, and started the season with ten straight victories, including a rugged overtime win against a difficult Oklahoma squad.

Nonconference opponents were not familiar with our style. Intimidation probably existed in facing two-time champions. Atlantic Coast Conference play started, and these teams, the ones we had been handing it to the last couple of seasons, salivated. For them, big brother was gone. Without the security blanket of Laettner, they imagined us vulnerable, no matter our record. Their coaches knew our tendencies, our sets, the spots we gravitated to on the floor.

In the recent past, a lot of conference games had been decided before the first possession. We could tell in the body language of our opponent when they took the court. Other times, especially on the road, we focused on opening strong, choking wills, deflating any lingering excitement in the building. Then there were the games we had that I'll compare to when I watched Jordan's Bulls teams. An opponent would always be up for those games and play the Bulls close at a game's start. Then Jordan would ignite a quick run of six or seven points just before halftime. The Bulls usually opened the second half with a similar spurt. Now the Bulls had carved out a double-digit lead. They became caretakers from there, managing the game until the end. At Duke, we were so used to being in that position for the last six minutes that we instinctively knew the pivot points, the moments when we needed a stop, when to tighten the defensive screws and execute.

In a game against Georgia Tech in Atlanta, we started flat. They scored the game's first dozen points, and it was uphill from there. We finally took a lead in the second half on my layup. I was able to score, amassing twenty-nine points, but it was not enough. We lost by a point, our first defeat in twenty-three games. The game was more evidence for me that, yes, this team was different. The responsibility was on me, Bobby, Thomas, and Tony to produce each and every game. Cherokee, for all his potential, just wasn't at the level we needed him to be yet. For the most part, our second unit was young, untested.

We bounced back with a statement win at Wake Forest. The game was even at halftime. In the second half, their crowd taunted Bobby. At an earlier point, older opponents and a hostile crowd could intimidate and irritate Bobby. No longer. Just like against Michigan, he absorbed everything and used it as fuel for his play. Bobby scored twenty points in the second half, baiting the crowd along the way, and we coasted the rest of the game. After another exhausting win over Iowa, we hoped that we were settling into a real groove.

Basketball karma caught us. We dropped games against Virginia at Cameron and an overtime effort at Florida State. It's not like we were just showing up, thinking that because we were Duke and defending champions, we were automatically going to win. We were struggling, competing, searching for ourselves, our identity, as our opponents stirred, conscious that this was their first legitimate shot against us in years.

Coach had inched us along my freshman year, almost pushing us over that finish line as we learned the characteristics of a championship team. The same group returned my sophomore year. We had already passed the test and he mostly managed us, ensuring that we didn't lose our sanity in trying to live up to expectations. If he coached every season, every team differently, this season was a blend of the previous two experiences.

A lot of the expectations and pressure existed even without Laettner. Coach knew that. As we struggled in January, he started pushing us harder. Practices became longer and more physical.

We showed resolve, finding our footing, and carved out a six-game win streak, including a convincing win over Carolina. That season is one of the only ones where we opened with the state's attention, the spotlight, on us in Durham. No one was expecting much from the Tar Heels after the program lost Hubert Davis, their best player, and replaced him with a freshman in Donald Williams.

We had won nineteen of twenty-two games. This, I started to allow myself to think, could be another special season.

———

Those hopes were dashed when I guarded my friend Rodney Rogers in a game against Wake Forest. We were competitive early. He kept Wake in the game by himself. I knew if I grinded and limited his impact, the game would be ours.

I planted my foot, turning to follow him as he darted through the paint. Something in my left big toe buckled. The pain was immediate, excruciating, acute. It radiated from just under the toe, the tiny mound of muscles that held everything together. The toe connected to the foot, ankle, and leg. It was beautiful when everything worked in symmetry. Remove one component, the whole structure folded.

I begged and bargained with my body, pleading with it to allow me back on the court. No luck. I retreated to the back to have it examined as Rodney powered Wake to the upset victory with a career-high thirty-five points.

My mom, in town for the game, drove me back to my apartment. A mix of concern and recognition crossed her face. Your injury, the way you fell, she said, looked exactly like how your dad broke his toe when he played football.

I was not hearing it. I didn't want to even speculate that it was broken. The internal haggling continued. I'd be out a game or two max, and our pursuit of another championship would continue unabated.

Further comfort arrived when the images returned.

Turf toe, I was told.

In my absence, the guys battled. Chris Collins was producing. We dropped an ugly game at Virginia following the Wake loss before piecing together a four-game win streak, including another win over UCLA, this time at Cameron. Bobby's jersey was lifted to the rafters before the game, another jersey retirement I took in while in street clothes.

By now, I had become uncomfortably familiar with injuries at Duke. The mask I wore after breaking my nose annoyingly obstructed my view, but I could still run and jump.

Now I couldn't do anything. The toe, that little appendage, was the final body part to land when I jumped and the first that departed on my ascent.

I'm someone lucky enough—or, more accurately, unlucky enough— to have been injured at different points and witnessed firsthand the evolution of sports medicine. In those days, we did not do a lot of preventive exercises. If someone got hurt, the training staff—all great guys— looked at the injury. If not, we got taped and went out there. Everything was reactive; the field remained essentially in the same state as when my dad had played in the 1970s and 1980s.

Being around the guys at practice, in the locker room, provided some semblance of routine and normalcy. It was a balancing act. My nature was to please, and I worried that I was letting them down. Their camaraderie was uplifting. I just didn't want my melancholy to rub off on them.

A doctor tells a player that an injury is expected to sideline him for two weeks. How the player reacts is telling. No one hears the two weeks. Some strive to return in one. Others respond by checking themselves out for at least a month.

A week slipped into two. With my previous injuries, small improvements offered signals of hope, the belief that each day was a step forward and would eventually lead to the freedom of again running on the open court. Goals, no matter how small or large, provided purpose. That purpose led to a destination. The journey to that destination involved milestone markers that afforded a sense of accomplishment and self-worth. That was the driving force behind so much of sports, the push to continue when a confluence of factors blocked your path.

Days passed without my toe feeling any better.

It was that time of the year—winter was turning into spring, when everything needed to be in sync in order for us to have a chance. The success of the previous years led me to believe that this was just one of the hurdles, a checkpoint, on the path to glory. This was supposed to be no different from Bobby's foot or my ankle the previous season. We had rallied to find our way then and could do it now if this toe would start cooperating.

I negotiated with my mind, telling myself that it was all right to be hurt now. Come the end of conference play, I needed to be back on the court. That should allow enough prep time to be ready for the NCAA tournament. We missed Laettner and what he brought to our team. We also wanted to prove that we could win a championship without him.

Occasionally, Coach K asked motivational speakers to talk to us. One day, I was caught off guard when David Cooks singled me out while addressing the team. At the age of fifteen, David had experienced a spinal aneurysm that left him in a wheelchair. Admirably, he didn't allow the injury to sidetrack him. He was a graduate student, usually encouraging, eternally optimistic.

You guys have a chance to accomplish something really special, he said, but you need to get it together, give it your all, and be out there for one another.

Grant, I'm paralyzed. I wish I just had a hurt toe.

I looked up, stunned. The accusation had landed out of nowhere. The thought that I had babied my toe immediately made me uncomfortable. Frustrated, I questioned whether I was trusted when I said that I couldn't go.

Thoughts of betrayal invaded my mind. I wondered if Coach K had put David up to levying the criticism as a way to discreetly rush my return. My mind became a battlefield. In sports, you are drilled from a young age to suck it up, to battle through discomfort—no gain without pain. The court was my haven, a sanctuary above anywhere else. Sitting out agonized me more than this toe ever could. It was not like I had done anything reckless. I hadn't even landed on someone's foot or rolled my ankle.

Part of the issue was that I could walk without the support of crutches. Our medical staff had fitted me for orthotics and inserted a carbon shank into the sole of the shoe. The shank didn't allow my foot to bend inside it, alleviating the pressure on my toe. The fitted shoe allowed me to walk without crutches and prevented my leg from atrophying. To the naked eye, I looked myself. My teammates, the student body, everyone, saw me walking around campus without any visible support. But when I removed the fitted footwear and placed weight on my foot, the pain returned with a vengeance.

I rehabbed every day, cycling through treatments of ice and elevation.

The carbon shank was replaced with a metal one inside my Adidas.

When I gave it a go at practice, the pain spiraled from my toe with every step.

I didn't allow myself the option of sitting out again after we closed conference play with a loss to Carolina, all of a sudden the nation's top team.

Mind over body. Team over self. Now or never.

The ACC Tournament would need to be my tune-up before the dance.

I loaded up on anti-inflammatories, suppressing nagging concerns. We faced Georgia Tech in the opener of the tournament. I was a spectator in my own body as I watched James Forrest, another friend, send us home early from the tournament with a 69–66 loss.

Two games. Two losses. We were not exactly entering the NCAA tournament with momentum.

Pundits ranked us tenth in the country, which meant that we were no longer able to enjoy home cooking to start the tournament. The powers that be exported us as the third seed in the Midwest Regional. We were great in the opener, pounding Southern Illinois, 105–70.

Cal loomed on the horizon after their surprising upset over Kansas. I knew their freshman point guard, Jason Kidd, touted as an out-of-world distributor. We were teammates a couple years earlier at Nike Camp when, as I recall, he hoisted a crooked jumper and seldom passed the rock at all.

That game, that second-round matchup, stood as Jason's national coming-out party. He played his behind off against us. Bobby more than held his own against him throughout. He was always destined to go out firing.

Lamond Murray proved to be the difference maker. I guarded him, aware that he was a capable player. He kicked my limited behind. To this day, I cringe at the memory of Lamond cutting back door for a lob, my mind aware he was going for the ball, my body incapable of reacting.

We were conditioned to make the plays, the winning choices, down the stretch. Cal, instead, asserted control, handing us an 82–77 loss. I shook hands with Jason and Lamond. The experience of losing while the tournament continued was completely foreign, utterly disorienting.

No more Bobby or Thomas Hill? On top of already losing Laettner and Brian Davis? They were my college experience. I couldn't help but feel as though I had failed everyone, my coach, my team, myself. And why was this toe still hurting so badly?

We flew home. Our seats on the plane were based on seniority. Tony Lang sat with me in first class. Coach ambled over to us. Maybe he had seen the defeat coming, knowing how much we had exhausted ourselves over the last couple of years.

No offense, Jason. Had I been healthy, we'd have handled Cal. We would have probably been a higher seed and bypassed them entirely in the early rounds. That season, we never got the chance to put it together, to figure it all out.

Coach tried pulling our minds from Cal, our early exit, the overwhelming disappointment.

Keep this between us, he said. We're switching our gear to Nike next year from Adidas. Three stripes, you're out.

Honestly, a little of the pain was alleviated. We were still teenagers who wanted to look cool. Nike was king. Nike was Jordan. And next year, we were going to be outfitted in them.

———

A couple of weeks later, my toe was still causing pain. I made an appointment with Dr. Frank Bassett. He performed some more imaging. I was shocked when he told me that my sesamoid bone was fractured.

Huh?

For weeks, I had blamed myself, cursed my body, clenched through pain, shouldered the disappointing ending to our season, only to find out that my gut had screamed the truth as I tried silencing it. In that moment, I allowed my mind to wander and the frustration to mount. I even naively speculated whether the medical staff and coaches knew it had been broken the entire time.

Years later, I came to realize that the break might have occurred after I resumed playing following the original turf toe diagnosis.

Reason, in the moment, eluded me. Dr. Bassett relayed that I needed surgery for the toe to properly heal. I was upset, frustrated that I had possibly not received the correct medical treatment since the beginning of the injury.

My mom, per usual, had been right. A sesamoid facture was the same injury my dad had sustained. He had received negligent medical treatment and never regained his full agility. You got my feet, because you don't hear too many people breaking the sesamoid, he told me.

I didn't laugh.

My parents offered me space to solicit additional medical opinions. They knew, better than most, that Duke possessed some of the nation's best sports medicine facilities. But I was adamant. I didn't want my surgery performed at the university.

Fool me once.

I flew home, scheduling a couple appointments based on my parents' recommendations. I met with a doctor in Charlotte, and another who was visiting Myrtle Beach for a conference. All the specialists agreed that my sesamoid needed surgery. Of course, they could perform the procedure, they said, before mentioning that Dr. Bassett had trained them himself.

I didn't appreciate or understand at the time that Dr. Bassett was regarded as one of the forefathers of sports medicine. Here I was, fuming at Duke, visiting other specialists, and they all encouraged me to undergo the procedure at Duke.

Somewhat sheepish, I returned to Dr. Bassett. He successfully performed the surgery.

The procedure left me on crutches, and I navigated summer school classes with the bolsters sinking deep into my armpits. I was out indefinitely, divorced from the sanctum of the court, searching for an act of defiance, somewhere to project my burgeoning bitterness.

Honestly, I just didn't feel or act myself a lot during those months. Earlier, I had found out that I had won the NABC Defensive Player of the Year that season, which meant flying down to Louisiana for the Final Four at the Superdome. I was joined by Thomas, there to play in the Senior All-Star Game. Our seats weren't great as Carolina beat Kansas and Michigan topped Kentucky. I had pulled for Michigan to take out Carolina in the championship game, hoping that Chris would finally win one. I felt awful for him as he tried summoning the time-out that Michigan didn't have, not realizing how that one moment, an innocent mistake, would trail him for years afterward.

In Louisiana, Thomas and I shared a hotel room. After the game, he called his girlfriend. She asked Thomas if I had lent the Land Cruiser to anyone.

Of course not.

Thomas passed me the phone. She relayed that she had spotted a couple guys driving my car around Durham, a pair of North Carolina Central University students who lived in our apartment complex. They were normally a friendly duo with lots of personality, and we were all constantly in and out of each other's places.

But no. I had never lent them or anyone else my car.

Hurriedly, I called Tony Lang. Can you check to see if the Land Cruiser is out front?

It was gone.

Tony thought for a moment, piecing the puzzle together. We had another friend, a cocky Duke student a year younger than us, whom we let do his laundry at our place instead of finding quarters and dragging his clothes all the way to campus. He had dropped by earlier that day and had to have swiped my keys off the counter.

Look, I'll get it back, Tony said.

He made a couple of calls.

I found the car in its place by the time I had arrived back in Durham.

By that point, I didn't care. The students were not about to get away with their little joyride so easily. I don't even remember dropping my luggage off. I left the apartment almost as soon as I entered, headed to their place in search of a fight.

Hey, Tony called after me. If you're going to fight them, you can't be in your flip-flops.

I looked down, noticing I was still in my blue Adidas slides. I didn't break stride. I planned to serve that whupping no matter the footwear.

Tony rushed to catch up with me. Now Tony was already about it, looking for any excuse. These same guys had raided our fridge and devoured his pizza a year earlier, and, along with a couple other transgressions, he didn't need any persuading to roll up on them.

They opened the door after I pounded on it. I burst in, yelling at them, while canvassing their apartment.

Is that my Brand Nubian CD?

I claimed it, along with several others, and scattered their possessions all over the place.

They were not ready for a confrontation.

My point had been made. Tony and I bounced.

They called us about ten minutes later. They felt disrespected, vowed to get their boys, and demanded that we meet them in an hour. That worked for us.

Tony decided to round up a friend, just in case. We drove to the guy's house, and he walked out with a couple of pistols.

I was pissed, but not pistol pissed. We persuaded him to bring himself, not the guns.

I knocked on their door again. Our boys aren't here yet, the tennis players answered. Tony went around the back, searching for a tree branch to wield. That time, they wisely didn't open the door.

We noticed police at the apartment entrance as we navigated the short drive back to our place at the opposite end of the complex. The tennis players had to have called them on us. The situation was defused once I explained to the officers that they had taken my car without permission. They asked if I wanted to file a report. I let it slide.

It was Easter Sunday, after all.

God, have mercy on us, Tony said after the cops had left.

———

The notion of me headed there, seeking a fight, wasn't my style, even if they deserved to be handled. I already had my car back. I could have asked Tony to get my CDs. Things could have spiraled quickly. It just spoke to my level of frustration at the time and not knowing where to aim it.

During the summer, my thoughts returned often to our season, my injury, the early exit. I found a target, pinning most of my frustration on Coach K and the medical staff.

I can admit that I'm probably off on this, but at some point during that season I sensed that Coach had started training his energy and efforts toward inflating Bobby's NBA draft stock. I had picked up on little things here and there that I subconsciously internalized and probably could have quashed with an open discussion and the benefit of maturity. But at the time, it seemed Coach sometimes had one set of rules for Bobby, another for the rest of us. I also had not liked the way Coach had been treating Tony. Joey Beard, who had played with me during his freshman year of high school at South Lakes, had since blossomed into one of the nation's top big men, and Coach had landed him as a top recruit. I had jokingly teased Tony that my Reston boy would be coming soon to take away all his playing time.

It was one thing for a roommate to pick at his roommate. It was another for Coach to do the same, which was what happened. Coach warned Tony that mistakes would cost him minutes once Joey got to campus and that he may as well start learning a foreign language because he'd only be playing professionally overseas.

No player headed into his senior year wanted to hear that a freshman who hadn't even arrived yet was going to siphon off his minutes. Sensing that it bothered Tony, I backed off my own ribbing and held my tongue when Coach got on him.

I was concerned for him. Meanwhile, Tony had noticed my constant stewing around our apartment and offered me space. One day, he asked if I had thought about leaving for the NBA. Honestly, the association hadn't even landed on my radar. I knew rehabilitation was going to take awhile, and I couldn't be auditioning for the league on one good foot.

Right or wrong—probably wrong—my frustration needed and found an outlet. I called my dad—I know this is sacrilegious, but I'm being real and this was me as a twenty-one-year-old—and absurdly declared to him that I was transferring to Carolina for my senior season. Why not hit them where it hurt? My dad, as I recall, didn't take the pledge seriously, although I am sure he was concerned about the GPS of my headspace.

Regardless, it was time for another silent protest.

I had agreed to attend an all-night graduation party for Durham high schools. On the day of the event, I made a detour, slipping inside a Foot Locker at the South Square Mall and purchasing a Carolina Tar Heels hat.

Now you couldn't pay me enough to wear Carolina blue. Back then, I curved the lid and wore it boldly, proudly, most of the night. It was liberating, a means to act out without lasting consequences or direct confrontation. Some folks caught it, appreciating the irony, offering a smirk or a snicker. I was used to carrying the weight of acting responsibly. This was my mild version of breaking bad.

Perhaps surprisingly, given the world we now occupy, there's no evidence of me in the hat. I've never seen any pictures, and you would've thought that someone, even back then, would have snapped a Kodak moment to remember.

During that span, I hadn't had many interactions with Coach. I don't know how he found out or if he ever knew of my frustrations. Tommy Amaker remained a sounding board. It would've made sense for him to relay my grievances.

Coach asked to meet for coffee on campus. I arrived without the Carolina hat.

He didn't apologize, nor do I think he needed to. He conceded that changes needed to occur, progression needed to be made. He told me that

I was about to be a senior, time to be hungry on the court and elsewhere: if my parents offered me one roll at dinner to take two.

Many of the specifics during the talk are lost and really aren't overly important. So often with Coach, it was not what he said but how he said it. He was gifted at leavening moments of grave seriousness and bringing seriousness to times of levity. I'm only writing about these moments now because they deepened my bond with Coach. Today, we're closer than ever. In all my years in basketball, Steve Kerr is still the only person I've come across who shared some of that DNA, that combination of presence and sensitivity.

That season was personally challenging for him. Years later, I realized the toll it had to have taken on Coach. His friend and confidant Jim Valvano had started dropping by that season. I knew Valvano as ACC royalty, the coach who steered North Carolina State to a magic championship, only to subsequently receive a raw deal when the school's administration pried him from his role following some questionable allegations. He resurfaced on television and often paired with Dick Vitale, calling games as the Killer Vees.

Valvano had recently been diagnosed with metastatic adenocarcinoma, a type of glandular cancer, and received his medical treatment at Duke University Medical Center. Often, he'd show up at practice, checking in on us, chatting with Coach.

I didn't grasp that he was nearing the end of a hard-fought battle.

I watched the first ESPYs that March, broadcast from Madison Square Garden. Coach, to my surprise, was there, tenderly aiding Valvano onto the stage. Valvano offered a dramatic, stirring speech of living each day to your fullest.

He passed away at Duke the following month.

He had shared a rivalry and respect with Coach K. Once they stopped playing each other, a true friendship had blossomed. In retrospect, to know that his friend was hurting, fighting, and struggling had to put an immeasurable weight over him.

———

I left our meeting. Kool-Aid sipped, slate cleansed. I was back on board.

The team was going to be different. We were onboarding a strong class. Most of the championship core had now departed after Bobby and Thomas graduated.

This squad, for the first time ever, would be my team.

9

A sincere, symbiotic partnership between Coach K and me sprouted my final season at Duke, the type of relationship, I believe, that he had always desired. Looking back, so did I. The roller coaster of three years of highs—the championships, the pass, the celebrations—and lows—my doubts and anger following the toe injury and rehabilitation, our early exit—built calluses and hardened resolve.

Coach planned to put the ball in my hands, entrusting me with our offense. He envisioned me in the mold of Magic Johnson, a big guard capable of surveying defenses and facilitating an offense. He was again that Coach K who had visited me at my parents' home, urging me to be great, telling me to trust my instincts and that I possessed intangibles that could not be taught. Our relationship was battle tested, and we were united, through to that other side. We were acclimated, accustomed to any possible scenario tossed at us.

Coach had those types of rapports with certain players who arrived in Durham. They left impressions on him, imprints on the program. One of his strengths was that he adapted, learning from players like Johnny

Dawkins, Tommy Amaker, Danny Ferry, Christian Laettner, and Bobby Hurley.

I probably could not have handled that level of responsibility earlier in my college career. I understood now that part of being on a team and building trust involved difficult dialogue and honesty. He solicited my observations, and I was comfortable respectfully pushing back as needed. He encouraged me to shoot, to go out and try to score thirty-five points.

For this team, you being unselfish is a selfish act, he said.

I accepted that in order for us to win in my senior season, one of my primary responsibilities was scoring, that sometimes a contested shot from me could be a better option for us than an open shot from others.

That desire to please others first remained. Possibly, in the recent past, I found comfort in having Laettner, Bobby, or even Brian Davis step into the spotlight. They were gone. I was exposed. It took Coach K three years of pushing, but I appreciated the suggestion that perhaps I was not destined for just a role—*take two dinner rolls*—but perhaps the role.

Better yet, my body was finally feeling like itself again as I transitioned from crutches to a boot to finally walking again. Thomas Hill had dipped in and out of our apartment between visits to NBA teams, preparing for the draft. He always returned with gear from whatever organization he had visited. That'll hopefully be me next year, I daydreamed.

I couldn't train at Card Gym yet with the guys. Instead, I imagined how we'd look, how I needed to play. I devoured an old VHS tape of Magic, *Always Showtime*, trying to memorize his mesmerizing moves, studying how he protected the ball by using his body and how he left people in his wake with an array of spin moves.

I was happy when the Pacers selected Thomas in the second round of the draft. With him leaving, I opted to live alone for the first time, settling in a fly apartment with a bedroom upstairs that overlooked the kitchen and living room. I kind of felt like Eddie Murphy's character in

Boomerang. Maybe it was not that extravagant, but it was a palace after living in dorms and apartments with roommates the last couple of years.

For the first time, no outside outsized expectations arrived with the new season. There were no discussions about the need to take another step forward after a Final Four appearance. We did not enter with the strain of defending a national title. No one expected us to win it all or even compete in the tournament. The spotlight was solely on Chapel Hill. Carolina had just claimed the championship and returned everyone except George Lynch, while importing a dynamic freshman class that featured Rasheed Wallace, Jeff McInnis, and Jerry Stackhouse.

Our roster was a hodgepodge. We flexed an experienced front line between me, Cherokee Parks, and Tony Lang. Jeff Capel was a talented freshman addition. He was a born baller. Kenny Blakeney, Marty Clark, and Chris Collins could all expect more playing time in the backcourt.

I had cultivated a deeper relationship with Chris over the summer. Coach asked freshmen to return home after the school year, to exhale and enjoy some familiar cooking after a whirlwind first college year. I had visited Chris in Chicago, the same way that Laettner and the others came to my home after my freshman year. Chris's dad, Doug, worked as an NBA analyst and had coached Michael Jordan's Bulls just prior to Chicago's championship years. While in Chicago, Doug had invited us to watch an Eastern Conference Finals game in the old Chicago Stadium. We enjoyed watching Jordan send the Knicks home on his way to a third straight championship. Doug, I was aware, had played some in the NBA. I didn't know his full history. After the game, inside his home, he had asked if I wanted to see one of his old games.

Sure.

He popped in a VHS cassette of the 1977 NBA Finals, his Philadelphia 76ers against the Portland Trail Blazers.

A different, more physical NBA roared to life. I immediately appreciated the depth of those 76ers. They had Dr. J, Darryl Dawkins, George McGinnis. They even brought Kobe Bryant's dad, Joe, off the bench. I was focusing on a younger, spry Doug on the court when a fight suddenly erupted. Dawkins and Portland's Bob Gross wrestled before squaring up. Maurice Lucas lured Dawkins's attention away from Gross with a slap. Dawkins launched a punch that missed Lucas and connected with Doug, leaving him dazed and in need of stitches.

Doug next inserted another classic, this time a game against the Celtics.

Grant, how many points do you think I scored?

I don't know. Eight?

Doug gave a wry smile as we watched his younger self make bucket after bucket.

He was like my dad, I thought. He enjoyed taking video strolls down memory lane. My dad was exactly the person I called to ask about Doug once I returned home.

You didn't know about Doug? He was the first pick of his draft.

I just hoped that Chris had inherited some of that shooting DNA. Most of the trip consisted of us forecasting our season. I tried building him up, aware that we were going to need his shooting. We're the Lakers and you can be my Byron Scott, I joked with him, not so slyly implying that I had the Magic responsibilities handled.

Beyond Chris taking the next step, I was excited about Joey Beard finally joining the program.

I believed he would make an impact. Instead, Tony took the jokes about playing time to heart and in the process ripped out Joey's. For all I knew, Coach was the Oracle in *The Matrix*. The ribbing might have been hard to receive at the time, but it lit a fire inside Tony.

Tony was the best player on the court those couple of months as I finally ran with the guys again, regaining my form. He made sure, demanded, that he guarded Joey during open runs and offered him no room to operate. I was excited that Tony not only was ready for our next season but also had elevated his game, although I was concerned about Joey's competitive spirit. Some guys wilted under the internal competition at Duke.

From the outside, Duke was a private, preppy, elite university. We liked to imagine that we were Ivy League–esque. Our basketball program, to casual spectators, was a reflection of that stereotype. No question, a lot of great white players were Duke products before, during, and after my four years at the school.

But the program's reality didn't align with the perception. Coach had recruited Chris Webber. He visited with Kenny Anderson. He went after Jerry Stackhouse. After me, he landed players like Elton Brand, Corey Maggette, Kyrie Irving, and Zion Williamson.

The list went on and on.

Can you ball or not?

To me, someone who lived and breathed Duke basketball for four years, the program was a reflection of hard work, of diving on the floor, of bloodying knees and elbows, of fighting, scraping, clawing for just one more possession, all rooted in Coach K's Chicago upbringing.

Some guys weren't cut out for it. Black, white, or in between, those guys were weeded out.

Publicly, Billy McCaffrey might have said he transferred after my freshman year because he wanted to play point guard and couldn't with Bobby Hurley firmly entrenched in the role at Duke. In my opinion, he left because Thomas took it to him daily in practice and he would have had to fight for minutes.

Joey arrived as a freshman with a lot of fanfare. He could have stuck it out. I assumed he couldn't handle Tony's intensity and left, later learning that he had other issues he was confronting before he transferred.

That thirst for loose balls, the will to fight through screens, the eagerness to take charges? The competition just for the privilege of being on the court, to be part of that ungainly battle?

That was Coach.

That was Duke basketball.

———

I was settling back into a school routine when I received an interview request from our Black Student Alliance. The television news program *60 Minutes* had asked for my participation in a segment about being a Black student at Duke.

No problem. I was more comfortable now in trusting my thoughts to make it successfully from my mind to my mouth speaking with the media. I had played in high-profile games, spoken at countless youth camps. I had watched closely how my older teammates conducted themselves with reporters. If they could do it, I figured, so could I. I knew how to tell myself to slow down, to project my voice. I could always express myself through sports. Now I could express myself through words as well.

I joined a couple other African American students, and we answered a few softball questions about our time on campus. I hoped to relay an entirely positive experience.

I watched the hit from my apartment, and "hit" was an entirely accurate description. Lesley Stahl narrated a scene that opened with students of color congregating at the Black bench.

What's going on here? This is 1993 and college campuses shouldn't look like this. Who decreed that Black students should keep to themselves? The White Citizens' Councils, David Duke, the Ku Klux Klan? No, the Black students did it on their own. If separate but equal was ruled out by the Supreme Court years ago, why are Black students now ruling in equal but separate?

The segment portrayed Black students as self-segregating themselves on campus, disinterested in investing or participating in Duke's larger social community. The story was nowhere near an accurate reflection of my time on campus. They had approached us with a story already in mind and looked for some B-roll footage and interviews that rounded out their thesis. They didn't even include my responses. I guess they didn't fit the narrative.

Most of the students on campus, Black, white, and everyone else, were outraged. Students of color convened a town hall meeting where everyone voiced agitation and disappointment.

Did we find a sense of strength among ourselves? Of course. It was human nature to gravitate toward the familiar. We shared in the communal journey of our ancestors. At times, we attended Black Greek parties and met up at a bench between classes. Part of that was an effort to preserve our sense of identity within our own culture. Hip-hop music was diverse, eclectic, and Afrocentric. Spike Lee had just dropped his *Malcolm X* movie. We were proud to be Black. If we had genuinely wanted to self-segregate, I was sure all of us would have been ecstatic to attend a historically Black university. We had made a conscious decision to enroll at Duke.

White students—Laettner, as usual, was the exception—usually didn't attend parties at the Black Greek fraternities. I had so many friends who were Kappas and I was at their house so often that I felt like one, even though I never pledged. The parties were fun, certainly, a large piece of the allure. There was also an expectation, a demand, to succeed in school, to capitalize on an opportunity that we were afforded. Iron sharpened iron. People, especially young ones transitioning into adulthood, yearned to play a part in something meaningful. To me, it was no different from playing on a basketball team.

We frequented other fraternities. I'd be lying if I didn't admit that the keg parties hosted by white fraternities were a big draw, even though I refrained from drinking after hearing one too many horror stories of athletes and drug and alcohol abuse from my dad.

Often, those parties played a little too much Young MC, Vanilla Ice, or whatever the mainstream hip-hop act of the day was.

How many times could you really bust a move?

I crafted my own cassette mix from the likes of X Clan and EPMD, popping it into the stereo at the parties. When it was time to go to the next place, the tape came with us, and so did a lot of the revelers. After a while, we became the party.

For students of color, every day was an act of folding ourselves into Duke's social fabric. We were living, learning, socializing, eating on campus. Our presence alone was integration.

Code switching was probably easier for me because I played basketball. We enjoyed an added level of recognizability. I was horrible at recalling names. Yet everyone, it seemed, knew mine. I simply called everyone dog.

I embraced Duke. Duke embraced me. Beyond campus, Tony and I became rooted in the city of Durham itself. Duke's campus was mostly sectioned off into three parts. West Campus hosted the pristine chapel and beautiful Gothic architecture designed by Julian Abele. Central Campus housed the apartments where we lived our sophomore year—1708 Pace. By design or not, it seemed like all the Black students lived there, so much so that we jokingly referred to it as the ghetto. Trinity College, an all-girls school, once anchored East Campus. Then it was home to all the university's freshmen. A wall, not a very tall one, but still a barrier, enclosed the entire campus.

Durham existed beyond the wall. Many students seldom crossed it in their four years, figuring that there was not much to do beyond campus.

Beyond practice and class, Tony and I lived outside the wall. We tied the university to the adjacent community, especially after we both had possession of our own cars. We were at barbershops—just with a different barber from my freshman year—sat in the stands at high school basketball games, dropped in at the fast-food joints, ate barbecue at community cookouts, and mentored kids in grade school.

When I reflect on my time at Duke now, basketball memories flood forward. I also warmly recall the campus life, the friendships forged, the experiences gained in the classroom, in the community, and, yes, at the Black bench.

I'm thankful that we were never secluded as athletes. The beauty was we had different life experiences that strengthened our bonds.

I shared an incredible journey with my teammates. That brotherhood and connection is eternal.

Still, the people with whom I speak most frequently from those days didn't play basketball. They were the students who helped me come out of my shell, who enlightened me about politics and awakened me to the importance of community.

What made Duke a special place then and why I'm still tethered now, not just to the basketball program but to the entire university, is a strong sense of community, a sense of family. There was an expectation of excellence, not just in the athletic program, but throughout the campus. Even then, I was aware that I was just a slice of what made Duke, as a whole, exceptional for everybody.

———

That season, the NCAA abolished the rule mandating that ball handlers were limited to five seconds to either shoot, pass, or dribble. Our first practice, Coach called us to mid-court and explained the new guidelines.

Grant, he said, come to the top of the key and dribble.

This, he said, is our "going to Charlotte" offense.

Charlotte, of course, would be hosting the Final Four, and he was directing me to hold on to the ball as my teammates ran action away from me, to kill the shot clock until I spotted a favorable matchup or driving lane. *Be great.*

In retrospect, he conceded that he should have coined it the "winning a championship" offense.

We started the season with ten straight wins, a stretch that included a key victory over Xavier. Coach challenged me in front of the team before that game. I was still searching for my comfort zone, but I responded by cobbling together a quality game. For the first time in a long time, in a big game in front of the Cameron Crazies, I felt as though I could fully trust again in my toe and myself.

We beat Michigan, again and always, although that time without Chris Webber, who had declared for the NBA and became the top overall pick. Jalen Rose and Juwan Howard were still Wolverines and played aggressively. Cherokee impressed. The rest of us rallied to the occasion.

This is not a well-oiled machine like two years ago, Coach K told the media afterward. In fact, I'm not sure we have a machine of any kind at this point.

Two days later, I woke up, fumbling for the remote to flip on *Sports-Center* out of habit. The show led with a story on Bobby. The previous night, he had been in a car collision. A bad one. A terrible one.

He had just been in Durham a couple months earlier, training for his debut NBA season with the Sacramento Kings. A motorist driving his truck without his lights on had plowed into Bobby's Toyota 4Runner as he returned home following a game at ARCO Arena. The impact had ejected him from his car, severing his trachea, collapsing his lungs, shattering his body.

Bobby? My brother? Will he live?

We reconvened a couple weeks later after splitting for the holidays. Bobby showed up at one of our practices. Doctors later said that the impact of the crash would have killed ninety-nine people out of a hundred. Bobby, of course, was that one survivor. He didn't know how or when to quit. He survived, only he was frail and moved gingerly, slowly, while dressed in a sweat suit and dark sunglasses. I was thrilled to see him. Yet I already mourned the death of his NBA career. His professional journey had just started, but in that moment I was certain he would never ball again.

Bobby being Bobby, he laced his sneakers and resumed his NBA career the following season.

———

Around our team, the atmosphere was carefree, light. It was a fun group. Together, we attended football games, ate, hung out. We were from all over the place with different perspectives and experiences: Me, a Black kid from the DMV suburbs. Chris, a white Chicagoan. Cherokee, a laid-back Californian. Tony, Black and from the Deep South.

Coach again molded us into one with a singular objective.

Earlier, with Coach on us my freshman year and the personalities of Laettner and Brian Davis, everything could feel aggressive, steeped in juvenile testosterone. The rest of us kind of fell in line, resorting to constant trash-talking and slap boxing.

College teams, especially back then, took on the personalities of their upperclassmen. We were going to need this group, somewhat experienced, mostly young and untested, to quickly coalesce. I tried empowering them, encouraging the younger guys at practice and in games.

Slowly, Jeff developed into a two-way force. Marty played well. At long last, Cherokee was taking that giant step forward. Tony was competing every game as though Joey Beard were coming for his minutes.

My dad called me early in the season. We were catching up when he casually dropped that Glenn Robinson, over at Purdue, was off to a heck of a start, dropping thirty points a game.

He paused.

Grant, don't you want to be player of the year? If so, you better start taking some more shots.

It was always balance. Give and take. The game's individual rhythm dictated how I played. Coach, my dad, part of me—everyone, wanted me to be that guy.

I'm trying to win another national championship, I said. I'm going to need Jeff, Chris, and Marty.

Those guys were going to have to be tested and battle ready if we were going to have a chance.

Maybe he thought I needed the GPS of my headspace examined again. But I really did think we had a shot.

———

Rodney Rogers was off to the NBA, but Wake Forest remained a problem. Randolph Childress, my old AAU teammate, was going off for them nightly early in conference play. We teasingly talked trash back and forth during our matchup. Typically, I could keep up with smaller guards, my length allowing me to harass them. This time, Randolph had the audacity to launch a step-back three-pointer right in my face that found pay dirt and clinched the game for Wake.

It was a loss, our first, but thankfully just a blip. We were the aggressors in our next game against Virginia. Beforehand, I caught whispers that Cornel Parker, their forward whom I had played against in high school, was upset, believing that he should have been the defensive player of the year instead of me the previous season. I felt in command that game, pulling the strings of our offense, influencing the game without having to score. We put them away early and easily. The media crafted a narrative afterward that Parker had wrapped me up and we won despite my play.

Okay, I thought, promising to remember that one for down the road.

Collectively, this group of guys wasn't the most talented squad I had played with. We were not deep, but we were connected and cohesive. I guess Chris did get some of his dad's hooping genes. He developed into a marksman, one of the first players I saw who ran to the three-point line during fast breaks, spotting up from there, instead of continuing for a layup. Jeff, Marty, Cherokee, Tony, all continued their reliable play.

Coach K, I sensed, was enjoying us, realizing that this group offered their all every game. We were no longer the silent assassins and rode a five-game win streak that catapulted us back to the country's top ranking.

It didn't last long.

The stars aligned along Tobacco Road. Carolina, the top-ranked team much of the season, nipped at our heels as the nation's second-ranked team. We had crisscrossed each other the past couple seasons, sharing in dominance but never really dominant at the same time. We had won some matchups. They had won some matchups.

See? A rivalry.

As we warmed up in front of their basket inside the Dean Dome, the man himself quietly motioned me over.

You know, Coach Dean Smith said, you can come sit over here on our bench if you'd like.

A faint smirk formed on my face. I couldn't help it. Those were probably the first words he had spoken to me since he left our house four years earlier, knowing before I was even certain myself that I would be attending Duke over Carolina.

We were close in the first half. They were too much of everything in the end: too athletic, too big, too deep, too good. They resembled our teams of recent years, arriving in waves. They were so deep that Jerry Stackhouse, one of the top freshmen in the nation, came off their bench.

I was chasing, hounding Randolph again a couple of games later against Wake Forest. I was on early, still trying to strike that balance between facilitating and scoring. An awkward, gangly freshman stood in the lane, blocking my path. I rose over him for a dunk, a moment I casually reminded Tim Duncan about occasionally once we were both in the NBA. Wake, for whatever reason, was always a challenge, especially at their place. The commute to Winston-Salem from Durham—too close for a flight, just far enough away to warrant a long bus ride—always took something out of us. This game was no different once I tired a little from pursuing Randolph, although I would never admit it to him. He stirred, nailing a couple dagger shots, and grinned my way. The final score wasn't all that close. It was my last game against the Demon Deacons. I didn't mind saying good riddance to them.

Another loss to Wake. Another tails-between-our-legs bus ride home. Again, as soon as the bus stopped, Coach told us to get taped and ready. This time, I was not fooled. He had pulled this a couple years earlier. I was a senior, aware the rules were different and thankful that teams were no longer allowed to practice following a game. Coach rounded us up in the stands, lasering his scorn at me, saying that he needed more for us to be successful.

Man, I thought, I'm guarding the other team's best player every game most of the time, initiating our offense, rebounding, scoring. I'm still not doing enough?

Maybe you'd have been better off in the NBA instead of coming back this year, he added.

That's when it dawned on me. That was the exact chastising he laced Laettner with a couple of years earlier. The message was more for my teammates than me. They watched, waiting to see how, if, I reacted. Motivate a team's leader and watch the results trickle down. Laettner took it then and the team responded. I would accept it now.

Thankfully, we could take it out at home against Virginia, and I could extract some revenge on their self-proclaimed defensive wizard, Cornel Parker. Inside Cameron, I gave the ball up early in our offense, shrugged off Parker by curling off screens, and hunted for the ball again. If most games started with me in search of the game's tempo, for once I came out with a lasso, hog-tying the cadence, hauling it toward me. It was probably the only college game that I could be credibly accused of tracking down my own looks. The matchup was personal, even more so following Coach K's dressing-down. After every bucket I glanced over and slyly smiled at Cory Alexander, a friend and their injured star, who sat out. He knew the deal. I was scoring. So were Tony and Jeff. Parker frustratingly fouled out as we trounced the Cavaliers by thirty points.

Against North Carolina State, Coach prepped us to be mentally ready, to maintain our focus. He knew that we were a better team than them, having discarded State earlier in conference play. This game, he said, isn't about your opponent; it's about you and maintaining your standard.

In my four years under him, Coach was skillful at finding the meaning of each individual game. Sometimes, some games, the challenge was the opponent. Other times, he preached to stay on the attack, to keep pressing forward, to play beyond the level of our opponents. Directive received. We handled State almost as easily as we beat Virginia.

I didn't need any motivation from Coach a few games later. It was a jersey-retirement ceremony I'd actually be able to play in, my own. Our opponent was Temple, a capable team that flexed a formidable zone defense and featured the future NBA players Eddie Jones, Rick Brunson, and Aaron McKie.

As crazy as it sounds, my first concern was that the hoopla over the ceremony and a surplus of family and friends in town would disrupt my routine.

I had become a creature of habit since forgetting my shoes a couple years earlier, a believer that rituals settled nerves, tempered excitement, silenced doubt. The anality was an often-futile attempt at control over a sport that confoundingly, ultimately came down to luck, be it a good bounce on a rim or a well-timed pass.

My game days were meticulously mapped out, from when I dressed, ate, and napped to the time I left for the arena and the route I took to get there.

Oh, it didn't stop there.

I was particular about what time my ankles were taped, what I was doing in the locker room before Coach talked to us, the moment I started stretching outside our locker room, and where I shot from on the court once we broke our layup line.

The ceremony arrived, sweeping away my concerns. So much of the season was a journey, the grind from one game to the next. The jersey retirement forced me to pause, appreciate, and reflect on those days, games, and moments with Laettner, Bobby, Brian, and Thomas. Taking my framed No. 33 jersey, I cradled it, lifting it toward the Crazies. I hugged my beaming parents, who stood near a proud Coach K.

There is little doubt about the origins of my rigidity about routines. That night, my dad was wearing the same outfit he did to all our games, a white turtleneck, tan khaki pants, and a blue hat. If he had worn it to a Friday game during a tournament and we won, he'd take the clothes off, hang them up, and put the same clothes on for our next game. On the road, he'd frequent the same restaurant, sit in the same booth, order the same meal.

In honor of the evening, several Crazies dressed in my dad's likeness, turtlenecks, fake mustaches, and all.

I was grateful to share most of my college experience with my parents. They finagled time out of their busy schedules to attend a lot of our games and wove themselves into Duke's community. My mom sat on several Duke boards long after I departed campus.

My teammates called my dad Cool Cal ever since we had visited the White House following our first championship. As we toured the grounds and walked past the Oval Office, we spotted my dad already inside, speaking with Marvin Pierce Bush, the son of President George H. W. Bush.

Most of the team's parents were a constant, comforting presence. We were a unit on the court. They were a unit off it. Jeff's dad coached at North Carolina A&T in nearby Greensboro. Chris's dad broadcast NBA games. Tony's dad was a schoolteacher in Mobile. My parents worked demanding jobs. Despite everyone's full-time job and commitments, they made time to see us play. They were not helicopter parents, though. My parents never questioned Coach over my playing time or when I was frustrated coming off the bench.

I realized that my basketball knowledge might have surpassed my dad's early on at Duke when Tommy Amaker approached me during a game. Grant, he said, your dad wants me to tell you that you should try to bank in your free throws. Now, I wouldn't advise that you do that. But you can tell him that I passed it on.

They were always there, to pick me up, whenever I felt low or down, to steady me if I was too full of myself or overconfident.

It had been a ride. The end was nearing.

The marathon continued.

That year, we played more zone defense than all my previous seasons at Duke combined. The defense protected our short rotation from foul trouble and shielded some of the younger guys still learning our principles.

At times, we maintained elements of man-to-man, and the game against Temple was one such time; Tony and I guarded Aaron and Eddie, while Chris Collins battled one of their bigs. Coach was innovative in his schemes, confident that we could quickly adapt. For the most part, we were a capable bunch. It's little wonder that Chris, Tony, and Jeff are all gifted coaches today.

Temple was a chore, Iowa-like in their stubbornness not to beat themselves. They made us sweat out a close win.

My final game at Cameron was fittingly against Carolina. Neither of us held the top spot anymore, though we were still both ranked in the top five. The night before, I teased Tony and Marty that neither better cry when they acknowledged the seniors before the game.

Again, Carolina's depth and athleticism prevailed as they turned a once-close game into an easy win.

We all knew the story of Gene Banks, a senior during Coach K's first year at Duke who hit a legendary game-winning shot over Carolina, capping his career at Cameron. If not a shot like that, I'd at least have settled for going out with a win. It was not the ending of my dreams, and I was discombobulated when administrators corralled me, Tony, and Marty, telling us we needed to address the crowd. I hadn't realized that Laettner and Bobby did the same following their last games at Cameron. Of course, they hadn't just suffered a loss.

Marty grabbed the microphone and quickly passed it to Tony. Tony's speech was even shorter. Mic in hand, still distraught over the defeat, I fumbled for words of gratitude. Whatever I said, I doubt it made any sense. All losses stung. That one, my final time in Cameron, hurt the most. It was hard summing up four years of many highs, and a couple lows, on the spot.

Looking back on it, I wish I had the chance to soak in more of Duke's academic offerings. Don't get me wrong. I wouldn't change much about the experience. A lot of my professors and classmates left enduring impressions through their lessons, shared experiences, and fellowship. The anatomy class provided me with an early and ultimately crucial understanding of my body. The public speaking course helped me to be comfortable in allowing my thoughts to flow freely.

I had entered Duke sincerely believing that law school would be in my future. Ambitions and plans shifted once the NBA became a possibility. I did what I had to do to maintain a decent grade point average.

I can't even find any lingering remorse about having to divide my attention between basketball, school, and other aspects of life. I wanted, in some ways needed, to learn how to be social, and that was how I spent a good chunk of time in Durham. I remember once, as a freshman, my dad called our dorm on a Wednesday night asking for me. Tony informed him I was on a date.

The next day, my mom called me.

Your dad was beyond livid that you were out on a school night instead of being at the library, she said. Tell Tony the next time he calls, no matter where you are, to say that you're at the library.

She recognized that the college experience spanned far outside the classroom. She had not finished at the top of her class at Wellesley. She watched some of her classmates who did struggle in life, while she continued rising in the corporate world. You can live without Chaucer and you can live without calculus, but you cannot make it in the wide, wide world without common sense, was one of her many bits of advice that I took with me throughout my life.

Coach shrugged off the Carolina loss, allowing the rest of us to do the same.

We handled Clemson in the opener of the ACC Tournament in Charlotte, setting up another matchup against Virginia. Beating a team three times consecutively, Coach K reminded us, was never easy (unless the opponent was Michigan—just couldn't help myself there).

They played loose. A freshman from Queens, Jamal Robinson, caught us off guard with a great game. I missed a couple layups, and the game slipped away.

We stayed the night in the Queen City's Adam's Mark hotel. Coach K summoned the seniors to his suite. His door was barely closed before he started admonishing us for our approach against Virginia, alleging that we hadn't arrived prepared and that we needed to be ready for the approaching NCAA tournament.

We're in that bad habit of wanting to stay back with success, instead of pursuing the next opportunity for it, he said.

Initially, we wondered why he had decided to come at us so hard. His message of urgency settled in with breakfast the next morning. We were all together, a team on the road with no game before us. Other schools had matchups waiting for them. We just had a long bus ride home in our immediate future.

As we departed Charlotte, I was reminded that it would be the site of the Final Four. I was not sure if we would be back for it. We called for a team meeting somewhere between Charlotte and Durham. The guys who had been through the tournament detailed their experiences. We talked of expectations, the need to play with one another, for one another, the importance of constant focus.

Motivate a team's leader and watch the results trickle down.

Jeff and Chris, we need your defense to take a step forward.

I didn't confront them. I challenged them, inviting them to take ownership, confident that they would take the charge as motivation.

We had lost two games in a week.

It would take a circuitous route if we did make our way back to Charlotte.

We started the NCAA tournament in the Southeast Regional by traveling to St. Petersburg. We breezed past Texas Southern in the opener, knowing that Michigan State would provide a challenge. Their star, Shawn Respert, was on a scoring frenzy. In the game, I was on him, another personal challenge. Whenever he slipped by me through a screen, Marty or Chris met him. Just like in earlier years, we were communicating, working as one. By the time Respert broke free, it was too late. They didn't have an answer for me or Cherokee on offense, and we gained separation in a comfortable win.

We had a few days of preparation before heading to Knoxville to face Marquette in the Sweet 16. Watching their film, they conjured memories of Kentucky. They were not a team I was overly familiar with, but they appeared deep and formidable and were anchored by Jim McIlvaine, a fierce presence in the post.

Marquette jabbed us a little at the game's outset, gaining an early lead. I was matched against a sophomore, a guard named Roney Eford.

He could ball a little bit. By the way he ran his mouth, he thought he could ball a lot.

I didn't need the motivation. I was trying to keep my senior season alive. By that point, Roney might as well have changed his name to Cornel Parker or for that matter Ron Burt.

I started the second half on a mission, demanding the ball, peeling off screens, finishing off alley-oops.

After the win, we filed into the Thompson-Boling Arena stands for a glimpse at whom we would play next between Purdue and Kansas. In the matchup, Glenn Robinson put on a clinic. He had been unstoppable the entire season and dropped thirty points on Kansas—in the first half—including dumping all over their tree of a center, Greg Ostertag.

I don't know if I've ever seen a college player of my era dominate a game so demonstratively.

I guess Coach didn't want us too wary. We left at halftime. I knew Glenn would be my primary assignment in the Regional Final. Cherokee Parks, my roommate on the trip, tried hyping me up that night.

If they call him Big Dog, he said, then you're a dogcatcher.

The moment would soon arrive when I would see just how true I was being with myself and my dad earlier in the season. Glenn was on his way to winning player of the year. He had put up the numbers. But I believed we had the better team.

I was pumped, buzzing from adrenaline and belief. So was Cherokee. We ended the evening performing defensive slides throughout the hotel's hallway.

Glenn and I played it coy with each other the following day when reporters corralled us for a joint interview. Each of us heaped praise on the other. Media billed the game solely as Glenn versus Grant, Grant versus Glenn.

I knew his game. He was a power forward who could shoot, a relative rarity at that time. He was not going to finesse me with his handles. He would look to find his shot following a dribble or two. I hoped to stay in front of him, invade his space, funnel him to my help.

Early in the game, Glenn shook me on a screen, nailing a baseline jumper. I pledged to dig deeper, to make it difficult for him. He didn't need much operating room, but we started suffocating him, denying him angles. Neither team pulled away. Tony clamped down on another one of their scorers, Cuonzo Martin. I took pride that Jeff and Chris were ready for the moment, impacting the game.

You're the guy in the second half, Coach K told Jeff at halftime. You're playing a great game.

That's right, Jeff, I added. Coach is right. Be great today. You can beat this guy.

Jeff opened the second half with five points, providing us with a slim lead. I was tacked with a fourth foul with about ten minutes left. Coach yanked me from the game. Doubt crept in. That could be it.

God, thank you, I said to myself. It's been a good run.

Instead, Jeff pulled everyone together, rallying our team. He told them that I had carried everyone this far. It was time for everyone else to step up.

They maintained the lead when I checked back in with about four minutes left. We grinded out the win, knowing the steps we needed to take to drag us over the finish line. Glenn was limited to just thirteen points and spent nearly half the game without a field goal.

We were going back to Charlotte after all. It would be my third Final Four in four years, Duke's seventh in nine.

We were nearly through cutting down the nets when Coach found me.

I almost screwed up with all those fouls, I told him.

Are you kidding me? You won the game for us at halftime when you told Jeff he could be great today. And he was. He was the difference when you were out. I'm proud of you.

I looked at him, nodding.

The reframing worked.

Glenn could be player of the year. He would be watching us, I was sure, along with Carolina, who had unexpectedly bowed out in the East Regional's second round against Boston College.

We were still playing.

———

That season, that team, was rejuvenating. When the previous season had expired against Cal, it felt like the weight and gravity of three entire seasons—the constant heaviness of expectations during the entire run with Laettner, Bobby, and Brian Davis—had come crashing to the ground.

We were not a great team. We were a good team with great heart, a combination that often overcomes adversity.

In the Final Four, we faced the Florida Gators, who had made a surprising, sprinting run after just squeaking past James Madison in the opening round by two points.

They featured another quality big, Andrew DeClercq. I remembered that we had recruited DeClercq and Cherokee at the same time a few years back. The pair had sat in the stands together, flanked by Mrs. K during one of our intra-squad games, as the Crazies cheered for both.

On defense, I faced another challenge in chasing Craig Brown, someone who never tired and used his teammates as roadblocks to free up space.

We practiced for a week, learning our responsibilities, vowing to stick to our principles, ready for the moment as we bused back down to Charlotte.

We were not.

Before we knew it, we were down by thirteen points. Was it us or Florida that had played in all those recent Final Fours? I gifted them possessions through turnovers, again watching my college career expire in real time.

Coach K called a time-out early in the second half.

Stay in the moment. Don't dwell on earlier plays or worry about the plays to come. Focus on this one.

With both nothing and everything to lose, I found my shot, located my rhythm, and drilled a couple three-pointers. Okay, I finally found you, tempo. I scored on putbacks, tip-ins, and jumpers. On defense, I denied Brown and hauled in rebounds. They assumed a one-point lead off DeClercq's bucket with just under three minutes left. From there, we made the right plays.

I connected on free throws. Marty stole a pass. Cherokee put home his miss. Tony drew a charge.

Little plays. Winning plays. Duke plays.

We escaped with a narrow win and a date against Arkansas in the championship game.

———

Just watching Arkansas film was overwhelming. We were in Coach's hotel suite the night before the championship. Their coach, Nolan Richardson, was someone I respected who had shaped his program in his image. Arkansas was long, like Carolina. They pressured full court, full time like Iowa. Like Purdue, they possessed an immense talent in the All-American Corliss Williamson. He was an updated Charles Barkley, an undersized pit bull as an interior force. Unlike Glenn Robinson and Purdue, Arkansas had surrounded Corliss with a squad. Scotty Thurman was a forward with long arms who could play on the perimeter. Corey Beck served as a crafty guard.

They brought reinforcements off their bench more than comfortable pulling up from beyond the NBA three-point line.

Yep, forty minutes of hell, indeed.

I left Coach's room, pondering how and if we could find a way to beat these guys. It was probably the only time a thought like that had crossed my mind the entire season.

I calmed myself by remembering that no one had thought we could beat Vegas a few years earlier.

We needed to play smart yet aggressive. We had to attack yet stay within ourselves.

Another delicate balance.

A couple years earlier with Laettner, we would have passed over their press. Last year with Bobby, we would have used him to slice through it with his dribbling. Now we didn't want to get into a track meet with them. We wanted, needed to control the game's pace.

I woke up the morning of the championship, trying to dismiss thoughts that win or lose, this was it.

The game didn't tip until late in the evening, allowing the day to drag. Coaches broke the monotony with meetings and meals. Downtime filled the gaps, and with every shuffle to and from every session I realized that this would be our final time eating together, our last bus ride, my last time putting on this jersey, representing this school, playing for Coach K.

Stay in the moment.

I was in it some twenty seconds into the game when, as I leaped for a rebound, Corliss bumped me in the back while I jumped for a board. I crashed hard onto the court. The arena turned ghastly silent. With help, I exited briefly, allowing the pain and emotions to subside before checking back in. Arkansas started a guy, Ken Biley, who had seldom played for them. I guess his job was to bother me, because he picked me up full court, talking trash and hand checking me the entire length. Two quick fouls and I didn't see Biley for the rest of the game. They were trying to dictate the game's tempo and yank it in their direction early.

Arkansas threw bodies at us, trying to trap and tire us. Coach preached patience as we established ourselves and our presence early, letting them know this would be a game. On defense, I remained conscious of getting back in transition early to meet Corliss, allowing Cherokee enough time to meander back.

Hands down, they were the best team we had played all season. They were smart and well coached, blitzing us at random times from awkward angles.

Zone. Double-teams. Man-to-man.

To outsiders, their defense might have seemed erratic, indiscriminate. Clearly, internally, they were united, knowing when to trap and funnel us to their preferred spots on the floor. They were committed to getting the ball from my hands.

We carved a ten-point advantage in the second half. Our own defense was resilient, limiting Corliss. Desperate, they surged, cutting into our lead. With under a minute left, Scotty Thurman broke a 70-all game, his shot arcing over Tony's outstretched hand and splashing through as the shot clock expired. I joke now that if Tony hadn't cut his fingernails beforehand, he would have blocked the shot. The moments, the plays, we were used to making eluded us in the final seconds as we watched Arkansas celebrate a 76–72 victory.

Players sometimes debate whether the psyche rested easier following a blowout loss or a slim defeat. I hated that Cal loss my junior season. I was over it—somewhat.

But being so teasingly close to another crown, accomplishing history, rising from the discarded to depart on top? That overwhelming sentiment of unfinished business resurfaced every single time I returned to Charlotte's locker room when I was in the NBA.

Jim Nantz pulled me aside as I left the court, my college basketball career behind me. Nantz and other national announcers like Billy Packer and Dick Vitale were a presence throughout my college days. I was a fan and conscious of who called each game. However, we didn't interact often with the announcers. Nantz quickly told me that he had enjoyed covering me throughout those four years and that I possessed a bright future.

Who would have thought that it would one day involve him and this sport?

Finally, I finished with the media and made my way back to the locker room. Some cried. I had been a leader all season. I tried being one then.

We should be proud. We needed to feel accomplished. Everyone had exhausted everything.

My next thought?

I was no longer playing for free.

10

I was true to my word.

Back then, the area's graduating seniors participated in a barnstorming circuit. We were hoopers for hire, college behind us, the NBA, for some of us, on the horizon. I crisscrossed ACC Country, hopscotching through cities like Asheville, Hickory, and Wilmington with Tony Lang and Marty Clark, along with seniors from Wake, Carolina, and State. The organizers paid us some change to play. Sometimes, we scrimmaged one another. Other times, we played against some of the local talent. Often, we capped the night with a dunk contest or a three-point shootout, the winner departing with an added half a grand in cash.

Let the record show that my first basketball payment arrived from these games and not the NBA.

We took it a step (or two) further by tapping into our entrepreneurial sides and cultivating a lucrative side hustle. We raided the Duke basketball offices, emptying them of posters and pictures before hitting the road. A buddy drove, while Tony, Marty, and I signed the memorabilia. The friend set up a booth outside whatever random high school arena we were at that evening. While we played, he hawked the souvenirs for twenty-five dollars a pop. We even designed T-shirts with our faces plastered on them, earning dollars on the pennies.

I don't want the IRS retroactively on my case. Let's just say we walked out with our pockets a little heavier, to the point where Tony upgraded from his ancient jalopy to a Pathfinder.

Marketing had moved more to my mind's forefront as the NBA draft approached. Duke was a successful program prior to my arrival. Through our memorable deep runs and sustained excellence, it had evolved into a national staple. I was occasionally conscious that the program generated millions of dollars in revenue that bypassed the players. Those moments settled at unexpected times like when Brian Davis teased the football players that basketball fattened the university's athletic purse or when I once tried buying my own jersey for my dad and couldn't afford the hefty price. Those moments were rare but stayed in the back of my mind. The discrepancies had not diminished my college experience or the bonds we had formed.

Between barnstorming games, Coach K hosted a senior dinner at the University Club to bid farewell to our class. We rode an elevator to the sky, gathering inside the restaurant on the penthouse floor of a towering building that offered sweeping, panoramic views of Durham and Chapel Hill.

Mrs. K addressed us proudly, advising us to bask in our accomplishments.

Of the 130 games that this class played in, 124 of them were on national television, she proudly declared. That's as much prime-time television visibility as the cast of *Cheers*.

Maybe I was just in my own cozy cocoon those four years, not fully aware of Duke's nationwide impact. Mrs. K's perspective hit home, crystallizing Duke's reach and pop-star-like popularity. People yelled and clamored for Christian Laettner like he was a teen idol, because that's exactly what he was to them.

The comparison started shaping my vision for how I hoped to enter the NBA as a known figure. I started appreciating just how far I had come in those four years, that I had put together a college career few others could claim. People would be on the lookout for me as I entered the pros. Laettner, I felt, had missed an opportunity to capitalize on his college popularity as a professional. I doubted any other rookie had entered the league with as high a Q-Rating as Laettner. He had played in four Final Fours and with the Dream Team and had sat on Arsenio Hall's couch. *People* magazine had featured him as one of the world's "50 Most Beautiful People," and long before we plastered our faces on some cheap T-shirts, *GQ* plastered his on its cover. He was everywhere, larger than life.

Laettner had put up decent numbers his first couple of NBA seasons. As a draft mate, Shaquille O'Neal, with his game, presence, and personality, had almost drowned him out; plus he was tucked away in Minneapolis, one of the NBA's smaller markets. I had never asked him, but from afar it appeared that he had tired of the spotlight and celebrity.

I probably didn't reach the levels of popularity that Laettner did while he was in college. No one did. But perhaps I could appreciate more fully, thanks to Mrs. K, that my Duke years provided me with some cachet to leverage as I started my NBA career.

I had no idea what that clout meant, just that I hoped to figure it out.

Each of the seniors—me, Tony, and Marty—had ambitions of playing professional basketball. At the dinner, Coach addressed the class collectively. At different points, he pulled us aside individually. I didn't recall having ever previously discussed playing in the NBA with Coach K, even though we both knew it was a long-standing goal of mine. He told me that the feedback NBA teams had relayed to him regarding my professional prospects was all positive.

He asked if I had decided on representation. I had felt the increasing presence of agents throughout my senior season. Nothing illicit or underhanded occurred. I was already friends with Charles Whitfield through our shared love of music. He had attended North Carolina Central University, and his brother, Fred, was working as a deputy for the superagent David Falk. The rest of the agents, I knew, were not trying to buddy up to me simply because I was a great guy. One agent had basically moved his family to Durham and stayed around my apartment complex constantly.

They knew I had no interest in conversations during the season.

The floodgates cracked once the season ended, and I would have to decide on representation soon.

With some, I had already had preliminary talks. A conversation with David Falk had ended with him offering to arrange a call with his client of clients, Michael Jordan.

I called Jordan at the designated time from the Land Cruiser while signing some posters on the way to another barnstorming game. He was in Lang country, Birmingham, Alabama, having surprised the world by retiring from basketball to play minor-league baseball. I could hear a cacophony of balls cracking off wood echoing in the background.

Hello?

It was Michael freakin' Jordan. I'd recognize that deep baritone voice anywhere, even if he was submerged underwater instead of surrounded by baseballs. Yes, I had scrimmaged against him a couple years earlier. This was a different interaction. He was invested in my future. Everyone in the car turned giddy. I shushed them as Jordan detailed the benefits of aligning with Falk.

Think big, he advised.

For a while, I had thought I'd been balling, driving an SUV, living in a warehouse apartment, being the BMOC. In truth, I had never needed much as a college student. I relied on my parents whenever I wanted to eat at a restaurant, attend a movie, or take a girl out on a date.

Maybe, possibly, I could fill a toe in Jordan's shoes while his own were in cleats. We could all dream, right?

I was weighing my agent options when my dad, one of his business friends, and Tommy Amaker accompanied me on a trip to Oregon. We were headed to the motherland, Beaverton, Oregon, the home of Nike, the land of Jordan, the kingdom of Phil Knight. They wanted to pitch me on an endorsement deal.

They led our group inside their employee store, offering us each a cart to fill. I grabbed boxes with both hands and clutched clothes off racks. They could've handed me a pen and paper to sign then and there and we'd be good.

Next, Knight invited us into his spacious office. This, I thought, was the man who laid the blueprint for Jordan's success. He presented a grandiose one for me, outlining Nike's potential, pinpointing the Far East and China as untapped markets primed for growth. At dinner, he suggested the idea of Nike flying me to the Great Wall of China, where I could appear live via satellite during the NBA draft.

The thought of all that exposure left everyone at the table awed. That could be *Cheers* and *Seinfeld* combined. Knight was a visionary then and now. I was a budding businessman, yes, but also just a kid on the cusp of a dream. My own draft night vision involved being there in person to shake hands with David Stern.

First, I needed to finally solve my agent riddle. Duke possessed a screening committee. We consulted with all the known names, bigwigs, heavy hitters. They were all capable. Yet none achieved separation.

My parents, of course, recognized that I was torn with the decision. My dad scheduled me a visit with Larry Lucchino. He was a partner at a law firm that churned out eventual Supreme Court justices. The firm's founder, Edward Bennett Williams, had shared an ownership interest in Washington's football team and the Baltimore Orioles, where Lucchino worked alongside my dad as the baseball team's president.

Lucchino was warm, inviting. He asked if I had made a decision.

No, I said.

He suggested that I speak with Lon Babby, another partner at the firm.

Lon was prepared, aware that Larry was hosting us. He was thoughtful, focused. Lon, I thought, could be helpful as I cycled through options. I had to make a long-term decision, and I wanted to be viewed as a businessman. Businessmen didn't hire agents. They employed attorneys to negotiate deals. I had a couple on the horizon that Lon could help navigate.

I asked him to take over the Nike negotiations; those should be easy enough. His first work on my behalf was handling a trading card deal that featured me in a Duke jersey. The pact brought in six figures. The windfall didn't change my lifestyle, although it certainly meant that I would never be asking my parents for movie money again.

That May, I watched the NBA's draft lottery unfold from my apartment. The Ping-Pong balls bounced in favor of the Milwaukee Bucks. Their coach, Mike Dunleavy, doubled as the team's general manager.

Excitedly, he showcased a Bucks jersey with Robinson's name already stitched on the back. Robinson, as in Glenn.

As in, we are taking him.

Well, I guess there went any hope I had of being picked first.

The Dallas Mavericks landed the second pick. The Detroit Pistons would select third.

Today, players train for months before their draft workouts. I didn't even have an agent yet. My preparation was limited to Durham pickup games. I had dropped the barnstorming circuit after we drove to Asheville to play Athletes in Action, an organization centered on growing their Christian faith and spreading it to others. I supported the organization. That night, in a packed high school gym, I didn't feel that love reciprocated. They played physically, nearly undercutting me a couple of times, and I had to yank myself in the third quarter. Those guys thought they were in a championship game. I couldn't risk injury so close to the draft.

The Pistons requested a private workout. They booked me a flight to Detroit, and I visited their home, the Palace of Auburn Hills, before leaving for the session at Oakland University. I was eager to build up a sweat, put in some work, show them my worth. The team's coach, Don Chaney, and general manager, Billy McKinney, walked me through a warm-up.

Nonchalantly, I converted a couple layups, shot a couple free throws, sank a few jump shots.

That's enough, Chaney said.

Huh?

We know what you can do.

Changing out of the workout clothes I didn't work out in, I joined my dad and met them for dinner at a Greek spot that would become a favorite.

We were joined by Joe Dumars, the masterful guard who tied those current Pistons to the era of the Bad Boys and Isiah Thomas. He was smart and soft-spoken, reminiscent of Tommy Amaker and Billy King during my Duke visit. He discussed his time in Michigan, how the team and organization were on the verge of becoming special again.

The whole visit felt right, familiar.

It didn't take an expert to know Milwaukee planned to take Glenn. The Mavericks already possessed a couple young wings in Jamal Mashburn and Jimmy Jackson. Jason Kidd, I figured, was the better fit there. I wasn't mad. I had grown up watching the Pistons battle the Lakers and Celtics. Detroit was a franchise with a rich history, one that could re-emerge with a quick injection of talent. They had laid a backcourt foundation the previous summer by drafting Lindsey Hunter and my La Jolla mate Allan Houston.

McKinney promised, if you're there, we're taking you.

Lon called shortly after I arrived back in Durham. Dallas wanted a visit. What's the point? They had a logjam. They were just doing due diligence. I politely declined.

Nike negotiations, Lon added, hit a snag. Howard Slusher, one of their main negotiators, had followed the incredible Knight meeting with a lowball offer.

Talks broke down. I was crestfallen.

My parents had an uncanny way of knowing my path before I could spot it myself.

My dad suggested we check out Fila's Baltimore offices while visiting my grandmother. He had a friend who worked for the company.

They were a high-end sports brand, dabbling in fashion sensibility. I was a tennis fan and recalled Björn Borg looking regal, decked out in Fila outfits. Some of the elite rappers like Doug E. Fresh and Rakim and their crews wore Fila sweat suits. I had wanted my own badly in high school, only for my parents to scoff at the price tag.

They were a legitimate company, just not in the basketball world. Reluctantly, I accepted the invite. Maybe we would at least walk away with an offer that lured Nike back to the table.

Have an open mind, my dad told me.

Fila had just ended a tumultuous deal with the boxer Riddick Bowe. He had gotten into a fight at a press conference, outfitted in their gear, a long journey from how Borg previously represented the company. They wanted stability, someone reliable and marketable. I later learned that they had tossed around the names of three rookie basketball players to target: Glenn, Jason, and me. Glenn, according to murmurs, was on the lookout for a massive payday. Jason was recently linked to some type of automobile accident in California.

That left just me.

I was impressed, even if I didn't want to admit it, at the array of shoes and apparel as we toured the massive factory. Red, white, and blue. Those were some classic colors. Olympic colors. American colors.

Still, at lunch, I was more interested in devouring the delicious plate of crab cakes in front of me than listening to a pitch meeting. If Knight had offered the Great Wall, what could they possibly present?

A couple of Fila executives got my full attention. Like Knight, they had a vision. But not just for an evening. For years. For a partnership. A line of shoes. A line of apparel. A specific, committed number of days for photo shoots, commercials, press. They even trotted out a mock logo with my silhouette shooting a basketball and the logo "hill."

They had certainly put more time into this presentation than I had anticipated. Mashburn, I knew, was on their small roster of basketball clients. I was skeptical, partly because his rookie commercials had come off to me as kind of cheesy.

They were persistent, still going on, selling me on not just rounding out their foray into basketball but being the face of their basketball division.

I just might have to do this, I thought.

They smiled. I was engaged. They knew they had my attention when they presented an offer, because my eyes opened wide.

Welp, I'm definitely doing this.

Soon, I called Lon. He had quickly proven himself a reliable negotiator and charged by the hour when traditional agents demanded a percentage from every contract. Lon and I made our arrangement official. He was my guy, although he had so far mostly taken the baton on deals that had already been fleshed out. He headed the Fila discussions, and we landed on a five-year agreement somewhere close to their original proposal.

Duke over Carolina. Fila over Nike. Lon over a traditional agent.

The agents I had met with earlier all told me that they'd handle everything—my investments, my contracts, my taxes—and I could just focus on playing. When most athletes become professionals, the thought of being forty and retired is unfathomable. I was already obsessing about my retirement. Somehow, Coach K's mandate about staying in the present was lost when I started thinking about my post-basketball career. My dad called it transitioning into civilian life. He had options once he had stopped playing football. A lot of his contemporaries had struggled in retirement. I had read enough stories concerning athletes who had lost their money after their playing days and faced bankruptcy and foreclosures that it worried me.

Look, my mom would say, trying to ease my racing mind. You don't really understand who you are and the opportunities that you will have waiting for you.

She would be right, of course. I just didn't want to wait on them. I was conscious, nearly to the point of paranoia, that my NBA career arrived with an expiration date. I wanted to continue growing and evolving. I wasn't necessarily the brightest cat at twenty-one, but I realized that what was being sold and offered from a lot of the agents held little appeal. The thought of granting one person autonomy over my life without any checks and balances didn't make sense.

I wasn't trying to find a way to be different or do something no one else had done with my decisions. I'm still shocked and surprised that I realized at that young age those were the right ones for me. Attending Duke, I believe, played a role in my thought process. I had been surrounded by so many other students who harbored lofty dreams and aspirations. Among my Black friends, we understood the sacrifices of our parents and of those who invested in us to have an opportunity to attend a school like Duke. In between our championships, someone like Brian Davis had interned for Senator Terry Sanford and at Morgan Stanley under John J. Mack. An unspoken energy motivated us to seek out the best versions of ourselves.

Someone, at some point in one of the cycles of meetings—maybe Lon, possibly my mom—said that I had an opportunity for multiple endorsement deals just by being who I was, playing the way I did, showing the character that I had displayed.

You have a chance to be a brand.

There was a disconnect. A brand wasn't a person. Brands were global, iconic, omnipresent.

Nike. Coca-Cola. McDonald's. Those were brands.

Think of it as someone like Michael Jordan.

I was about to enter a league without Jordan. He had extended the league's tentacles beyond the court, vaulting it into the corporate hemisphere through marketing and sponsor partnerships.

You have to give a lot of yourself in order to be a brand, Lon said.

Are you prepared to do that?

I was on crutches at this point a year earlier, the NBA the furthest target from my mind. Now I was in daily meetings after my mom advised me to take stewardship of my career, to attend every session and hire an assistant to help with the scheduling. The largest marketing firms in the world told me that I possessed the intangibles that companies wanted to align with. If I had been asked that question a year earlier, I don't think I would have been comfortable putting myself out there. My senior season had afforded me a lot of confidence. It was like someone who had large feet and looked clumsy had suddenly hit a growth spurt and looked well proportioned. I made the focused effort to embrace the idea of being a pitchman. It would be a whirlwind. But I was also very intentional and strategic. I spent time with the advertising agencies and designers. I wanted them to know me so I could project my authentic self.

I wanted to feel how Jordan felt.

The trading card and the shoe deals were locked in.

More were on the way. First, Milwaukee wanted a visit, Lon informed me.

I didn't want to waste my time. Nothing against the city of Milwaukee. Everyone knew they planned to take Glenn. Glenn knew they were taking Glenn.

Lon, though, was adamant. Don't you want to try for the top pick? Really, this is one of those things you can't decline.

Another reluctant visit. Fine, if this was half as fruitful as the one to Fila, it would be worth it.

It was not.

I promise you, Mike Dunleavy tried to make me throw up during the workout. He insisted on a series of drills, sprints, and defensive slides over the course of ninety minutes. I wondered if I had somehow ended up back at Duke, enduring one of Coach K's marathon practices after a loss. Dunleavy probably saw in my body language that I would have rather been somewhere else. I didn't sabotage the workout. It was just obvious I wanted it to be over. Maybe I should have fought harder to be the first pick, but I had already started envisioning a future in Detroit.

I grabbed my shorts, trying to catch my breath. Dunleavy asked to play one-on-one.

Now? Against you?

I dragged myself back onto the court, checked the ball to him, and planted myself several feet away in the paint.

You aren't going to guard me?

I don't think you can make that shot.

At that point, I knew Dunleavy as the former coach of the Lakers. His team had lost to Jordan's Bulls in the finals. I had no clue that he had actually played in the NBA and even engineered a few decent seasons.

He made the shot. He sank eight in a row without me guarding him to win the game.

To me, it was a silly exercise to boost his ego. I doubt the organization would have changed course and taken me had I beat him in a one-on-one game.

I'm writing this only because we later developed a relationship.

Then?

I was happy to head back to the airport. The visit only reinforced my hope that I'd be on the board when the Pistons selected.

———

Warm memories of our first championship, the surreal thrill of topping Vegas, the ecstasy of downing Kansas, flooded back the day of the draft when we headed to Indianapolis. We ducked inside the same karaoke joint where we had knocked out a few off-tune songs before that life-altering Final Four game against Vegas.

There was no time for an encore.

My parents, of course, were with me. So was Lon and a cabal of close friends—Michael Ellison, Mario Joyner, Rob Robinson, and Mark Williams. I wore a fresh suit I had bought while in Los Angeles for the presentation of the John R. Wooden Award.

Officials outlined the evening's itinerary. Butterflies hopped and leaped. This was it. The moment when dreams become reality. Jason Kidd and I hung close among the draft mates; I was glad a true friendship was blossoming between us.

They shuffled us into the greenroom. David Stern emerged. Milwaukee, no surprise, took Glenn. At least Dunleavy got his one-on-one game out of me.

The clock reset with Dallas next. I panicked, worrying that they would take me, sight unseen. I was born in Dallas. My dad had played for the Cowboys. They may see me as a fit, even if I didn't.

Stern announced the franchise had selected Jason. The burst of applause from my table might have drowned the one from his.

Okay, I thought. We know it's Detroit. They had promised to take me if I lasted through the first two picks. I was still nervous, even though I knew my destination. I felt for some of the other players who were really in the dark about their future.

Each second felt like a minute.

Finally, Stern walked back to the lectern, announcing that the Pistons had selected me, Grant Hill, out of Duke University.

I was not walking. I floated to greet him.

Don't trip. Don't fall. Don't trip. Don't fall.

I was there, finally, clutching his hand, cheesing wide.

Immediately, I was shepherded to and fro, whisked through a series of interviews and photo ops. *Smile here, talk there.* The frenetic atmosphere resembled a Final Four win. It would've been overwhelming if I actually had the opportunity to contemplate the gravity of the evening in the moment.

I would always remember the couple of phone calls I received that evening. Bill Clinton, the politician from down South who my mom had predicted would one day be president? That day was now. He called, offering his congratulations, although I knew that only a couple months earlier he had rooted for his Arkansas Razorbacks in the title game.

Exhausted, I finally returned to my hotel room at the Westin. I saw the light on the phone, checked the voice mail, and was surprised to hear a man who needed no introduction introducing himself.

Hey, Grant, this is Isiah Thomas. Congratulations. You had an amazing college career. You have a great career in front of you, and you just joined a fantastic organization, the Pistons.

I had never met Isiah. By that time, he had already retired to join the fledgling Toronto Raptors as a part owner and executive. That he had reached out to me on behalf of an organization he capably piloted for so many years spoke volumes about him and my new organization.

I rounded up my longtime friends the next morning.

We sat around and listened to the message again. Yes, we had Jordan on the line a few weeks earlier. But this was Isiah, the Piston of Pistons, welcoming me to my new home, Detroit. It was important to share the moment with my friends. I had played basketball with Michael and Rob for forever. We all harbored dreams of being drafted into the NBA since we took turns at the park trying to see if we could dunk.

Now we were all coming of age. Michael had graduated from Virginia and had started working for the United States Tennis Association. Rob had played collegiately at Niagara University and was trying to get a professional career going overseas. Mario, whom I met through Tommy

Amaker at Durham, was a year behind me in school and had a lot of possibilities that awaited him. Mark Williams was well on his way to becoming a successful businessman.

It was a time of communal celebration. But it was also the moment the dynamics of our friendship began to shift.

My paternal grandparents, Henry and
Elizabeth Hill.

My mom at eight years old, probably around the time
she used to switch the signs of white and colored only
water fountains for fun.

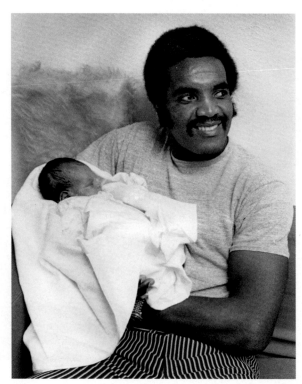

Dad started his bond
with me at my birth.

With my parents in Hawaii in 1975. My dad spent a season playing for The Hawaiians of the World Football League.

Dad with the cool pose and threads in the 1970s.

My mom with her parents, Malcolm and Vivian McDonald.

With my grandmother, Vivian McDonald, outside her front porch in New Orleans. She and my grandfather Malcolm ran a successful business, McDonald Laboratories, crafting dentures from the basement of their home.

Basking in my mom's love.

Definitely a 1970s holiday family photo.

I didn't use the Betamax in our basement just to watch sports. I replayed *Motown 25* repeatedly to mimic Michael Jackson's electrifying dance moves.

Soccer was my first sports love. The open fields provided freedom—I imagined myself the next Pelé.

I'm surprised my eyes are even open here. I stayed up all night to finish a paper the night before we traveled to play Georgetown my freshman season.

Facing capable players like Larry Johnson at the Final Four in 1991 offered seeds of confidence that my game would translate on the next level.

Coach K no doubt telling me to stay in the present moment.

This was about the moment I knew Christian Laettner's shot was going in. Afterward, it felt like everyone had been shot out of a cannon.

Christian Laettner's passion could have been the accelerant that torched a program. Instead, he was always the fire that fueled our runs.

Looking for some daylight against Chris Webber and Jalen Rose in the 1992 championship game.

I didn't even register how high I leaped for this dunk against Kansas in the 1991 championship game until Brian Davis mentioned it afterward.

Nike pitched broadcasting me from China on draft night, but there was no way I was going to miss shaking David Stern's hand in person.

Every season is a grinding journey. My jersey retirement allowed a brief pause to appreciate all that we had accomplished in four years at Duke.

Going one-on-many with the press at my first All-Star weekend in 1995. I was the first rookie to lead the league in All-Star voting, but still questioned whether I belonged in the same locker room with players I looked up to.

Coach John Thompson, Patrick Ewing, and the Georgetown Hoyas sparked my early passion for basketball.

The All-Star Game is always a chance to debut your newest shoe. The 1998 game at Madison Square Garden was no exception. I'm wearing my fourth Fila signature shoe, while Michael Jordan flexes his Air Jordan XIII's. Glen Rice . . . well, he must have had a sweet deal to rock those Nauticas.

I wanted to know what it was like to be Michael Jordan away from the court. I treasure the few times I competed against him on it.

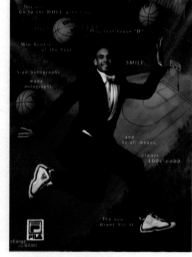

A mold-breaking partnership with Italian sportswear company Fila proved to be one of my most important and lasting business relationships.

Sometimes, you can't imagine how your life will be improved until you experience it firsthand. I expected to settle down after my NBA career ended. Tamia thankfully changed that perspective early on.

My dad told me how he felt weak watching my mom walk down the aisle on their wedding day. I could relate as soon as I laid eyes on Tamia in her dress.

Tamia with my mom and her mom, Barbara Peden, at our wedding reception.

Are you hurt or are you injured? In the NBA, they are two different things.

I had no idea that a long road of recovery would await me as I departed my final press conference as a member of the Detroit Pistons in 2000.

I never had the opportunity to play to my abilities in Orlando, but I was determined to get back onto the court despite many setbacks.

Tamia with Myla on the way. I had no idea how to be a parent back then. Thankfully, Tamia, here with my mom and grandmother, was a natural caretaker.

My mom attended Wellesley College the same time as Hillary Rodham Clinton, and the Clintons watched me play basketball when I was a child.

Myla, at the age of three, with her uncle Trey, who was eight at the time.

I felt a sense of accomplishment that was lost since my college days when we claimed the gold medal at the 1996 Olympics. Our combination of size, speed, and youth made us one of the most talented squads ever assembled.

These photos are separated by a couple of decades and a lot of medical procedures. I can see the kid who loved competing in both.

I gazed at Andrew Young, the civil rights icon, during the news conference announcing my purchase of the Atlanta Hawks with Tony Ressler, and noticed the sense of pride he reflected.

Later in my career, I enjoyed the challenge of guarding players younger than me like Tayshaun Prince.

With my new talented team, Jim Nantz and Bill Raftery, at the Final Four in 2015.

Joined by Coach K and Patrick Ewing during my Naismith Memorial Basketball Hall of Fame enshrinement.

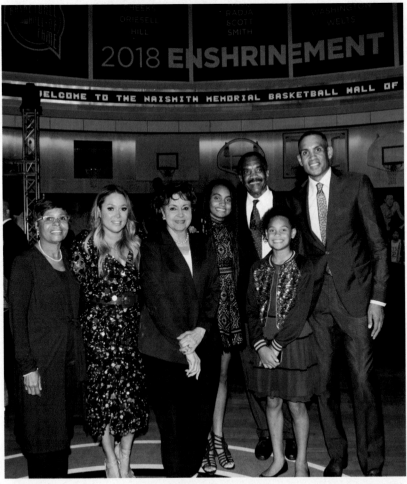

I reflected on my journey during the months leading to my induction into the Naismith Memorial Basketball Hall of Fame. I'm glad I had my family with me on a basketball ride that culminated that evening. From left to right: Barbara Peden, Tamia, mom, Myla, dad, Lael, and myself.

I I

N O matter how many times I told myself that I was now an NBA player, it didn't feel real. Maybe, partly because nothing had immediately changed. After the draft, I returned to my same apartment in Durham, greeted the same people in the lobby, slept in the same bed.

My parents counseled me that I should be prepared. Things might have felt the same, but change loomed on the horizon. Soon, I would possess a considerable amount of money. I needed to show discretion.

I was an only child with no cousins, uncles, or aunts. My circle was small, and there was not room for people who weren't already in my corner.

Still, they cautioned, navigating even familiar friendships may be more difficult. My dad had seen it repeatedly among his own friends who had entered pro sports and encountered tugs and challenges over the juggling of careers, money, and relationships.

If your friends have fifty dollars in their pockets, then you make sure you have fifty dollars in your pocket, my dad told me. It took me a little while to understand what he meant, but the advice made more and more sense over time.

Keeping their guidance in mind, I attended the rookie transition program at the Orlando World Center Marriott. There, the NBA presented a curriculum that was essentially a crash course on everything that could go wrong when you were young with money: sessions on the risks of blowing through it on elaborate purchases, the illegalities of gambling, and the troubles that can be had with groupies. The days were informative, although I was not sure how much I needed the reinforcement having grown up under the General's jurisdiction.

Next, my parents met me in Michigan for my Pistons introductory press conference. That morning, we sat for breakfast at a hotel near the Palace. As I excitedly caught them up on the program, I noticed a couple side glances from my dad. He advised me to shave before the conference.

Fine, goodbye, peach fuzz.

My dad bought a razor from the hotel's gift shop after I told him I had left my electric clipper at home.

It's easy, he said. Just put the shaving cream on and shave it.

No problem.

I hurried back up to my room and came down clean shaven. We headed over to a concourse inside the Palace, where I shook hands for the first time with Mr. Bill Davidson, the team's owner, who amassed his fortune by operating one of the world's largest glassmaking businesses.

The conference opened and Billy McKinney said he had become emotional when he realized the franchise would land me.

Hopefully, you didn't cry because you were disappointed that you got me, I joked as the flash of cameras popped in the room.

I don't think I realized in the moment how difficult the previous year had been on Billy as one of the league's only Black general managers, to lose so many games and not only retain his job but also wind up with the player he had targeted for months.

A lot of responsibility rested on my shoulders. The day was another whirlwind, just like draft night. I was introduced to all the people who made the Detroit Pistons go, the coaches and trainers, people in the marketing and public relations departments. I vowed to get better at learning names.

Somewhere, in the middle of it all, I signed the absurd contract that Lon Babby had negotiated, one for eight years and forty-five million dollars. That was the era of bonkers rookie contracts, when players entered the league and could command more than veteran players, benefiting off the league's increasing popularity and growing revenue. Chris Webber, Shawn Bradley, and Penny Hardaway had signed lengthy, lucrative contracts a season earlier. When the Pistons had made me an opening offer of twenty-five million dollars, it was more money than I could have ever fathomed. I had wanted to sign immediately.

Lon laughed. You're not signing that. You can get double.

I understood. His reasoning made sense. Yet at some point, it all sounded like Monopoly money.

Jason Kidd had signed first, setting the market, inching Detroit to the offer I signed. Glenn Robinson was still holding out for a tremendous contract in Milwaukee. I guess it would take a lot for him to play Mike Dunleavy one-on-one.

Back at the hotel, my new reality settled in. I had signed a contract. It was official.

Suddenly my face started burning. I had obviously not shaved correctly earlier.

I might have been a signed and delivered NBA player, but I still had a few things to learn.

A couple weeks later, I took a house-hunting trip to Michigan. The arena was a haul from downtown Detroit. A realtor showed me a few places in the Bloomfield area. I settled for renting a town house with a basement and ordered some furniture. Hopefully, the place would be good to go by the time training camp arrived.

As I flew back to Durham, my goal was to be a better player when that time came.

I was playing some of the best basketball of my life, lifted by the confidence gained in my senior season, equipped with the burgeoning confidence of being a professional. I dominated those Card Gym open runs when Duke's NBA alumni made the early fall pilgrimage back to Durham and mixed it up with the current college crop.

In one of those sessions, Quin Snyder pulled me aside, offering some advice that carried through the years.

Quin had noticed that I had the tendency, like most big ball handlers of that era, to sometimes protect the ball by reflexively turning my body to the defender.

You don't need to turn your back, he said. You should face up and attack. You can cross up and go at people.

Attacking instead of reacting.

That September, I followed the suggestion. The results were evident. I was meeting defenders downhill, momentum on my side. A quick inside-out dribble later, I was past nearly anyone guarding me and at the rim.

My game had taken a similar leap in these same open runs just before my sophomore season. The gains came in those quiet moments, outside the spotlight, among my peers. Hands down, I felt like I was the best player on a court I shared with guys like Johnny Dawkins, Christian Laettner, Danny Ferry, and others who had already played in the promised land. I probably wouldn't have been as comfortable acknowledging that realization a year or two earlier.

Maybe my game's development was syncing with my mindset of being comfortable with dominating a game. Possibly, my craft just needed time to get to that point. Whatever it was, the timing couldn't have worked out better when I headed to Michigan a few days before training camp.

Hey, Smitty, someone called as I walked through the airport to baggage claim upon my arrival. I kept it moving, not really catching the reference. It happened again. I realized that I was being mistaken for Steve Smith, the talented Michigan State product who had been taken by the Miami Heat a couple years earlier.

I planned to soon make a name for myself in Michigan. The funny thing is that now, decades later, we work together as analysts for NBA TV. On set, we're called twins. Everyone always gets us confused. I guess we have similar frames. He'll be called Grant. Someone yells Smitty at me. And occasionally, people call me Reggie Miller, which I don't really understand at all.

I finally bade farewell to the Land Cruiser, giving it to a distant cousin in South Carolina. Driving a Toyota in Detroit would have been sacrilegious. My sponsorship deal with General Motors was done, and they thankfully provided me with a ride for an extended period.

Despite my efforts, the town house wasn't ready. I checked in to a Holiday Inn, which quickly became cluttered with boxes from Fila, more gear than I ever could've imagined as a kid when I had begged for a single Fila outfit. Lindsey Hunter, entering his second season, picked me up and we played pickup with some of the other early arrivals. I played confidently, my performance reflecting my summer gains.

You're going to help us, Lindsey said as we drove to meet up with Allan Houston for dinner at a Thai restaurant.

We're going to be better with you.

I didn't know Lindsey well yet. I was quickly enjoying his personality. He was easygoing, fun loving. His early stamp of approval offered reassurance.

I couldn't help but think that we were the future as I sat with Lindsey and Allan and we passed around heaping plates of pad thai and sticky rice. We were the new Pistons, the evolution of Isiah Thomas, Joe Dumars, and Vinnie Johnson—even though Joe was still on our team as the veteran presence. I knew what Allan could do. Lindsey was talented. We were going to be just fine.

———

Training camp was easier than I envisioned, a few notches below a Coach K practice. I had connected with Don Chaney, my coach, during my pre-draft visit. He was an affable guy, in his day a guard who had played on the Celtics and was known for his defense.

Camp broke on a Saturday. To that point, I hadn't gone out socially, preferring to fully focus on the two-a-day sessions. Oliver Miller, a teammate, insisted we celebrate the end of camp. I had faced him as a college freshman when he played at Arkansas. He was a large guy with just as big a personality.

He had my stomach hurting, telling jokes, as he maneuvered his Lexus coupe across the Ambassador Bridge and into Windsor, the Canadian city on the south bank of the Detroit River.

We arrived at a club. Oliver, ignoring my objections, decided to park his car directly in front of a fully visible no parking sign.

We ducked inside for a couple of hours. Of course, when we came out, the car was nowhere to be found. Frantically, we found a parking lot attendant who thumbed through a phone book and located the number for a towing service. A cab took us to a junk yard. We spotted his pearl green car through a barbed wire fence. Midnight was approaching. Some lonely dogs barked in the distance.

Oliver, there's no one here. We've got to figure a way to get back to Auburn Hills.

He banged on the fence anyway. Somehow, someway, someone

emerged. Oliver pulled out a wad of cash, much more than necessary, and handed it over to the tow truck operator.

Something like that happens, you count your blessings, call it a night, and head home, right?

No.

To Oliver, the night was just getting started. I was essentially helpless, being shuttled around shotgun. I had insisted on driving everywhere in high school and college. I didn't drink and I unilaterally ended the night if I wasn't feeling a situation. I kicked myself for violating my own rule my first real time going out as a pro. I was in a city and area I didn't know well yet. The only person I barely knew was Oliver and I was starting to see him as someone who created the crisis, instead of solving it.

We drove back to Detroit, ping-ponging through different nightclubs. Legends. Currency Exchange. The State Theatre. Every place was crowded. People recognized us and offered support. Maybe, Oliver had salvaged the night.

The evening lurched toward two in the morning. Oliver asked if I was ready to head out and, of course, I was. He stopped at a fast-food joint on the lengthy drive back to Auburn Hills. There, a woman appeared seemingly out of nowhere. Oliver started talking to her, and from their conversation I ascertained they were in some type of relationship. He invited her into the car. I crammed my frame into the backseat. By that point, I just wanted to do whatever it took to get back to my room. Exhausted, I started dozing off.

I stirred when the car suddenly swerved. Oliver was flying that thing down Interstate 75, driving with his legs, laughing while his hands were in the air. The woman, who I thought had to be his girlfriend, told him to calm down and the two argued.

I did my best to calm them down by cracking a couple jokes, silently exhaling when we pulled into the hotel's parking lot.

Peace.

I raced into the lobby when I heard the woman calling my name.

Grant, what room are you in? He's acting crazy.

I didn't know the extent of their relationship. Whatever it was or wasn't, I didn't break stride on the way to my room. I don't know what else happened that night between the two. My own evening was over. A memorable, draining first one as an NBA player. Oliver, Allan, and Lindsey all lived near one another in a row of town houses. I soon found out that he had called me only because they wouldn't go out with him anymore. They had already experienced similar Oliver outings.

I just didn't know any better yet.

I had learned my first rookie lesson.

———

Nerves over playing in my first NBA exhibition were quickly alleviated. We hosted the New Jersey Nets at the Palace. A teammate batted the jump ball to Joe. I streaked down the court, and he found me for an alley-oop about three seconds into the game.

The rest of the preseason was like that, a steady momentum building toward opening night. Our team was a collage of players at various stages of their NBA careers. The young guys like Lindsey, Allan, and me mixed in with veteran players like Joe and our center, Mark West—older, thoughtful guys with more reflective personalities. For Joe, I was sure the last few seasons had taxed him. The franchise had traveled from being annual contenders to one routinely in the lottery. He offered advice now and then in his own quiet way, although, I admit, I had wanted a full downloading about the league from him that I never received. On the court, though, he was still smart, resourceful. I learned a lot simply through observing him maneuver.

My game, that early, was translating better than I could have anticipated. I played through contact, found paths to the rim, and facilitated for my teammates.

I called my friends back home.

The NBA, I boasted, is easy. If anything, I was now overconfident, which might have wound up being a bit of fool's gold.

For that first month, we won as much as we lost. It was not like college when we could go months without a loss. Still, the franchise was in a much better place now than a season earlier. Everyone voiced optimism. Meanwhile, I settled into a rhythm. The town house was finally ready. I moved in, decorating the house with paintings and art that reminded me of the home I grew up in.

I had said I wanted to know how Michael Jordan felt. I didn't know I'd get a peek inside that life so early into my pro career. Then and now, the league is enamored with potential.

The brands wanted me to be a brand. Coca-Cola called. McDonald's made inquiries. Schick, the razor company, recruited me. I could have used them at my press conference. The immediate attention was overwhelming. Thankfully, my teammates were supportive and, in some instances, protective of me. I was a young guy on the team, but also a focal point of the franchise. Team dynamics, the survival of the locker room, as I called it, were important for me to manage. As much as the NBA liked to promote and market individuals, I was very much aware that it took a team and everybody playing for one another to accomplish anything. I tried to be a glue guy before I even knew what that term meant and show that despite any type of external attention I was one of the guys. To accomplish that, I brought it. Before anything, I had to prove myself on the court, and I tried doing that at each practice and each game. I didn't take plays off, a mindset that didn't change for as long as I played in the league. My highlights started leading *SportsCenter*. I received interview requests from all over and not just from the usual suspects like *Sports Illustrated*.

GQ wanted to do a cover piece.

A writer by the name of Tom Junod flew into town that winter, introducing himself at a practice. While we shot the breeze in the training room, Terry Mills, a veteran teammate, asked if I planned on attending his birthday party that evening.

I must have missed the invite. Tom and I were scheduled to have a quiet dinner and talk for the story.

Just bring him, Terry said.

I picked up Tom and we snaked downtown, arriving at the State Theatre. Every single person inside the venue was Black, with Tom being the exception.

We were in Detroit smack in the middle of the cold winter. Everyone wore their best mink coat. I was putting up numbers in the league. More people recognized me now than during my first outing at the club with Oliver. They approached me, congratulated me, dapped me. We only stayed a few minutes before bouncing to sit down for the actual interview.

I was stunned when I read the magazine's cover with a headline blaring, CAN GRANT HILL SAVE SPORTS?

Save sports from what exactly? I was just trying to be my best for the Pistons.

It got worse. I thumbed through to find the story. Tom led it with a mocking scene of the party and labeled me a fish out of water.

There were these guys in these long mink coats, wearing these big mink hats, and you just know they had guns stuffed in their pockets, he wrote. *There were these crazy women running around, who were with the hoodlums but who were all drunk and lubricious and ready to go. And in the middle of this chaos was none other than Grant Hill.*

I hated every word. The story wasn't a reflection of the Detroit I was starting to embrace and be embraced by. It was absolutely demeaning, dehumanizing, to the people he described. Even some of my quotes, I felt, were taken out of context. My teammates understood the circumstances of how the article came to be. I pledged to be more careful with reporters moving forward. I had thought the *60 Minutes* story wasn't accurate. Somehow, *GQ* went out and topped it.

I had wanted to come to Detroit and play for the Pistons, but had not known much about the city beyond the broad historic strokes. I recognized Detroit as the home of the auto industry, that it had once been a city of opportunity, especially for people of color. The riots of 1967 and the flight to suburbia roiled Detroit and eroded its tax base.

I immediately felt the residue of those scars. I arrived in Detroit right after Coleman Young's sometimes defiant tenure.

Often, in those early days, I inhabited different, divided worlds. My teammates and I lived in the suburbs, near the arena, to cut our commute. But we frequented Detroit as often as possible to socialize. I had grown up in a progressive area in Northern Virginia and attended college in North Carolina. Yet I almost felt like Detroit represented the South more than those two environments. Pockets and enclaves of different ethnicities often stayed to themselves.

But over the days, I also sensed growing optimism. Dennis Archer, Coleman's successor, attempted to bridge the gap and heal the city in returning businesses and jobs. The car industry was thriving. General Motors committed to moving its global headquarters back to downtown. New restaurants were popping up. Quickly, I grew to love the city of Detroit. I even debated securing a downtown condo or penthouse to stay in the mix.

It was a place I thought I could spend a fulfilling career and retire, maybe even developing a next act somewhere inside the auto industry.

———

The freeze of my first midwestern winter arrived in full force. My game turned cold as well. So this was that rookie wall. I was seeing teams for a second time. My scouting report was out. I learned the hard way that pros were pros not just because of their amazing athletic ability but because they were also capable of making quick, needed adjustments. I drove by one defender, only to find another blocking my path. My numbers dipped; the team collectively stumbled. Lindsey went out, breaking a bone in his leg.

We landed Johnny Dawkins. He was a welcome, familiar presence nearing the end of his playing career. He probably expected to sign and play a few minutes here and there. In one layup line, he looked like how I did at that Georgetown game my freshman year. He could've gone to sleep, then and there. Instead, he played forty-something minutes. We battled a rash of injuries, myself included.

Still, the attention away from the court continued. Matt Dobek, our public relations director, was the first to suggest that I could make the All-Star Game.

The Rookie Challenge? I knew that the league had just implemented the junior varsity game a year earlier.

No, he said, the actual All-Star Game.

I laughed him off.

Soon after, the league revealed the first results of fan voting for the game's starters. I somehow ranked first. The thought of starting in the game as a rookie was unfathomable. I allowed myself to gradually acknowledge the possibility when I maintained my poll position with each subsequent release.

To that point, Fila had outfitted me in an edition of a shoe named the Spoiler, while we worked on a signature edition. Sketches in October evolved into prototypes to try out in November. They were clean and slick, nearly universally white with some splashes of red and blue. It felt like I was wearing a sleek Italian sports car on my feet. My teammates served as my ultimate focus group and voiced universal approval.

When the final votes were released, I became the first rookie to lead the league in All-Star voting. Fila wisely decided that a better moment wouldn't arrive than for us to debut the signature shoe at the game.

Following our last game before the All-Star break, Fila chartered me a flight to New Mexico to shoot my first major commercial with the company. We were in the heart of the Tularosa Basin, marveling at one of the world's great natural wonders, the glistening white sands. The sands were marvelous, an endless beach with no ocean. The setting immediately resonated with me. Boyz II Men had just shot their "Water Runs Dry" video here.

Fila had plopped a basketball court in the middle of it all. For eight hours, I dribbled and dunked, dunked and dribbled, as different shots were captured. *Run. Jump. Jump. Run.* I was exhausted. The league took a break for a reason. The sun set and the temperature dived. Meanwhile, I was in a tank top and shorts.

You have to give a lot of yourself in order to be that brand.

Cut!

I was off to Phoenix for the game of games, sharing a locker room with guys I still looked up to. By then, I had played against most of these guys.

Joe was also here. So was Patrick Ewing, still stiffing me my pizza money. There were Alonzo Mourning and Larry Johnson, guys I played against in college. But I was no longer that college kid in La Jolla, scrimmaging against Scottie Pippen. I was on his team. There he was, with a locker near mine.

That Friday, both teams met and I found myself sharing a room with players like Shawn Kemp, Gary Payton, and Karl Malone.

I knew I was leading my team in points, assists, and rebounds as a rookie. I still felt out of place, wondering if I belonged with these guys. I didn't flex the same résumé yet and worried whether my place in the game was just the result of a popularity contest.

Should I call Tommy Amaker again?

Confidence was a tricky state of mind. I had come to think of it as a finite resource, something that allowed me to come this far, only to tell me that this was as far as we could go. We had run out of gas.

I was good, probably too good, at projecting a level of confidence that didn't match my insides. My parents, my close friends, could probably recognize my moments of anxiety. They only had to look at my stubby fingernails.

I hid it from everyone else.

Coach K used to tell the story of the bull and the matador. The bull could sense whether a matador was scared or nervous. Part of the elegance of the matador was projecting poise and confidence even as he trembled internally. His life depended on it.

Nerves should be held inside. Strangle them long enough, and the fear, the anxiety, the doubts, the uncertainty, they all eventually dissipated, like Bobby, suddenly transforming from a jittery freshman to a confident sophomore against the same Vegas team.

I hoped my doubts would similarly, simultaneously disappear. I did my best to shrug the concerns away. I was inspired to be on the same level as these guys as soon as possible, to carve out my own list of accomplishments.

The doubt didn't prevent me from enjoying the weekend's festivities. Only six years earlier, my dad had taken me to All-Star weekend in Houston. We had hung out in the hotel lobby and watched my idols walk back and forth.

Now I was partaking in the spectacle, meeting celebrities, being pulled in different directions. I made appearances on behalf of new marketing partners like McDonald's and Sprite while trying to ensure that my friends were also enjoying themselves. Sometime that weekend, my first Sprite commercial aired. The game itself was a blur.

The shoe started selling through the roof, surpassing Fila's projections and expectations and far exceeding my own. We sold more than one and a half million pairs my rookie season, the most since the Air Jordan 1 a decade earlier. Even now, those numbers amaze me.

Deals continued pouring in. Nestlé Crunch. TAG Heuer. Kellogg's. Most of the companies were already aligned with the NBA through league sponsorships. The NBA, I realized, was already a global marketer. The league was good at promoting their players, particularly the good young players. I had seen it before I entered the league with guys like Shaq, Chris Webber, and Penny Hardaway. I dissolved the partnership with my marketing firm. Offers, from my perspective, were arriving on their own. I wanted to leverage these opportunities in hopes that cultivating the relationships would serve me once my career ended.

I acquired some office space near my house, on the corner of Square Lake and Telegraph, and hired a couple associates to help cycle through offers, engage with advertising agents, design campaigns. Basketball never strayed from my top priority. Still, it was me, not a surrogate, who met with Steve Koonin at Sprite and Rick Wagoner at General Motors. We talked business and basketball, the present and future, establishing ties and relationships that would span decades.

———

I worked through the rookie wall, adjusting to how teams schemed against me. It was not enough. We struggled throughout the second half of the season.

Coach Chaney was a nice guy. He believed in me, positioning me to succeed. He designed a play for me, three-shake, where my teammates cleared out and I engaged the defense one-on-one. The offensive freedom, at first, was liberating. But when defenses countered, piling defenders on my side of the court, our offense remained stagnant.

I'll admit, it was tough departing from the level of coaching and the expectations of a season earlier when everything revolved around vying for a championship.

The traits of an excellent college coach and a professional one are different. To be sure, some qualities are shared in terms of the need for any coach to focus a team toward one goal in order to be successful. The elite college coaches of my era—Coach K, John Thompson, Dean Smith— all cultivated a presence around them. There's something slightly un- usual about grown men selling themselves to teenagers, but if you think about it, that's essentially what a college coach has to do. They recruited players to their programs and schools, but most important, they sold themselves. They were truly authority figures. They dealt with teenag- ers, and at their core they were teachers. They wanted to win and estab- lish their programs, but they also used basketball as a vessel to instill life lessons.

We've all seen talented college coaches who could not replicate that same success in the NBA. It's a different game. A player arrives as a more finished product. An expectation of understanding the fundamentals ex- ists. An NBA coach's job is to mold the talent and personalities around a successful game plan. Their coaching involves less teaching and more strategy. The power dynamics are also different because players rou- tinely earn more than coaches. Coaches have to pick and choose their moments to lay down the hammer throughout the course of a long sea- son. Players can and do tune them out. Buy-in from the team's best player has always been crucial. I was always mindful of the story of Red Auer- bach and Bill Russell in Boston. Every year, on the first day of training camp, Auerbach laced into Russell, who was in on the charade and will- fully took the scolding. Auerbach showed that if he could scream at Rus- sell, the league's most valuable player, then no other player had the right to complain.

But a general malaise had settled into the Pistons' culture. Little things surprised me, like having to pay the equipment manager to wash our practice clothes. I didn't know if it was a hustle or not, but that was the only year in the NBA in which I encountered such a policy.

Luckily, my teammates were professionals and enjoyable to be around. Occasionally, we grabbed dinner as a team, but those meals took only a sliver of the evening, and, well, I couldn't risk going out with Oliver again.

I missed the social outlet that college had naturally provided. Most of Duke and Durham existed in a protective bubble. I mostly felt free to be a college kid without constant scrutiny. I didn't have to be skeptical when confronted with a new face. My wariness probably prevented me from knowing a lot of great people, but I couldn't help questioning the intentions of those I didn't know.

My suspicions rose when I was followed home a couple times after games. I always entered the town house through the garage, seldom through the front door. Occasionally, when I spotted a tail, I circled around until I knew I was in the clear.

Practice ended in the early afternoon. The rest of the day was mine. The isolation provided moments of reflection, time to recharge.

However, I was not used to so much of it. I could no longer walk to see what Tony Lang was up to, what Mark Williams was doing. Now I rounded out the days by watching sports, listening to music, and reading books. My childhood friends flew in occasionally and broke the monotony.

Finally, Michael and Rob moved in with me. No single man was an island. Coach Chaney allowed for open practices, and often players brought along a couple of friends, who'd watch and wait for it to end. Rob, still trying to get his pro career going overseas, began training with me at the facility.

The friendly faces helped. Commercials or not, I was still a kid who grew up in blissful isolation.

The struggle adjusting away from the court highlighted basketball's importance, which deepened the frustration over losing so often. At one point, earlier in the season, I felt I had a lock on rookie of the year. Suddenly Jason Kidd gained momentum.

I noted his performances on a nightly basis. Players on a team headed nowhere typically couldn't wait for the season to end. You battled your own expectations against the reality of the situation. I found motivation in aspiring to be named the league's top rookie.

Our final games of the season consisted of a swing through Atlanta and Miami. First, we played an early afternoon tilt against the Hawks. Freaknik, Atlanta's gigantic annual spring break, engulfed the city. Coach Chaney offered us the option of either flying out after the game with the staff or traveling separately and rejoining the group in Miami.

This would've never been the case at Duke, I thought.

Tired, I decided to spend the night in Atlanta.

The game ended. I handled my media obligations, got dressed, and readied to leave. Everyone had already departed. The players, the coaches, the staff, the bus. Oliver and I were the last of the team still in Atlanta.

We opted to try to get back to our hotel, the Marquis, on foot. Oliver, in the middle of Freaknik, was in his element, offering hugs and fist bumps to everyone who recognized us. It was too much for me. A car pulled up. I had no idea who was inside. I didn't care. I hopped in just to escape the surrounding madness. Thankfully, the driver had no problem dropping us off at the hotel.

We flew to Miami, where I needed only twenty-three points to finish the season averaging a cool twenty a game.

Neither team was playing for much, other than to play out the string. I planned on getting those points, to shoot every time I got the ball as though Cornel Parker were guarding me.

Only, I couldn't buy a bucket. I missed everything—jumpers, layups, free throws. I ended with twenty-one ugly points on twenty-three shot attempts. It still pains me that I didn't get one more bucket to end the season with a twenty-point-per-game average my rookie season.

The next month, Jason and I were named co-rookies of the year. We were hanging out at the draft almost a year earlier. We were together again, this time in New York, accepting the award, catching a Knicks playoff game courtside against the Pacers, the one where Reggie Miller scored eight points in the final few seconds to rally Indiana from a six-point deficit.

Now, it would take some fluky math for the voting to work out the way it did. I'll be honest, I wanted the award for myself. But if I had to share it with anyone, I'm glad it was with Jason. It was not the first time he had caught me by surprise.

12

STABILITY had always been my bedrock, my foundation for comfort and success. I was the kid who didn't have to leave my neighborhood as I matriculated through elementary, middle, and high school. On the court, I played for the same coaches, year after year, in AAU, in high school, at Duke. The NBA, though, was the land of impermanence. The league was a results-oriented business.

We didn't show enough progress my rookie season, seldom sustaining momentum. For the brass, it was one year too many in the basement. The Pistons cleaned house, firing Coach Don Chaney, Billy McKinney, and the athletic trainer, Tony Harris. Tom Wilson, the team's president, who mostly focused on business, headed the search for our next coach. He filled the dual jobs of coach and general manager with one person, Doug Collins, the father of my former teammate at Duke and the eager viewer of his own highlight videos. He hired Rick Sund to handle some of the day-to-day work, but Doug maintained the final say on the court and off it.

We had an existing relationship, and I was sure Doug would have a positive impact on the organization. He was knowledgeable. I learned a new thing or two whenever I listened to Doug call a game on television. He was also hungry to succeed. The opportunity presented a chance to make up for how he had left Chicago. As a young coach, he had molded Scottie Pippen and Horace Grant, helped evolve Michael Jordan into a superstar, and led the Bulls to the brink of contention, only to be relieved of his duties, shelved as Phil Jackson nudged the organization to a string of championships.

What better way for Doug to prove himself than by leading another youthful crop of talented players on the cusp of a breakthrough? There was also some irony. In Detroit, he was now in charge of the franchise that had once bulldozed and bullied his Bulls teams.

Doug, at his opening press conference, vowed to push me. I was not exactly sure what that would entail. He bristled when reporters suggested that I played any role in him landing the job. It was true. As much as I liked and respected Coach Chaney, I had agreed with the decision that we needed a new voice. But I wasn't in the loop or aware of the pending change. Nobody within the organization had consulted me concerning Chaney's dismissal or Doug's hiring.

———

The NBA endured its first lockout that summer. Owners wanted to rein in the skyrocketing rookie contracts by implementing a sliding scale for debuting players.

The standoff barred players from entering facilities or meeting with team employees, which of course made it a less than optimal time to be onboarding a new coaching staff. I played when and where I could, visiting Allan Houston in Louisville between stops back home and in Durham.

I had a break in my schedule when a television executive called, asking if I'd be up for a guest spot on Queen Latifah's show *Living Single*. I had caught the sitcom a couple of times. Latifah was hip-hop royalty. I had already made an in-and-out appearance on another television show, NBC's *Hang Time*, which starred the former NBA player Reggie Theus. It didn't take much effort on my part, a couple days, a couple scenes without a live audience.

I expected the same routine when I flew to Los Angeles to prep for the *Living Single* appearance.

The script arrived at my hotel. I flipped through it.

Oh crap.

They had written me into a lot of scenes, doing a lot of things. Did they think I was a professional?

All the actors, producers, and writers sat around a table for the reading the next day. The actors were fluid, hitting a switch, turning into character. It was intimidating. I was nervous, back in middle school, speaking low, stumbling over words. I looked haplessly and helplessly at the writers. No doubt, they were already thinking of how to write my lines out.

Luckily, we had three days of rehearsals before taping in front of a crowd.

With each rehearsal, I found my footing. We gathered in the mornings, leaving time to kill in the afternoons. One day, while I read the script again, someone hit me up. Michael Jordan was in town, filming his movie *Space Jam* on the Warner Bros. lot.

They had built him his own court to practice on when they weren't shooting. A lot of NBA players were getting runs in. You should come out.

Toward the end of my rookie season, Jordan had hung up the baseball spikes and made a celebrated return to the NBA. That March, while we were in Oakland to play the Warriors, I rushed to my hotel room to catch his first game back, against the Indiana Pacers. In it, he looked foreign wearing the number 45 on his jersey and rusty in bouncing shots off the rim, although he certainly wasn't shy in taking twenty-eight shots.

Michael being Michael, of course, put up fifty-five points a few games later, against the Knicks in Madison Square Garden.

We caught the Bulls at home a couple weeks later. Before the game, Vinnie Johnson, the former Bad Boys stalwart and now one of our radio analysts, pulled me aside.

Don't give that guy too much respect. He's a great player and all, but you've got to make sure you go at him.

We didn't match against each other often in the game. I did cross him over nicely on one drive to the rim. We played undermanned, without Allan, Joe Dumars, and Lindsey Hunter, and were unable to muster much of a fight. I sensed that Jordan needed time to round himself back into basketball form. His Bulls later collapsed against Penny Hardaway and Shaquille O'Neal's Orlando Magic in the playoffs.

The approaching season would mark Jordan's true comeback tour.

Guess I've still got a ways to go to be Jordan, I told myself, pulling past Warner Bros. security for the pickup game. I was stressing over a couple of sitcom scenes. He was co-starring with Bugs Bunny in a blockbuster movie.

I entered a gigantic bubble surrounding a court brought down from the University of California, Santa Barbara. It was elaborately constructed and even featured a weight room. Some of the UCLA players fresh off a championship—Charles O'Bannon, Toby Bailey, Kris Johnson—were on the court, sprinkled among pro players like Reggie Miller, Lamond Murray, and Muggsy Bogues.

We broke out into some runs. Jordan matched up against me. He was already slimmer, quicker than when he had returned to the game at the end of the season.

I couldn't have dreamed up what happened next. I gave Jordan the business, attacking him, scoring against him again and again. The ball was on a string. I crossed him up. My jumper was wet, and I didn't even consider myself a shooter. Everything flowed. I did whatever I wanted on the court against the best to ever do it. I wish someone had captured those moments on film.

He motioned for me to sit with him afterward. He was wearing his patent leather Jordan 11s. He asked me about my own midsole blue patent leathers on my feet, the Fila Hills.

His trainer suggested that I return for the next day's run. Sure, I said giddily. I barely closed the door on my rental before calling my boys, telling them that I had just played Jordan and he couldn't stop me.

I had talked signature shoes with Michael Jordan after outplaying him on his own court? It felt surreal then and now. It was a more singular experience than playing against him in a scrimmage while in college or even talking to him on the phone on the brink of entering the league.

Of course, if I had learned anything after scrimmaging with him in college, I should have known to stop after that first day.

Instead, I worked on some lines that evening, waking up the next day for another round of rehearsals before rushing back to the court at Warner Bros. There, Jordan was Jordan again. His trainer had probably only invited me back for his superstar client to claim his vengeance. Maybe, the previous day, he had filmed the scene where the Monstars steal the power of the NBA players, and he had just wanted to act it out during our scrimmage.

Either way, let's just say that I was not quite as eager to call my boys after that run.

We taped the show the next day. One scene with Queen Latifah's character involved us on the couch talking, exchanging awkward glances. Finally, we were to kiss as the scene faded out. We had rehearsed everything, except the kiss. Beforehand, the producers said they would cue us to stop when the scene ended. I was, of course, jittery and not much of a PDA guy. The scene arrived, we kissed, and I didn't hear a cue. We continued, only to look up after an eternity had passed to a lot of stifled laughs and grins.

They had conveniently forgotten to tell us the scene was over.

The lockout ended. Facilities reopened. In evaluating my rookie season, I planned to strengthen in a couple areas away from the court.

Despite the occasional tails from games, I never felt unsafe in the town house, but I decided to move just to be on the safe side. I also realized that I wanted my friends close to me, just not that close. I was young and still relatively new to the NBA. Long-standing friendships were becoming a little difficult to juggle. I certainly didn't do the best job establishing boundaries. Michael, who had become the director of marketing at the sports field house that Joe Dumars built, and Rob had started bringing people over and treating my place like it was their own. I won't say I kicked them out, but I did encourage them to find their own residence.

Still, I wanted them to share in my experiences. There was an expectation to spread the wealth among a circle of friends when an athlete suddenly came into a lot of money and even a sense of guilt that you were the one who made it. They came along if I went to a steak house after the game. I respected that they could not afford the check on a nightly basis like I could. I often picked up the tab until it started to become an expectation and then an obligation. It was a ritual that I couldn't help but come to resent. My dad's warning about friends having the same amount of money in their wallet meant that everyone should pay their own way whenever we went out. I learned that lesson the hard way, and we experienced a slow straining of our relationships.

I settled on a home inside a community with a lengthy drive from the gate and a security guard who watched over the neighborhood. The spacious home was recently built with the basement unfinished. For the first time, I spent some of the money I had earned and outfitted the space with a weight room, a jacuzzi area, and a game room.

I also wanted to improve my diet and energy levels. The fatigue of cycling through practices, games, and travel had caught me off guard my rookie season. Will Robinson, a legendary Pistons scout and a former coach at Illinois State, sometimes slyly strolled by me in the corridors of the Palace, offering a couple words of wisdom and keeping it moving.

If you want to shoot, fake the pass. You want to pass, fake the shot.

Young man, you got to take care of yourself. You got to eat right. You got to sleep right.

The last message stuck. That first year, I'd often depart shootaround and head home for a pregame nap. First, I'd come to a major thoroughfare containing every fast-food joint imaginable. My big meal deliberation of the day consisted of deciding which drive-through to enter.

Being on the road worsened my dietary habits. Allan, Lindsey, and I often gathered to watch a movie inside one of our hotel rooms post-shootaround. I'd sometimes call room service and order a couple appetizers, an entrée, and an apple pie à la mode.

Man, you can eat all that?

Yeah, I need that fuel.

Obviously, I was finding ammunition in the wrong places, weighed down in games by dense calories. With the new house, I also needed a chef to right my nutrition. I could simultaneously consume healthier meals and not worry about where I would eat on a daily basis. My heart was in the right place. My stomach was getting there. I still had to keep my mind on my corporate sponsors.

A journalist, one day, asked about my summer priorities.

Well, I said, I noticed I was eating nothing but fast food. I want to try to eat healthier, so I hired a chef.

It didn't take long before the suits at McDonald's called me. I earned myself a long media training session that day.

Another lesson learned. I had tried to be forthcoming in the interview. But I was no longer just speaking for myself. I also spoke for the companies I represented.

———

Training camp opened with a noticeable buzz. Doug possessed the frenetic energy of a former NBA player. He was on the court, running with us, enduring the same drills we were.

He planned to put the ball in my hands and allow me to dissect defenses. Yes, he said, he would challenge me. He expected me to rise to those expectations, to be in top condition, to dominate games. I was ready for it, I believed. The greatest players accepted coaching that guided them to new heights.

From the outset, he wanted us to know that this was a different season under a new regime. The closing off of practices to friends and spectators was among his first policy changes. He pushed us at training camp through drills and conditioning. He didn't just challenge me. He confronted everyone daily in trying to shift the culture. He recognized the difficulty in trying to sustain a winning mentality after losing had settled into the franchise.

We were horrible in a preseason game in Knoxville against a Magic team fresh off a championship appearance.

We were pros. It was an exhibition and didn't really count, right?

It counted for Doug. We flew home and the next day participated in a practice worse than a post-loss session at Duke and a Mike Dunleavy workout combined. Doug divided us into teams he branded the softies and the competitors.

He grouped me with the softies, along with Allan, Lindsey, Mark West, and a couple other guys nursing injuries. We started with relay races. The softies lost. Our punishment involved thirty push-ups and converting several free throws. We must have dropped about eight races in a row before finally tying in the last race.

Tie, Doug said, goes to the competitors.

My deltoids, pectorals, and triceps were all on fire when Doug announced we were moving on to a scrimmage. I was game, hoping to take out some frustration. On my way to the rim, I got hammered again and again. The coaches swallowed their whistles, ignoring the blatant fouls.

Chuck Daly, the coach of the Bad Boy teams, had dropped by to watch the practice. I approached him once it finally ended.

I'm never going to have a practice like that again, I told him. No one's ever going to question my competitiveness.

Thankfully, there was no need. We were a little slow at the season's start before finding some continuity. Lindsey began at point guard with Allan joining him in the backcourt, while I played small forward.

Slowly, as Doug had promised, I started playing more with the ball in my hands as a point forward with Joe supplanting Lindsey in the starting lineup. Allan hit his stride, becoming the player we knew he could be, and we developed an on-court synergy. I was the slasher, facilitator. He was the marksman, who could also put the ball on the floor. Our rookie, Theo Ratliff, flexed his potential as a big who defended the paint. Otis Thorpe, also a new addition, had arrived with championship pedigree. We developed as a solid pick-and-roll pairing.

We were winning as winter arrived, playing hard defense, executing our offense. Finally, I was learning what it took to win in this league.

———

All-Star weekend was another whirlwind. Somehow, I had again paced the league in fan voting, even though Jordan was back and had returned to his dominating form. He was, of course, voted in, part of a Bulls conglomerate that included Scottie Pippen and Phil Jackson as our conference's coach.

Brian Hill, Orlando's coach, had conducted a dummy practice prior to last season's game where we did some perfunctory layup drills in between smiling for cameras. I anticipated the same this season once I landed for the game in San Antonio.

Instead, Phil instructed us to get taped and prepare to get up and down the court. He divided the Eastern Conference group into two teams, and soon I was lost in the stellar competition, sweating, working hard to measure myself against the best of the best. At one point, I looked up. Michael and Scottie were both chilling on the sideline. That's a cagey coach, I thought, taking the opportunity to rest his players while challenging and exhausting the rest of us.

Finally, we got some water as Alonzo Mourning continued his conditioning, jogging from sideline to sideline. We've got a fitness test when we get back to Miami, he told me. Coach Pat Riley doesn't play.

The next day, Scottie pulled me aside inside the locker room. Neither of us wanted to guard Shawn Kemp, the Western Conference starting forward, who posterized people for fun. Charles Barkley was their other forward, undoubtedly still nursing himself from a long night along the San Antonio River Walk.

I know you got more votes, Scottie said, but I got to pull seniority. When he catches the ball, he's going to spin baseline. Just don't let him.

Seniority was seniority. Scottie was Scottie, the same person who had welcomed me in La Jolla. I accepted the challenge of trying not to be a poster, while Jordan earned MVP in his return to the game.

———

Shortly after the All-Star break, the Toronto Raptors arrived for a game at the Palace. I had looked forward to the evening, the night that the Pistons would officially retire the No. 11 graced by Isiah Thomas.

Before the game, Anita Baker, the legendary soulful singer, eloquently sang the national anthem.

During halftime, I loitered on our sideline watching the retirement ceremony, inspired to try to build as impactful a career. We finished off the Raptors, and I quickly showered and changed to meet everyone for a reception inside a restaurant at the Palace.

I was introduced to Anita and her then-husband, Walter Bridgforth Jr. I congratulated her on the performance. She deflected, making small talk, and asked if I was dating anyone.

No, you have to introduce me to someone, I joked.

I didn't think much more of the brief interaction. I had no idea that a short while later she would attend an awards show and meet an admirer of hers, a talented, beautiful young singer from Windsor.

———

We improved by sixteen wins over the previous season, a significant achievement. Doug deserved a lot of the credit for how he drove us and integrated the new players into our roster.

I was excited for my first playoffs; we drew Orlando. Penny and Shaq were at the height of their talents. They harbored championship aspirations, thoughts of correcting their finals loss a season earlier to Houston.

The sun shone in Orlando during our two blowout losses as I encountered a new level of ramped-up intensity. The best-of-five series shifted to Michigan afterward. We put up a fight but lost by a couple of points. Our season over, most of the team convened at our usual postgame spot, the Auburn Hills TGI Fridays, across the street from Oakland University.

The Magic, I guess, were staying overnight to celebrate. We spotted Shaq and Dennis Scott. I looked at them and then through the windows to the gray sky and the snow still piled on the ground outside, though

April was turning to May. We had just been in the clear skies of Florida a couple days earlier. It was a fitting end to a season full of bright, sunny days and dark, cloudy ones.

I sat with Doug for my exit meeting a few days later. I appreciated how he had improved our team. I was used to coaches pushing, but Doug, at times, could be a little much.

I wanted next season to be different, more of a collaboration.

———

Michael, Rob, and Mario, who had also moved into town, were planning to attend a talent show downtown. Andre Harrell, the new king of Motown, was hosting, searching for new acts to sign.

I was still in a funk over the end to our season. It didn't feel right to party.

Your loss, they told me heading out.

A short while later, Michael called me on the phone.

You should've come. You know that singer, Tamia?

Tamia, Tamia? Tamia from "You Put a Move on My Heart" on *Q's Jook Joint?*

Yeah, I know her.

Well, she's here.

Dang. Maybe I should have gone.

Hold on. I'm going to put her on.

I fumbled for my television remote, lowering the volume. A beautiful voice, her voice, *that* voice, said hello. We exchanged pleasantries. She passed the phone back to Michael.

Michael, I said, she probably won't think that it's actually me. You're some random guy handing her a phone. But just in case, give her my number.

My boys dropped by after the party. We were in my garage, listening to music, when she called.

I ducked inside a guest room. I obviously knew who she was. Maybe my ego hoped that she knew who I was as well.

You're that basketball player Anita was talking about?

Anita in the clutch. Tamia and I spent hours on the phone getting to know each other, discussing everything and nothing, our families, the pressures of feeling like we were on the verge of breaking through yet still wanting to prove ourselves, the intricacies of making a Michigan left.

The sun was rising before we knew it.

We made plans to meet up as soon as we caught a couple hours of sleep.

A little while later, I was on my way to pick her up for a movie. To me, that was the ideal first date, a safety outlet. I could tell when we were in the car together, buying the ticket, getting the popcorn, whether the conversation would carry through the actual film. If not? Cool. I could kick back and hopefully catch a good flick.

Pulling up to her home in Windsor, I spotted a couple of her family members peeking through the blinds. She opened the door. I had seen her before on television and in music videos. I should have known what to expect, right? Still, I was speechless. She was flawless, a dream in a green blouse and blue jeans.

We picked up where our conversation had left off that morning. In downtown Detroit, at the Renaissance Center, we were the only spectators for a showing of *Twister*.

We laughed, talking through the movie. I think the film was about hurricanes or tornadoes. A blockbuster about some type of natural disaster. Maybe.

The credits rolled. Already? I didn't want the date to end.

Dinner?

Soon, we were eating shrimp and gumbo at Fishbones, a Cajun joint in Detroit's Greektown.

I reached into my pockets when the waiter brought the check to our table.

Nothing.

My wallet must be in the car. Let me run out and get it.

Don't worry about it, she said. I got it.

Tamia pulled out a credit card from her pocketbook, a better credit card than I had, placing it on the table.

She's definitely a keeper, I thought, driving her back home.

I didn't want the date to end, and really it didn't. She was in town for a week before hitting the road again. I made the drive to Windsor again the next day. Her great-uncle, a gentleman named Bubbles, answered the door, squinting at me.

Grant Hill? What's he doing here? He's got money.

Tamia nudged him from the doorway. This time, she invited me inside. We were inseparable the next few days, visiting Detroit, hanging out in Windsor, finding ourselves in deep conversation, losing ourselves in each other. I had been in prior relationships, but nothing had felt so seamless, so early. I wished Tamia good luck as she headed to Chicago for a television spot on Oprah Winfrey's show before she flew to Las Vegas to continue her music career.

I summoned Michael, Rob, and Mario. Anyone feeling lucky?

We were off to Vegas, my first time in the City of Lights. As I stepped into the arid, sweltering heat, all I knew about the city was the vibrant nightlife and that one hotel with the pyramid, the Luxor. That was where we stayed, meeting up with Tamia. Kidada Jones, Tamia's friend and one of Quincy's daughters, also dropped by for a couple of days.

We explored the city together, a couple probably before we even knew we were a couple. I barely caught my breath before we left for Los Angeles, where she planned to work on her debut album while staying at a colossal mansion in Bel Air.

I thought I was doing all right for myself. People in the music industry, I found, operated in a different stratosphere. I jogged through the hills of Los Angeles, trying to maintain my conditioning, whenever Tamia went to the studio. When we were together, we bypassed the clubs on Sunset and spent our time at restaurants off the beaten track.

I had never wanted to be around someone as often as I wanted to be around her. But after a couple of weeks, we bade each other goodbye.

Participating in the Olympics was probably the only event that could have lured me away.

I had won a couple of college championships, participated in two NBA All-Star Games. The Olympics, to me, was a cut above. I was no longer representing a university or a franchise. The Olympics was the pinnacle of athletics and competition, the United States against the world. It conjured memories of being a mesmerized kid in 1984, watching Carl Lewis dominate track and field events at the Los Angeles Memorial Coliseum and Michael, or Mike back then, Jordan, Patrick Ewing, and Chris Mullin collaborating as collegians to take basketball's gold medal with Bobby Knight stalking the sidelines.

A high-ranking USA Basketball official at the 1991 Pan American Games had mentioned to me that pro players would take over the Olympics for just a cycle to restore America atop basketball's hierarchy following our loss to the Soviet Union. The Dream Team had accomplished the mission by dominating other countries and spreading the game globally. I was under the impression that the national team would subsequently again be plucked from the amateur ranks and that I had forever missed my Olympic opportunity.

That's messed up, I thought then. There goes my shot.

Instead, the Dream Team was such a success that NBA players would be selected for the foreseeable future. It took me less than a millisecond to agree to play in the 1996 Olympics in Atlanta. I was joined by a collection of stars from the Dream Team—Scottie Pippen, Karl Malone, Charles Barkley, David Robinson, John Stockton—and newcomers like Penny Hardaway, Hakeem Olajuwon, Mitch Richmond, Reggie Miller, Shaquille O'Neal, and Gary Payton, a late replacement for an injured Glenn Robinson.

We kicked off with a training camp in Chicago before a slate of exhibition games held around the country. I was the youngest on the team, eager to spend quality time with a group of players of that caliber. The All-Star Games were always in-and-out experiences and left little opportunity to develop relationships that went beyond the surface. There was also some of the 1980s residue still around. Joe Dumars, at my first All-Star Game, saw my giddiness over being in the presence of so many superstars. Calmly, in his lowered tone, he pulled me aside.

We're Pistons, he said. We just stay over here.

Joe wasn't around this time. I planned on enjoying this.

Our first scrimmage was at a familiar place, the Palace, against the U.S. Select squad, a team of collegians similar to the one I had played on with Bobby Hurley and Chris Webber against the Dream Team. No one had televised those games. This one aired live.

We were all new to playing with one another. No one wanted to be viewed as dominating the ball. Naturally, everyone deferred. Meanwhile, the college team played energized. Tim Duncan banked in shots from crazy angles. Austin Croshere held his own against Hakeem. Shea Seals somehow transformed into Superman and dunked over Shaq. They were free, loose, finding pay dirt. We were down seventeen points before we even knew it.

What goes around comes around.

Our coach, Lenny Wilkens, had seen enough. Scottie and Gary

checked into the game. Their harassing, suffocating defense disrupted the college team, allowing us to escape with a six-point win.

Witnessing Scottie's choking defense up close provided a deeper appreciation for his talents and efforts. That was an area where I planned on challenging myself. With the Pistons, I had to be our offensive fulcrum. At times, the burden stole from my defensive energy. I had evolved into a lockdown defender at Duke. I wanted to get back to being that guy, a player who caused chaos at both ends of the court.

We canvassed around, playing exhibitions in Cleveland, Phoenix, Salt Lake City, and Indianapolis before setting up shop in Orlando for a final Olympic tune-up.

At most of the stops, I posted up in my hotel room once the game was over, spending the rest of the evening with Tamia on the phone. I was surprised we hadn't run out of topics to discuss or that she wasn't tired of hearing my voice. We could both probably agree that we were falling for each other and falling quickly. I had nearly gone out with Reggie and Charles one night, deciding to stay in at the last second. That was the evening Charles supposedly got into it with someone at a club, and I made a note to myself to add Charles to the list with Oliver.

In Orlando, Scottie invited me and my boys to hang out with a couple of his visiting friends. We finished practice early, exiting to a sweltering day, and decided to hit up Disney's Blizzard Beach Water Park. Each line stretched as long as I could see. I found out there was nothing like traveling with Scottie. It was like rolling with Brian Davis, if BD had gone on to become a celebrated NBA champion. People clapped for us as I meekly apologized for skipping to the front of the line at rides. So this was what it was like to be an NBA champion with the Bulls.

That night, the Orlando duo, Penny and Shaq, hosted a party in their hometown. The entire team attended. We were all relaxing, joking. A few guys enjoyed some drinks. Scottie puffed on a cigar. I was still a teetotaler. I've got him at tomorrow's practice, I told myself. They were still picking up steam, playing cards, when I begged off at around three in the morning to get a couple hours of shut-eye.

The next morning, Scottie was as fresh as someone who had gone to sleep after watching the early evening news. To my disbelief, he ran circles around me. An observer would have thought I had been the one who pulled the all-nighter. The guy was just on a different level. Maybe his body was forced to evolve after all those long nights with Michael Jordan.

This team, I was finding, was full of personality, collectively loud, universally talented. Shaq, Gary, Charles, and Reggie were always making fun of one another. Their voices more than made up for the reserved players, Mitch, John, David. I enjoyed spending time with each player individually, discovering their personalities, appreciating their work ethic, discerning the unique characteristics to their games. Hakeem and I often played one-on-one after practices. The rules were that I couldn't shoot from the perimeter, and he couldn't draw from the paint. It didn't matter. I couldn't keep him in front of me. His footwork, full of spins and pivots, was pure basketball beauty, even more impressive because of his length.

It's no different from what you do on the perimeter, he said. I just do it in the post.

He had just offered me a secret window into his art and followed by asking how I pulled off my hesitation crossover. I happily walked him through the move.

That summer, we were together as the NBA shifted. A few guys on the national team, headlined by Shaq, had arrived at free agency. My teammate Allan Houston was also an unrestricted free agent. I expected him to stay in Detroit and wanted the Pistons to deliver every cent possible to him.

Don't let them tell you that I have to make the most money, I told

Allan earlier in the summer when we debuted the Pistons' new teal color scheme. I got my contract two years ago. This is a different market. You should naturally be getting more.

In a huff, Reggie returned to the bus after a practice. He was a free agent and expected to use the Knicks as leverage in his contract negotiations with the Indiana Pacers. Allan, he had just learned, had agreed to terms with the Knicks, throwing his main bargaining chip out the window. That's how I learned my running mate was leaving Detroit. I had no prior indication he had planned to depart, leaving me shocked and a little hurt. I probably should have phoned him to learn the backstory. But I was in my feelings in the moment.

Then Shaq lumbered onto the bus, grinning. The Miami Heat was rumored to be nearing a hundred-million-dollar deal with Alonzo Mourning. Guess there was a good reason he put up with all those conditioning mandates under Pat Riley.

If he's a BMW, I'm a Porsche, Shaq said. I should get more money than him.

A day later, he fumed, gripping and waving a copy of the *Orlando Sentinel* like he was Mr. Wilson agitated at Dennis the Menace. The paper had conducted a poll on whether the Magic should extend him a massive contract. Overwhelmingly, fans had voted against such an offer.

I can't believe they don't want to pay me, he said.

It didn't make much sense to me either. This was peak Shaq, a force that had never before been seen in the NBA. I just assumed the situation would be resolved. In Shaq and Penny, Orlando possessed the tandem of the future.

Shaq didn't accompany us on the short trip from Orlando to Atlanta for the start of the Olympics. I later learned that he used the window to meet with the Logo, Jerry West, and reach a deal to join the Lakers and head out west.

Good, I thought. Get that big dude out of the East. All of us in the Eastern Conference, I'm sure, thought the same thing: finally, we have a chance.

———

In Atlanta, we cycled through media sessions. Someone asked Reggie what it was like to stay at a hotel, the Omni, while the rest of the athletes holed up at the Olympic Village.

It's not like we're staying at a really nice hotel, he replied. It's the Omni.

Reggie found his hotel door locked after he returned from practice. For hours, he couldn't get inside. I told myself to never dis the Omni.

We were last for the game's opening ceremony as athletes and delegations from around the world formed a line that dwarfed the one at Blizzard Beach. I wished we could have bypassed that one too.

Flashbulbs popped from every direction when we finally walked into Centennial Olympic Stadium. The noise sounded like several Camerons at once. Then Muhammad Ali emerged with the torch. His hands shook. So did the flame. The toll from Parkinson's disease was visible. I worried whether he would be able to light the cauldron. He, of course, completed the task with noble dignity. It was a moment I would always remember, appreciating his history and life's sacrifices.

———

The world was still catching up to America's basketball prowess. We were not really challenged throughout the Olympics. Penny and I, the two youngest players, headed our second unit. The La Jolla scrimmage represented the only time we had previously played together. We developed a chemistry, utilizing our strength, speed, and athleticism.

Officials randomly drug tested two players following each game. We all questioned how indiscriminate the tests actually were when Karl was randomly selected after every game, along with our leading scorer. Karl was solid as an ox. I had seen his dedication firsthand after I joined his workout sessions throughout the summer at the crack of dawn. He lifted daily, spending an hour or two focused on the same group of muscles. But no one wanted to be tested alongside him after a game. Those tests took forever. Those moments when it looked like we were being unselfish late, playing hot potato with the ball on the perimeter? The ball got spread around because no one wanted to end the game as our leading scorer.

The games were more celebration than competition, enough so that Charles gained the biggest applause during a rout over China when he spelled out Y-M-C-A on our bench as the Village People bellowed from a speaker during a time-out.

It was a lot of fun, though, made more enjoyable when Tamia flew to Atlanta to visit and continue work on her album with different producers in the area.

We met for dinner one night, laughing, eating at Planet Hollywood with my parents and Perri "Pebbles" Reid, the architect of the hit R&B group TLC. Tamia put my parents at ease, just like she did with everyone in her orbit. Suddenly we heard a commotion and learned that an explosion had just occurred, not too far away, during the middle of a crowded concert at Centennial Olympic Park. People were hurt. Some badly.

We scrambled, leaving the restaurant, rushing back to the Omni. The hotel was transformed into Fort Knox. Security buzzed everywhere. We couldn't move a couple feet before being asked to flash our credentials again. Pebbles invited Tamia and me back to her house to escape the evening's uncertainty.

With practice called off, we returned to the Omni late the next day following a restless evening. Authorities had named a person of interest in the bombing. Officials said we were safe at the hotel, now fortified enough that we called it the Rock after the recently released Sean Connery flick. For the rest of the Olympics, we rarely left the hotel. All our venues were connected to the Omni through a maze of interconnecting skywalks and tunnels.

I distracted myself through conditioning, still trying to keep up with Karl in the morning. At that point, I was probably the strongest I had ever been. But I pushed through one too many sessions, upsetting my knee, making me unable to play in the gold medal game against Yugoslavia.

They didn't need me. The outing was like the others that summer, a coast-to-coast win. In the game, a healthy Shaq played about as much as me. As we readied to exit our locker room, stand on the podium, and accept our gold medals, Shaq held everyone up. He threatened to walk out with a Pepsi can in defiance of the team's beverage sponsor, Coca-Cola. Thankfully, an official talked him down. We accepted our medals with no issues over spilled soda.

In my opinion, we could have held our own against the Dream Team. Some of the players, of course, were crossovers, having played with both. Collectively, with Shaq and Hakeem, our team boasted more size, strength, and youth. We took pride in our suffocating defense. That 1996 team, for whatever reason, is often lost now in the conversation surrounding the best teams ever assembled.

When I was on that podium, completely in the moment, a wave of accomplishment crashed over me, a feeling lost since college. This is what it was all about. I wanted this for my team, to bring a title to Detroit.

Moving in the right direction was all about silencing that little doubt in your head that tells you you're not good enough, that you couldn't possibly reach that next plateau. Checkpoints of reaffirmation helped drown that apprehension. It withered when countered with an abundance of evidence.

I had patterned parts of my game after Scottie. He was the gold standard of small forwards. At the All-Star Games, I questioned if I deserved to be among all those amazing players.

Battling Scottie daily in practice, not relenting, giving as much as I took, I firmly, finally proved to myself that I could play with these guys.

I couldn't wait to see how it would all translate into my next NBA season.

———

Tamia and I returned to Los Angeles, where I rented a suite at the Hotel Bel-Air for the rest of the summer. One day, I grabbed lunch with Lon and Hollis Greenlaw, one of his Williams & Connolly associates. Fila wanted to renegotiate our deal after just two years. I had signed a pact for five years with a base salary and built-in royalties. The first signature shoe had surpassed projections. The second did even better. While Lon negotiated with Fila, Phil Knight realized that I was in Los Angeles and asked to get together. He proposed a lucrative five-year offer with Nike once my Fila contract expired in a couple of years. Knight acknowledged that Nike and Howard Slusher had botched my original recruitment to the company out of college. As I drove back to see Tamia, I was comforted by the apology. My ego probably needed to hear the mea culpa, and I seriously contemplated the secret Nike offer. But two years was a long time, and the offer wasn't guaranteed until then. Fila had shown early faith in me and was willing to increase their commitment. I decided to reciprocate that belief. Lon would negotiate with Fila throughout the approaching season, and I eventually landed on a new, seven-year deal with the company for eighty million dollars, one of the largest endorsement contracts signed to that point. Fila also named me chairman of the sports marketing and athletic committee, allowing me to advise the company on the athletes they considered for endorsements.

A few days after the meeting with Knight, Tamia and I were hanging out at the house she was staying in when she fielded a telephone call from Kidada Jones.

I guess Kidada didn't like my choice in Vegas hotels. She told Tamia that she was in Vegas for a Mike Tyson fight and at that crazy pyramid hotel again, this time with her boyfriend, the rapper Tupac Shakur. He was an impressive artist, a poet, capable of reaching everyone from the hustlers to the preachers. Recently, he had worn a pair of my signature shoes for a picture in the booklet of his album *All Eyez on Me*.

From an ego standpoint, things didn't get much better. We were still a few years away from Allen Iverson completing the game's synchronicity with hip-hop. But basketball and music had always intersected. Basketball's expression lends itself to music. One could trace the roots all the way back to the Harlem Globetrotters and the Harlem Rens and the influence of jazz. As time continued, basketball reflected the goings-on of society. Hip-hop emerged during Michael Jordan's rise. It might not have influenced Jordan. But he influenced hip-hop through his swagger, bald head, baggy clothes, and of course shoes. The Georgetown Hoyas, in a different way, impacted the culture as a dominant all-Black team. Back then, everyone had a Georgetown Starter jacket. The Fab Five's defiance and expression also embodied the spirit of hip-hop. Basketball and hip-hop traveled on somewhat parallel, sometimes intersecting journeys. When I was growing up, the NBA Finals played on tape delay, and hip-hop was an underground culture burgeoning in New York. Now they were both global and cultural phenomena.

Method Man had worn my first signature shoe in the "You're All I Need" music video with Mary J. Blige. I hadn't thought people would wear the shoe outside the basketball court like how people donned Jordans to both hoop and chill. Method Man, coming off his success with the Wu-Tang Clan, provided me the first indication that the shoes could possibly cross over beyond the basketball court. My mom and I crossed paths with Method Man about a year later at the MTV Video Music

Awards when we somehow shared a booth. My mom told Method Man that he had a nice face and advised him to stop looking down and scowling so much. Method Man couldn't have been nicer in our interaction, and on the rare occasions we ran into each other over the years he always asked me how my mom was doing.

I'd like to think that I was the one who delivered those shoes to Tupac for his album art. We frequented the same rim shop in Atlanta. I forwarded the guys who worked there some pairs. They said Tupac would love them and promised to send some to him. But really, I don't know if the shoes he had on for the shoot were the ones that had been sent.

We were devastated later that night when we learned Tupac had been shot. We thought he would pull through, heartbroken when he succumbed to the injuries a few days later.

Usually, Tamia and I spent our Los Angeles nights quietly with each other. One night, Tevin Campbell invited us to a listening party for his new album *Back to the World*. We decided to make an exception. We were both admirers of Tevin. Jay Brown, who worked artists and repertoire at Tamia's label, Qwest Records, joined us.

Somehow, after the party, Dalvin "Mr. Dalvin" DeGrate of the R&B group Jodeci hopped into my rented BMW. No issues there. I was a fan. We grabbed a bite to eat at Popeyes, then cruised along Sunset Boulevard, before ending the night.

Oh, there you go, Mr. Dalvin said out of nowhere from the backseat, while we were stopped at a red light in West Hollywood.

He jumped out of the car, leather jacket and all, darting inside a Pink Dot.

Jay raced after him and dragged him back to the car. Mr. Dalvin, upset, mumbled that he had spotted the guy and woman who had stolen the musical stylings of his brother, DeVanté Swing. He kept repeating a name, a boot brand made popular by New York hip-hop artists.

To that point, I had never heard of Timbaland and Missy Elliott. I promise, the next day we heard Ginuwine's "Pony," the megahit produced by Timbaland. They were all over the place after that, dominating the charts.

It's a story I didn't relay to Timbaland until the winter of 2016 at President Barack Obama's final party at the White House. We chopped it up, two Virginia guys, and I couldn't resist asking if he remembered that night when he was out and Mr. Dalvin jumped out of a car to confront him in the middle of West Hollywood. Instantly, he recalled the interaction.

He had no idea I was the one driving the car.

I'm not trying to be disrespectful or anything, but Timbaland and Missy advanced from that night to influential, impressive musical careers. I didn't hear much more from Mr. Dalvin after he leaped out of that car.

13

THIS was going to be the season we finally cleared the hurdle and pushed the Pistons back into playoff relevancy. I was better, bolstered by my Olympic experience. So was my team. Lindsey Hunter was prepared to move forward in the absence of Allan Houston. Joe Dumars looked spry. We were used to Doug Collins, ready to look over his occasionally grating tendencies.

Tamia was probably the first person I encountered with a schedule that could match mine. She was off to St. Martin, filming *Speed 2: Cruise Control* over the next few weeks with Sandra Bullock and Willem Dafoe. We have a chance to be really good, I told her before she left. I'm not saying we're ready to win a championship, but we're pretty close.

The season began and we clicked, starting with four straight wins. Then the Bulls arrived at the Palace. Michael Buffer delivered the pre-game introductions for the nationally televised game. Joe and I were the only ones in rhythm. We managed a fight, but Chicago handed us a loss. I took pride that we were mostly undeterred, reeling off another six wins after the setback.

Allan showed up the next month for his first return to Michigan. That night, we let the Knicks have it. Lindsey was on fire. Joe played well. My shot was a little off, but I still managed a triple-double. We won by around thirty points. Allan only scored a bucket. Afterward, his stats loomed big and large on the video board. It was petty. It was also Detroit, the city versus everybody, even back then. You didn't willfully leave Detroit without expecting the city to feel some type of way. I knew that then and would experience it firsthand later.

We were winning, playing intense defense, beating the teams we were supposed to, playing competitively against the teams that were supposed to be better than us. I hated that Allan had left. The departure of someone who complemented my game and personality so well was a sizable loss. Inadvertently, though, his exit had solved a logjam among the guards. Joe and Lindsey were more at ease, playing in their natural roles. They were both shooting well from beyond the three-point line, along with Terry Mills, stretching defenses, which allowed me wide driving lanes.

We didn't overwhelm teams with our talent. We were just a group of guys who knew what to do individually for our team to collectively win. We had lost just five of twenty-five games when we played the Bulls again, this time in Chicago. We knew we needed to play at our best, that any little slip could allow them to put a stranglehold on the game.

Dennis Rodman did what Dennis Rodman did. He found gaps in our defense, indecipherable to anyone else, slipping past our veteran big, Otis Thorpe, for three consecutive offensive rebounds in a single possession to start the third quarter.

Doug was livid. He immediately summoned a replacement off the bench for Otis. Alvin Gentry, an assistant coach, rushed over to try to soothe Otis, who took a seat as far away from Doug as possible.

That night, a fracture was created, one that increased as the season continued, slowly draining the energy from our locker room.

―――――

I stretched my calves on a slant board next to Michael Curry and Lindsey after a practice. We were scheduled to fly to Portland in a couple of hours, the first stop of a difficult, lengthy six-game trip out west.

You know, one of us surmised, Joe isn't going to play in one of these games. Which one do you think he'll sit out?

Sometimes, Joe would do that. It's no knock on him. He was our veteran, still putting up decent numbers. He listened to his body, sitting a game here and there when it told him he needed to rest.

We hit the road, splitting the first four games of our trip, taking the Lakers into overtime, where we prevailed. It was always fun playing in front of the stars at the Forum. I put up monster numbers, crafting one of my finest games to that point as a pro with thirty-eight points, fifteen rebounds, and nine assists.

Just like when I went against Glenn Robinson in college, personal accolades were never my goal. My ears did perk when I heard whispers that I was an early MVP candidate. The award was typically bestowed upon the best player on the top team. If we kept winning, I started thinking, I could possibly be in the running. I had pushed myself to score more. I was still happiest facilitating. A great win to me was when everyone contributed. I seldom thought about how I could beat a team, preferring to figure out how we as a team could combine to dismiss an opponent.

I was mindful of the trajectory Michael Jordan took before his cascade of championships. Doug was a walking reminder. Isiah Thomas also received his lumps early in his NBA career before winning titles. Players not named Magic Johnson didn't arrive in the league, snap their fingers, and win a championship. I was chasing ghosts and GOATs. Like at Duke, I was climbing the hill, learning how to win on this level. That season was the most optimistic I felt about the prospects of our team during my time in Detroit.

The opportunity to see Tamia was another reason why I looked forward to the Lakers game. Our relationship, at its core a deep friendship, continued growing through visits and phone calls.

When she was not available, my friends helped break the isolation I had felt during my rookie season even as strains in our relationships started becoming more apparent. We formed a bubble, frequenting the same couple of dining spots. I counted down the time until the mall was virtually empty and I knew we could duck inside without causing much of a stir. When I was recognized or approached, I tried to be the Grant Hill people expected from commercials. Some fans felt that they knew me intimately, that time with me was their right in exchange for supporting the Pistons, buying a pair of Filas, drinking a can of Sprite. Everything had its price. I smiled and tried to be gracious through interruptions, signing my signature at every interaction. But each time I thought I was getting closer to what Michael Jordan must have felt off the court, I couldn't help thinking that I'd also like to reel it in a little bit.

I guess, if I had wanted to, I could have walked away and left opportunities dangling. Around that time, Lon Babby told me that he would also represent Tim Duncan. Tim, he said, didn't want to do any marketing or promotions at all.

That's refreshing, I thought to myself. How liberating would it be to focus on nothing but the game?

Those ideas were nudged aside. Time in the spotlight was finite. I wanted to explore the opportunities while they were available.

In Sacramento, we neared the end of our trip. Michael, Joe's backup, figured that Joe would sit out the trip's finale against the Warriors. The Kings matchup would be nationally televised, and Golden State's Latrell

Sprewell wasn't the player anyone wanted to face on a back-to-back at the end of a long road haul.

I'm going to get a nice meal right now, Michael said when we sat with Lindsey at a Cheesecake Factory following shootaround. I'm not playing much tonight, so I'm going to get to the gym early and get a workout in. That way, I'll be ready to go tomorrow.

Sounded like a plan. I took the bus over to ARCO Arena for the game, where Joe was already on the training table with Arnie Kander, our strength and conditioning coach.

I liked Arnie. He had a background in physical therapy and was a bit ahead of his time. He believed in holistic healing and had practiced ballet, gymnastics, and martial arts. Isiah Thomas had sought Arnie to help with his chronic injuries late in his career. Eventually, Isiah started bringing Arnie in to work with him before games, and Arnie found a role within the organization. Arnie was the first person who explained to me the benefits of strengthening my core or, for that matter, what a core was. In college, I had focused on working out specific body parts—my shoulders, legs, and chest. When I first entered the league, I suffered hard falls nearly every time I drove to the basket. I sometimes braced the impact with my hands and inevitably hurt my wrist. Arnie illustrated to me how true strength comes from a strong base. We designed exercises that strengthened my core, which allowed me to absorb contact and land on two feet. Getting hit and watching a defender fall as I finished through the physicality became a badge of honor.

I didn't think Arnie's hiring sat well with Dr. Benjamin Paolucci, our team physician. But Arnie had developed a strong relationship with our team owner, Mr. Bill Davidson. By the time I had arrived in Detroit, the pair worked out as we practiced. Often, they played tennis on the indoor clay court that Mr. Davidson erected inside the facility.

You'd think after a hundred times of Mr. Davidson always winning that he'd get that I was throwing the games, Arnie confided in me. It's getting harder and harder to make sure he wins.

Occasionally, I'd join them on the tennis court for some added cardio. We'd bring along Tom Wilson for doubles. Tom refused to hit at Mr. Davidson, a decent player, but a bit elderly to be moving baseline to baseline. I took no pity, targeting Mr. Davidson for drop shots. Arnie, though, could beat both of us nearly single-handedly. Maybe one day you'll finally beat us, Mr. Davidson would say to me, while I offered a smirk at Arnie.

I greeted Arnie and Joe in Sacramento. Michael walked into the room, exhausted, dripping sweat, the product of an intensive pregame workout.

Suddenly Joe rolled on the table. Something in his back gave. Michael and I looked at each other. Uh-oh.

That game, a depleted Michael was sacrificed to Mitch Richmond. Mitch was one of those eternally underrated players. His team wasn't good. He was. Mitch dropped about forty points against a full-stomached Michael, amassing a triple-double.

Thankfully, Joe's back was improved the next night, when we beat Golden State easily. But I am sure Michael wished he had guessed the right game Joe was going to sit.

———

We reached the All-Star break with the second-best record in the Eastern Conference, just behind the Bulls. Chicago's staff had worked last season's game, so Doug and our assistant coaches earned the right to guide the stars at Cleveland's Gund Arena. Michael Jordan topped the vote getters. I was selected to start alongside him, along with Penny Hardaway, Scottie Pippen, and Patrick Ewing.

Joe joined us as a reserve. Christian Laettner was also on the team, a first-time All-Star, who now played for the Atlanta Hawks. I was happy for him, hopeful that his professional career was gaining traction.

I settled into the audience the night before the All-Star Game for the dunk contest. A skinny kid, Kobe Bryant, won with some amazing, athletic dunks. He was fresh out of high school and had played only a couple of minutes in our game against the Lakers.

Maybe, I thought, this kid is someone to watch.

It was early spring, the weather crisp and clear when we landed back in Los Angeles to play the Clippers. As much as I enjoyed playing the Lakers at the Forum, I also looked forward to playing the Clippers in the Sports Arena. The little brothers of Los Angeles provided a different energy, more akin to a summer league game than all the glitz and glamour in going up against their counterparts at the Forum.

Our team was staying in Los Angeles the night before flying to Seattle, which meant more quality time with Tamia. After we dispatched the Clippers, Tamia and I left the arena together in a stretch limousine with friends from her record label, snaking our way to her place. Someone popped in a CD featuring a new song from the Notorious B.I.G. His husky Brooklyn accent wafted through the air.

Pink gators, *my* Detroit players.

The song hit. We played it again and again. Pink gators? That's someone who knew Detroit inside out.

At Tamia's place, we readied ourselves for a rare night out. Beyond that eventful evening with Mr. Dalvin, we hadn't spent many nights out as a couple in Los Angeles. But her label was throwing an event that night, along with *VIBE* magazine.

We pulled up to a building along Wilshire Boulevard inside the city's Miracle Mile. People loitered everywhere, spilling outside, clamoring to get inside. Someone said that the Notorious B.I.G., Puff Daddy, and all of Bad Boy were already in the Petersen Automotive Museum. The group had had a beef with Tupac Shakur before Pac's killing. That's brazen, I thought, that they're out here, on his old turf, celebrating a record release.

Tamia and I held hands in an effort not to lose each other in the crowd. I felt people's eyes on my back as we maneuvered through the packed floor. People were seeing us paired for the first time, not knowing that we had been together about a year now. The whole vibe of the party, the glances and side eyes, made us uncomfortable.

We were inside for probably less than ten minutes before deciding to split.

By the time we were back at Tamia's, we learned that someone had shot up Biggie's car and that he wouldn't make it.

Two hip-hop titans gone in the span of a few months. I found out about both deaths at the home Tamia was staying in. At that point, no one knew whether the genre I loved would survive.

We started losing our momentum. We just were not the same team. I'm not blaming either one, but the deterioration of the relationship between Doug and Otis played a role in the season's downfall. They had stopped communicating with each other.

We didn't have a counter for Patrick Ewing, dropping a late March game against the Knicks at the Garden. Doug was rightfully upset. We didn't play well as a unit.

Some of you in here are with us, and some of you are against us, he said. Those of you who are with us, I want you on this side. And those of you who aren't, on this side.

Otis, of course, remained seated, mean mugging Doug with an icy stare.

Doug asked, What are you going to do? Are you with us or are you not?

Otis finally rose and approached Doug. Is this what you want?

The two were separated, led to the bus through different pathways. Disaster avoided. I changed clothes, intent on finding Allan in hopes of patching our relationship. I had heard rumors about why he left that didn't make sense and showed public indifference when queried by reporters about his departure earlier in the season. In a weird way, some of my public quotes probably further endeared me to Detroit's fan base. The city, the organization, had taken a lot of abuse in recent years. A player left, and another player, in this case me, had questioned his motives. Personally, I had felt scorned. I had enjoyed playing with Allan, envisioning us as a dynamic pairing through the prime of our careers.

We were cool, friends who had gotten along since high school. We hadn't addressed him leaving one-on-one, and it seemed foolish to allow speculation to manifest itself when a conversation could clear the air. Allan told me that he had no concerns over sharing a spotlight with me, but the Pistons had opened with a low offer and dared him to see what he could command on the open market. The Knicks had made Allan feel wanted. The Pistons didn't. Finally, I understood why he had left, and we let bygones be bygones.

———————

The tiny acts of antagonism between Doug and Otis continued as we neared the end of the season, putting the rest of the team in a difficult position. We liked and respected Doug. We liked and respected Otis. Neither liked or respected the other. They were both prideful, stubborn people who probably had more in common than they'd like to admit.

For instance, Doug wanted us all huddled together in the first five seats on the bench during time-outs.

I want to see everybody's face, he'd say.

Otis routinely made sure that he sat three chairs down from the rest of the group.

Or on our team plane, all the players received their meal before Otis obtained any of his food.

Back and forth they went, neither backing down. By the end of the season, we had lost the connective thread that enabled us to begin with unity and purpose.

Still, I was bullish that we could push everything aside for the playoffs and I could have a better showing in my second postseason. We drew the Atlanta Hawks, a well-rounded team with Steve Smith and Mookie Blaylock on the perimeter and Laettner and Dikembe Mutombo on the interior. They captured the first game before we rallied back, taking the next two in the best-of-five series. With the chance to close it at home, we fumbled the opportunity, laying an egg as the Hawks sent the series back to Atlanta.

In Atlanta, Laettner broke a tie with a shot from the top of the key as the shot clock expired. Where have I seen that before? They made clutch plays down the stretch, ending our season.

It was over, another learning experience, another chapter in our team's growth. At some point, though, we had to stop learning and be ready to win when it mattered most.

———

For the summer, Tamia and I rented a place in Malibu that overlooked the Pacific Ocean. The scenery, the weather—it was perfect. So was she. I found comfort waking next to her every morning after months of only sporadically spending time together.

From afar, I watched as the quick playoff exit initiated another round of wholesale change. Otis, no surprise, was traded. The front office refused to sacrifice future flexibility and allowed Michael Curry and Terry Mills to walk, taking a lot of our defensive grit and three-point shooting with them. Malik Sealy and Brian Williams, soon to be known as Bison Dele, joined the franchise on lucrative, short deals.

The season started on an ominous note when we hosted the Washington Wizards and Joe went down with a hamstring injury minutes into opening night. He would be sidelined the next two months, and suddenly Malibu already felt like a long time ago.

The roster struggled acclimating throughout the first couple months of the season. Brian was a nice guy and super talented, fresh off a successful stint with the Bulls. I was not sure he completely loved basketball. He was the type of guy who decided whether he would put forth a full effort upon arriving at the arena. Bringing in new players through trades, draft, or free agency, I was learning, was always a bit of a crapshoot. Sometimes it worked. Sometimes it didn't.

It's not even fair to say this season has been like a treadmill, I told reporters at one point. You can always get off a treadmill.

Frustration mounted, initiating more overhaul. Doug traded Theo Ratliff, a shot blocker, and Aaron McKie to Philadelphia for Jerry Stackhouse and Eric Montross, Laettner's once-scorned roommate.

Jerry was a confident gunslinger. Both of us were slashers. Meanwhile, Brian preferred posting up more than dancing in the pick-and-roll, which clogged our driving lanes. We needed time to find a healthy middle ground where all of us could operate to our strengths, and that was a luxury Doug didn't possess. He rightfully sensed pressure over his job security. We had won plenty of games the previous season, creating an enjoyable atmosphere that often made the tension between Doug and Otis tolerable. Now we were losing. There was no Otis to blame. The entire roster was miserable.

Regularly, I arrived at the Palace before shootarounds on game days to practice free throws. I was there one morning, in the middle of my rou-tine, when Tom Wilson, our team president, approached me with one of the team's penny counters, Ron Campbell.

You have a second?

Sure.

They got right to business. If you want Doug fired, we'll fire him, they said.

We were less than a year since Penny Hardaway had allegedly headed a player coup that led to the dismissal of Brian Hill, who had been a pop-ular coach in Orlando. Resentful fans had booed Penny and the entire team for weeks afterward.

The prideful side of me believed I could win with any coach. A re-sentful side was bothered that they even tried to put this decision on me.

You hired him. If you want him fired, you fire him.

Shortly after, I was doing an interview before a nationally televised game against the Utah Jazz. I was asked about Doug, the job he was doing, the rumors over his future. I responded the best I could.

I don't know. We're not playing well this year. We all are responsible for that, not just Doug. It's on me. It's on all of us. At the end of this year, the powers that be are going to sit down and evaluate everybody.

Doug watched the interview, later beckoning me into his office. He was upset that I didn't offer a full endorsement.

Michael Jordan endorses Phil Jackson. Karl Malone endorses Jerry Sloan, he said.

I was tired of hearing it from all sides. For the last couple months, Doug had been telling me that if I didn't want him to be the coach, he'd quit. To me, I just thought he was trying to ensure that we were on the same page. I had been supportive of him, both in private and in public.

Exhausted, I finally asked, Do you want to be here?

Later, I ran into Joe at a barbershop in Pontiac that we both fre-quented.

They're going to fire him while we're on the road, Joe said.

What?

I sat on the disclosure for a couple days and decided that I didn't want Doug fired. He had helped create this situation. The roster he coached were mostly players he had acquired. He should be the one to figure this thing out. Firing Doug would be letting him off the hook.

Maybe, I thought, Joe wasn't completely in the loop. We dropped a game in Cleveland before heading to Washington, D.C. Doug approached Joe as we walked into practice at Georgetown.

No! Joe screamed out. I figured that Doug must've just delivered news of his firing to Joe, but Joe's reaction surprised me. He was the one who told me Doug's dismissal was imminent.

After a quick practice, Arnie Kander spotted me in the hotel's lobby after I had grabbed a meal with my parents. Doug and the coaching staff are being let go, he said.

Doug, Arnie said, is blaming you for it.

I headed back to my room, distracting myself by leafing through a book on the background of Jerry Jones, the owner of the Dallas Cowboys. The book couldn't compete with my racing thoughts. I could sense what was happening. Featured players received the blame when a coach was fired. I was not going to be helped if the departing coach breathed life into those baseless beliefs. I had nothing to do with Doug's firing, just like I had nothing to do with his hiring. He had molded the roster and directed us through his schemes. We just hadn't had enough time to coalesce and reach the expectations of the previous season.

The team canceled the following morning's shootaround. Doug summoned everyone into his hotel suite. He fought back tears and tried to compose himself as he confirmed that he was being let go. He said that he had enjoyed coaching us, that we had a great run and had gotten better. To me, Doug's firing marked a sharp regression, really for the first time in my basketball life. We lost a lot my rookie season, but our team had still won eight more games than the team before my arrival. Doug's firing was far more difficult on me than Don Chaney being let go following a rookie season that had largely been a whirlwind. Doug and I were united through our Duke connection long before he became my NBA coach. I wanted the continuity that a franchise, coach, and player like the Jazz, Jerry Sloan, and Karl Malone shared, and that only came with time and through overcoming adversity. But Doug had helped me adopt a winner's approach in the NBA, and for that I'll forever be grateful.

Doug possessed as brilliant a basketball mind as I had ever encountered. He ended up being the best NBA coach I ever had, but he could also be difficult. He had an interesting entrance to the organization and an exit that I would never forget.

Back in my room, I barely had enough time to pick up my book before the phone rang. Rick Sund, the vice president of player personnel, announced himself on the other end. He asked that I come up to his room. When I arrived, Joe was already seated with Tom Wilson.

This is what we're going to do, Joe said. Alvin Gentry is going to be the interim coach. If things turn out well, we'll give him a two-year deal for three million.

Alvin was a young assistant, a player's coach whom I got along with. I had no problems with him assuming the big chair. I just didn't understand why Joe, a teammate, headed the meeting, discussing a coaching change and disclosing the financials, while the two front-office members sat back and took directives from him.

———

It was too late to rescue our season. At Duke, losses shook my inner being. The sun didn't shine as bright the days between games. Food didn't taste as good. I didn't want to be around anyone else until we had wiped off the stink of the defeat. In the NBA, we played every other night and sometimes back-to-back and often traveled when we were not playing. The games cycled past so frequently, losses piled up so fast, that a season could go off the rails before a team was even fully aware. After a bad game or after another loss, I'd take a shower, watching the water circle down the drain. Got to flush this game down with it, I told myself in an attempt to preserve my sanity.

I wish we could have flushed that whole season. We barreled toward another unwelcome spring break.

Toward the end of the season, with a game or two left, Joe approached me. We should both publicly endorse Alvin, he suggested.

No problem. I wanted as much stability as possible heading into next season. Alvin knew the players, I told reporters. He knows our strengths and weaknesses and what we need to do to get better.

A couple weeks later, I swear, Alvin signed a deal for the same amount of years and money that Joe had proposed back in that hotel room.

Until that point, I hadn't realized that I had been playing with my de facto general manager.

Our final game was like so many that season. Only the opponent and locale had changed. This time it was a loss against the New Jersey Nets. All season, we had not risen to our expectations. I had not met mine as an individual. Walking out of the arena, I promised to open myself up to criticism, to pinpoint smart, specific areas to better my game. I was determined to try to make something out of these trials, to not regress without gaining knowledge to use in the future, keeping in mind my dad's advice that there were always a lot of reasons, but there was never an excuse.

14

I was not the most organized person. I was a latchkey kid who misplaced keys so often that my parents joked I had holes in both of my pockets. In college, I once forgot where I had placed the keys to the Land Cruiser and phoned Tommy Amaker in a panic. He told me to calm down, that my mom had given him a spare set knowing that I'd inevitably lose them at some point.

So, I knew I would misplace this engagement ring for Tamia if I kept it in my possession too much longer. We had gone window-shopping for rings a few months earlier. I needed a feel for what she liked and had slipped back into the store a couple weeks later to buy the ring. I felt the weight of it in my pocket while we ate at Gladstones, a favorite restaurant of ours that overlooked the ocean where Sunset Boulevard met the Pacific Coast Highway. I debated dropping to a knee then and there between dinner and dessert. I had second thoughts about a public proposal and the moment passed, the ring still in place. Before Tamia, marriage had never entered my thoughts. Shy and under the General's watch, I didn't have much of a social life growing up in Reston. I had a girlfriend my last couple years of high school. I think each of us viewed the relationship as one of convenience. My mom was friends with the girl's parents, and her household was one of the few places she allowed me to visit. I don't think either of us thought we were built to last. I dated around in college, part of the journey in socializing and losing my awkwardness. Most relationships weren't serious. I didn't think I was in a mental space to allow myself to be vulnerable or open to falling for someone. I always thought I would settle down and marry once my career ended. The NBA required an unflinching commitment. When I first entered that world, it didn't make sense to bring a wife let alone children into that chaos. Most of my friends and teammates were single.

Tamia changed my perspective. Sometimes, you can't imagine how your life will be improved until you experience it firsthand. I couldn't envision not having Tamia as a partner, best friend, and confidant to offer her perspective and provide guidance and care as we journeyed through life together.

Michael and I were eating at a soul food joint sometime the previous season when I told him that I wanted to propose to Tamia. He looked at me as though I had just told him that I planned to quit basketball for fly-fishing.

Why?

He knew how I felt about Tamia. The thought of committing to someone forever at a young age didn't translate, or maybe he feared that my relationship with her would intrude upon our friendship.

But the thought of proposing didn't scare me. Every moment with Tamia felt right. We were young, supportive of each other, both early in our careers.

My hope to find the perfect setting and place bumped against a building anxiety that this ring would go the way of the Land Cruiser keys. I had an early flight one morning while we were at her West Los Angeles apartment, the Dorchester.

I couldn't keep this thing on me. I was going to lose it. What was I holding on to it for?

If you know what you want to do, make that decision.

That morning of July 24, 1998, I dropped to a knee, pulled out the ring, and popped the question. She held a hand over her mouth in shock and said yes. It was not the most planned-out romantic proposal, the one that I had tried engineering in my mind. No matter how I did it, though, it would have been perfect, because she was perfect. We were ready for the next, eternal step. We inhabited separate, crazy worlds filled with bright spotlights and inherent pressure. She was someone I could be honest and open with from the moment we met. We shared an intimacy, not just physically but emotionally and mentally.

I hugged her before dashing out the door to catch my flight, an engaged man.

———

We were locked out, the league and the players' union at a standstill. Owners wanted to curb player salaries. We naturally didn't want salaries lowered.

Neither side budged. Negotiations broke off. I planned to take advantage of the break, to fulfill my vow of bettering my game. To that point of my career, most of my off-season regimen had consisted of finding the best pickup game to play in. I kept active through competition, but never really narrowed in on any singular aspect to improve.

Time on my hands, I wanted to focus on my shooting. Opponents knew I wanted to get to the rim and jammed the lane in anticipation. I was tired of seeing two, three defenders collapse when I drove, like I was a magnet drawing them in. The constant contact took a toll. I wanted to make defenders pay if they sagged off me.

Shooting coaches, at the time, were a novelty. There was a guy who worked with Shaq on his free throws, and while this man might have been a renowned shooter himself, Shaq's performance at the line didn't reflect well on his ability to transfer his knowledge. I met with a different shooting guru who tinkered with my form. The advice made sense, except I began missing more shots the more I incorporated his lessons into my routine.

I was starting to get in my head again, doubting I would ever be the marksman I needed to be to elevate my game. I headed back to Durham: the start of the new school year summoned the pro players back to campus like we were all freshmen again. That year, Coach headed arguably his deepest roster since our last championship. I watched guys who would soon be on the next level—players like Elton Brand, Shane Battier, and Corey Maggette. I know that 1998–1999 squad gets lost in the shuffle of all-time great Duke teams because they ended up losing to Connecticut in the championship. To me, they are without question among the most talented Duke teams ever assembled.

In the runs, those guys came at me, testing themselves. They were mixed in with pros like Danny Ferry, Thomas Hill, and Christian Laettner. We always joked that Laettner couldn't jump over a piece of paper, and he was wearing these gimmicky jump shoes marketed to help strengthen a player's calves and increase his vertical.

On one play, Laettner planted weird, crumbling to the ground.

I tore my Achilles, he said immediately.

What are you talking about? Get up.

We helped him off the ground. He tried putting pressure on his foot and shouted in pain. I looked at his calf. The muscles looked rolled up like an accordion. I immediately felt for him. We shouldn't have even been here. We had both been selected to play for the national team at Greece's FIBA World Championship, but the lockout prevented NBA players from participating. He was a free agent, a recent All-Star, on the verge of turning his professional career around and landing a large contract. I knew that Detroit was looking at him as a candidate to help our frontcourt. He would need months of rehabilitation. He eventually joined us in Detroit, but his NBA career never gained the same traction as before the injury. I always hate people dismissing Laettner's pro career as a bust. He walked into the league and averaged eighteen points and nine rebounds as a rookie for a downtrodden franchise. Most of his NBA coaches just didn't know how to utilize him correctly. *Fire that warmed the building or the accelerant that burned it all down.* Before the injury, though, he had figured out how to be a successful pro and was becoming a force in the league.

Once Laettner was attended to, we returned to play a few more games. Afterward, Johnny Dawkins, who had completed his playing career and worked with Coach K as an assistant, put me through a shooting drill. Everything I threw up drew iron. Here I was, the All-Star, the Olympian, and I couldn't hit anything. Frustrated, I took a seat in the stands.

I think you should meet my guy Chip, Johnny said. He played at Duke with me and may be able to help straighten you out a bit.

The next day, Chip Engelland introduced himself. He was a Southern California guy, cool and confident. Apparently, after his Duke career had ended, Chip had spent some time playing minor-league basketball and now dabbled a bit in coaching. At that point, I was looking for all the help I could get. Johnny vouching for him provided an added incentive for me to see if he had any worthwhile guidance.

Chip, I soon found out, was a basketball scientist. Before we even stepped onto the court, he discussed the physics behind shooting, the importance of equal weight distribution throughout the body.

When you shoot, he told me, you're extending the ball too far in front of your face, and you aren't producing enough arc on your shot. When you shoot a flat ball, the rim gets real small. With more arc, the rim gets bigger, the more chance your shot has of falling. It's all physics.

I thought back to a coach a long time ago who told me that if a player practiced but missed most of his shots, then all he was doing was practicing missing.

Lately, I had been practicing missing.

Chip situated me a couple feet from the basket. Using one hand, over and over, I flicked the ball into the basket, harnessing my follow-through, recapturing what it felt like to see the ball go into the basket. He recognized before I did that my form required a complete overhaul. I offered to compensate him for his time. He refused, insisting that he shouldn't be paid before I saw the desired results. I appreciated the mindset. A couple years prior, I had worked with a trainer and asked the team to bring him on. The guy threatened to sue me when the Pistons declined. The incident left me disheartened. I had wanted to see it out, but my representatives told me to just swat away the nuisance and settle the dispute for a small amount. I was aware that some saw me as an opportunity to make money, but Chip was different.

He offered his phone number. If you need me, I'm here.

The lockout dragged on, long enough that Tim Duncan and I filmed probably one of his lone national commercials for Sprite, a funny spot that involved us taking on odd jobs like delivering newspapers and mowing lawns to fill our time. It didn't take long for me to take Chip up on his offer. I had a promotional shoot in New York, where Chip met me. I surprised him by arriving with just a basketball. We gained a lot of looks as we walked the city streets to a midtown Manhattan gym. Soon, Chip started flying in and out of Michigan to work with me.

I introduced Tamia to Chip one day as we headed out the door.

He's helping me with my shooting, I told her.

Tamia looked at Chip, sizing him up. She turned to me.

Why do you need a shooting coach? You're already an NBA All-Star player. How much better can he really make you?

Chip, I could see in his eyes, thought that our time together was all but over. Well, there's always room for improvement, I said to Tamia as we shuffled out the door. Thankfully, Chip and Tamia developed a strong friendship soon after. The two even have the same birthday.

We performed a lot of our work inside the paint, squaring up to the basket, widening my base, moving my index finger to the center of the ball, and shooting in one fluid motion. He left me with homework in between our sessions. On weekends, I ducked inside Franklin Athletic Club twice a day. The gym bustled and featured a couple basketball courts, plenty of indoor tennis courts, and a workout area. The chill of fall was settling in, and the club served as one of the few places people could go for a sweat. I took up one court, shooting nothing but set shots two or three feet away from the basket as kids on the other court engaged in energized pickup games. I knew these guys had to be wondering what in the world was going on with me. *Grant Hill drinks Sprite, but Grant Hill can't shoot a jumper?*

Man, I thought to myself more than once, was this going to translate when it counted?

I flicked the ball home again.

Hi, this is Grant. We're glad that we're back. And we're glad that you're still with us. Loy Vaught and Christian Laettner are going to be great additions to our team, and we're excited about the new year. Looking forward to seeing you at the Palace.

The Pistons had asked me to record the voice message for our season ticket holders. The game returned at about the time a regular All-Star Game would be taking place, the sides arriving at a deal that should have been hammered out in weeks, not months. Michael Jordan retired again, that time it seemed for good, and the Eastern Conference was finally, fully for the taking.

Before the season started, Joe Dumars announced that it would be his last. I respected everything about Joe's talents on the court. He was a basketball savant, tenacious and resourceful. I learned mostly from watching Joe.

His lessons were impactful when he did decide to directly impart knowledge. We had played the Hawks in Atlanta toward the end of that awful previous season. I drove to the hole one play and received the contact I had anticipated. Yet the official, Bill Spooner, didn't call anything. His whistle only shrieked when he handed me a technical for complaining. I attacked the basket even harder the next possession, and Atlanta hacked me again. Again, Spooner looked the other way. I made sure he saw the foul I committed to stop play. As we lined up for free throws, I summoned my best Coach K first day of practice energy and hurled every profanity I could think of at Spooner. Alan Henderson of the Hawks stood between us, swiveling his head at me, then to Spooner, in disbelief. I dared Spooner to toss me from the game, and he did in giving me my second technical and handing me the only regular-season ejection of my career.

I cooled down in the locker room and realized that that wasn't me, that I had gotten caught up in a season going nowhere. Joe pulled me aside as we walked to the bus.

Sometime before the next game he refs, go up and apologize. Tell him you were wrong and your emotions got the best of you. You guys will be good from there on out.

I did exactly that, and I never had another issue with Spooner. I passed on that knowledge from Joe to younger players for the rest of my career.

He's a special guy in his own special way, Lindsey Hunter would say at Joe's jersey retirement. Everyone within the organization could read the hidden message in Lindsey's speech. Away from the game, Joe's mannerisms could be difficult to interpret. I didn't think he ever wanted to be one of the guys.

To me, the relationship didn't have to be that way. He almost seemed to relish adding a layer of uncertainty. For example, Joe usually sat in front of me on our team bus. Most times, he'd be on the phone, whispering into a mouthpiece. I couldn't make out a word, and I was next to the guy. There was no way he could have been audible to anyone on the other end of the line. After a while, the team arrived at the consensus that he pretended to be on the phone to avoid talking to the rest of us. Then, once the bus parked at our hotel, guys usually lumbered around and lined up to receive our hotel keys from the athletic trainer, Mike Abdenour. Not Joe. He'd turn into a ghost once the bus pulled up. We used to think that he sprinted out of the bus as soon as the driver put the brake on.

I recognized that the NBA wasn't college. We did not hang out with one another every night, slap boxing like at Duke. Still, we often broke bread as teammates on the road or occasionally attended a movie together. Joe ate with us once in New Jersey. That was it. I couldn't help but sometimes wonder if it was just me he didn't want to foster a deeper relationship with. He had spent all those years under the shadow of Isiah Thomas. Isiah left and I arrived with a rush of fanfare, perhaps taking some of his overdue shine. But often, he just seemed like a quiet personality who didn't need, seek, or crave the spotlight.

In that hurried season, Washington came to town for an early game. Chip sat behind our bench. He had started coming around our organization a little bit as we continued working together. The Pistons, more or less, tolerated his presence at the Palace, while I flew him out to road games. That night, my first couple of free throws careened harmlessly off the rim. Joe hadn't even acknowledged Chip's presence that season until I missed a third consecutive free throw. He called Chip over in front of everyone during a time-out, asking, What are you going to do now, shooting coach?

Chip, surprised, froze and didn't know how to respond. But I hardly missed again that night, ending with a career-high forty-six points and finishing eighteen for twenty-two from the charity stripe.

I was improving, trusting in my developing pull-up jumper, even if my numbers didn't always reflect the ground I had gained. Chip and I fit in sessions as much as possible through the sprint of the season. We qualified for the playoffs, but—a recurring theme—we lost in the first round to Atlanta.

That postseason, Tim Duncan and San Antonio captured the championship in just his second NBA season. The rest of us had to keep grinding.

———

We set our wedding date for exactly a year after the impromptu proposal. Everyone complimented the scenic setting of a neo-French château in Battle Creek. I embraced it, although the wedding day marked my first time viewing the tent where our reception would be held. I had attended maybe one other wedding in my lifetime. Tamia had meticulously planned the day. I had just picked out my threads—a three-piece Richard Tyler tuxedo—and the shirt-and-tie combination for my groomsmen, Michael, Rob, Mario, Mark Williams, and one of Tamia's younger brothers, Tiras.

Every piece of my life, all the important ones at least, was falling into place. I was confident that I was moving in the right direction again on the basketball court. We didn't live together yet, but Tamia had spent more time in Michigan throughout our engagement, which deepened our ties and strengthened our connection.

Neither one of us had wanted a bachelor or bachelorette party. Instead, we had settled on a joint night out with the wedding party planned by Michael. I hadn't ever spent much time imagining my bachelor party, and apparently Michael hadn't either. He held it at a chain pizza joint that featured go-karts and miniature golf. At some point, Michael asked if I could sign a couple autographs to the owners as partial payment for the evening.

Thankfully, Tamia and I didn't mind. We were there mostly for our friends and viewed it as a stepping-stone to the point where I huddled in the basement of the château with my groomsmen. About an hour before the ceremony, my dad had everyone in stitches.

Grant, when I married your mother, every step she took walking down that aisle, I could feel myself getting weaker. I could feel the deal with every step she took. As she was getting closer, I was thinking I got to run. But I didn't have any energy left, so I just fainted.

My dad was like that at times, flexing the ability to cut through tension with humor.

A single man, he said, is like a lion roaming the plains and asserting his dominance. The engaged man is a peacock, scared, timid. A married man is a jackass. From one jackass to another, congratulations.

I shook his hand through fits of laughter. We walked upstairs and outside for pictures. Rain had pelted the rehearsal dinner a day earlier. A sweltering, borderline oppressive heat had now replaced it. The industrial fans that we brought in worked overtime, yet still didn't make much difference. Michael had been my best friend since childhood. That day, he was my best man. He handed me a cloth to wipe some of the perspiration.

All other thoughts were shoved aside when Tamia approached in a horse-drawn carriage and took my breath away. I could now relate to what my dad was talking about. My knees wobbled as she made her way down the aisle in a stunning Vera Wang dress.

A couple hundred of our friends and family celebrated with us. My dad's cousin, the Reverend John H. Grant, performed the ceremony where we exchanged our written vows that united us forever.

Tamia surprised me during the reception by leading me to a chair. I had playfully teased her that she sang for the world but never for me. She asked for a microphone and, in front of everyone, sang me a melodious Celine Dion song delivered equal parts from her vocal cords and her heart.

We had decided against a receiving line, so during dinner my mom suggested we stop over at each table to thank everyone for attending. As we neared the last table, we were summoned to the floor for our first dance. Next, a band played all the popular hits from Michael Jackson to Whitney Houston. I noticed and appreciated the wide array of attendees, people like Mr. Bill Davidson, Jerry Jones, Detroit's mayor, Dennis Archer, Roger Staubach, all our family and friends enjoying themselves. Soon, the band gave way to a DJ. The dance floor quickly emptied except for the younger crowd as Miami's own Trick Daddy's booming voice belted out, You don't know nann . . .

We danced the rest of the night away. Finally, as the perfect day wound down, we made our exit, planning to take a car back to the Ritz-Carlton in Dearborn before flying the next day to our honeymoon in Bali. We had spent hours trying to soak in every moment while entertaining, dancing, and posing for picture after picture during a heat wave when it dawned on me. We had never eaten beyond the sliver of cake Tamia fed me during the cutting. I asked if there was any food left. The caterers had already packed up and headed out. I had not gotten one bite of any of that steak or even a nibble of lobster. Both of us were famished. Spotting a 7-Eleven, we asked the driver to make a quick detour. We grabbed a couple chili dogs. I got a Slurpee. She drank a Big Gulp. We chomped the food down on the way to the rest of our lives.

———

You and Jerry are going to have to put up numbers, Alvin Gentry relayed in the fall of 1999. I need you guys to score fifty a game for us to have a chance.

I would reach free agency following the season. I didn't want my status to become a distraction for me or the team. I shoved the uncertainty to the back of my thoughts, ignoring it until reporters inevitably brought up my future. At one point, a journalist asked if my parents hoped that I signed with Washington to be closer to home.

When my mom wanted me to go to Georgetown and my dad wanted me to go to North Carolina, I went to Duke, I said.

I had the foresight to individually make that decision as a teenager. I hoped my present and my future remained in Detroit. I didn't know where I would wind up, just that I would be confident whenever I did settle on a decision.

Over the summer, I had fine-tuned my game with Chip, anticipating that I would play more off the ball. He had accompanied me throughout the hot months, enough so that Tamia joked that she was surprised he had not popped up with us in Bali. Chip was at my side throughout a promotional tour for Fila, Sprite, and McDonald's, and we hunted for whatever small gym or court we could in places like Germany, Greece, and Italy.

The Pistons hired Chip to a somewhat lukewarm reception. Alvin didn't bother introducing him to the rest of the team. They knew that I was Chip's priority, and organizations could turn possessive regarding players and external influences. I was aware that Chip's onboarding could be an effort to pacify me as I approached free agency. Whatever the motive, I appreciated the overture.

Chip and I spoke the same language. We enjoyed the specificity of slicing through layers, building from the ground up. We broke down my game into smaller parts, excavating for areas that I could revamp and master. We focused on my mid-range and postgame, the same areas in which Michael Jordan dominated as his career progressed, adding go-to moves, a jab here, a fake there, and counters for when a defense tried denying me. The Pistons' video coordinator spliced together highlight tapes featuring Hakeem Olajuwon, James Worthy, Adrian Dantley, and

Kevin McHale all dancing in the post. They were uniquely talented, and all possessed uncanny footwork. I studied the tapes like I had the Magic one while at Duke, adding bits and pieces from each. Eventually, almost as an afterthought, Chip and I drifted out to work on three-point shooting. Long range had never been part of my arsenal. But I was looking to turn whatever weaknesses existed into strengths. Who knew how or when it may come in handy?

New circuits formed. Muscle memory took hold. I reminded myself to not forsake my ability to get to the bucket. That would always be my bread and butter. My developing skills were akin to a fastball pitcher adding a curveball to his repertoire. The curve added a wrinkle that kept hitters off balance. But when he needed it, he would always have that fastball to rely on.

Around that time, I read a book by Rick Barry, the former Golden State Warrior guard who famously shot his free throws underhanded. In one passage, Barry dissected how he averaged so many points a game. First, he amassed a couple layups from back cuts and a couple more in transition. He could count on making at least six free throws. By then, he'd have fourteen points without taking one jump shot.

It was all a formula, individual components producing the whole. The passage spoke to me, so much so that I tinkered with it, developing my own blueprint for scoring. Every game, I wanted to produce a couple layups and dunks off transition and mix in an offensive rebound and a putback. If I was attacking, I'd be able to count on another couple easy baskets. Add in five or six free throws and a couple mid-range shots off the dribble, and I would be able to roll out of bed and collect eighteen points without forcing anything.

That was almost already my portion of the production Alvin expected between Jerry Stackhouse and me. We were part of a team again, transformed, with Joe now a member of the front office. Bison Dele had abruptly retired in the off-season. Laettner and Loy Vaught remained question marks as they recovered from significant injuries. A couple of my favorite teammates, though, Michael Curry and Terry Mills, returned to Detroit.

I was still figuring out how to coexist with Jerry. We were cool in college when—and I don't know if he'd ever admit this—he wanted to play for Duke instead of Carolina. He spent two years there before declaring for the draft, landing in Philadelphia. He had signed with Fila, where each of us had signature shoes, and seemed poised to be a 76er for a long, long time. Then the franchise drafted Allen Iverson and jettisoned him to Detroit. He went from being a focal point in Philadelphia to often coming off the bench for us in relief of Joe and Lindsey. He should have started, but by that point Alvin probably realized that Joe would soon be his boss and he needed to keep him happy.

In college, teams aimed for collective harmony. While ideal, the same mindset wasn't sustainable in the NBA. Too many variables conflicted. Basketball was no longer just a passion but also a livelihood. People played to reach that next contract. Egos needed massaging, including mine at times if I'm honest. Occasionally, I sensed Jerry wanted to be the guy atop the totem pole there. There was no single instance that I could pinpoint to justify my feelings, and they may just be a reflection of my own insecurity. But after undergoing one difficult stretch the previous season, I had told reporters that losing Allan Houston for nothing in return had caused our franchise to regress. Someone told me that Jerry found offense in the quote, although I had not intended it as a slight. For whatever reasons, Jerry and I never connected like I wish we had.

Opening night, against Miami, my instinct was to toss out everything Chip and I had worked on. I couldn't buy a bucket and fumbled around like I had at Card Gym the day Johnny took pity on me and first introduced me to Chip. Jerry, though, clicked and hit a three to send the game into overtime. There, my game snapped into place. The basket opened. I got to my spots and scored in a variety of ways. We dropped the game in double overtime, although I departed encouraged that I had not panicked. Miami was a potential contender, a rugged defensive team. I had not allowed them to dictate my play. I had trusted myself, and Chip, and patiently waited for the results. That night, I jotted down how Miami had played me in my journal. It was quickly becoming a habit, to scribble down the tendencies of opponents. The game could be broken down, just like the cadaver in that anatomy course back at Duke. The more knowledge, the better.

We're off to a decent start, I wrote in one of the early entries that season. *Tamia tells me that I say this every autumn, but this could be our year.*

I wish I would have stopped myself more often to appreciate those moments. If I had a great game and scored forty points, the first thing I did was look at the box score to find out how many free throws I had missed. I focused on the negatives in replaying what I had done wrong instead of what went right. I felt like I was always in a race to replicate what Isiah Thomas and other great players had accomplished.

———

Nasty falls were inevitable the way I played.

I was used to clenching my teeth, rising, and moving on to the next play. Usually, it was only the next morning, when inflammation kicked in, that I became aware of the toll I was absorbing.

We were in Chicago playing a suddenly sullen Bulls team lacking Jordan, Pippen, and friends. Toni Kukoč lofted a downcourt pass that I leaped to grab like a free safety hunting for an interception. Ron Artest, their rookie made of brick, collided with me. The impact sent me spiraling to the floor, hard enough that the thud echoed throughout the United Center. Pain shot down my back, coursed through my backside, and cycled through my legs. I cringed, rolling onto my stomach. Trainers rushed onto the court. I spotted Laettner and Lindsey, out of the corner of my eye, staring at me with looks of concern. With help, I rolled over and walked gingerly to the locker room.

Alvin was right. We needed Jerry and me together in order to have a chance. We struggled as I stayed in street clothes the next few games, hoping my backside recuperated. I returned just before the All-Star break when we met the Toronto Raptors in the midst of Vinsanity. Vince Carter and I threw haymakers. We came out on top in overtime. I was stunned afterward, holding the box score, realizing that I had played more than fifty minutes through pain.

That February of 2000, I made a silent vow to earn MVP at the All-Star Game. It was a goal of every player who had made a few appearances. I had spent my first few trips to the game in awe of the raw collection of star power and talent. In those games, the ball had always seemed to find Jordan's hands more than any other player.

He was off playing golf somewhere. The game in Oakland would be my chance to light up the scoreboard and take home some hardware.

I woke up early the Sunday morning of the game, yawning as I removed my disposable contact lenses from their case. One slipped as I went to transfer it to my finger. I picked it up and had to discard it after finding the lens torn.

Before every season, I gave boxes of my lenses to Mike Abdenour. He kept them close during games, and when they occasionally popped out, he was there at the ready. Mike was somewhere back in Michigan, and I had not brought any spare contacts with me.

I wore one lens during the All-Star Game, which was clearly not the best idea. I played discombobulated. I tried throwing an alley-oop to Vince early and nearly tossed the ball out of the arena. I stood at the free-throw line at one point, squinting at the basket.

So much for earning MVP. Well, I comforted myself, at least there was always next year.

＊

Everything hurts at some point during an NBA season. There's an old NBA adage: Are you hurt or are you injured? They were two different things.

I started missing more practices in an effort to preserve myself for games. Our team struggled. I tucked the nagging doubt somewhere deep inside my mind and continued playing. The effort was not enough to preserve Alvin's job. In my opinion, he was a great fit, an offensive-oriented coach who allowed us freedom in our play. And to be fair, we didn't possess the personnel to be defensive stoppers. George Irvine replaced Alvin in early March.

My ankle had been nagging me for months and started requiring more time and treatment with Arnie just to get on the court. I didn't want to miss a nationally televised game against Philadelphia near the end of the regular season. I usually played well in Philly, and Allen Iverson was gaining steam as one of the league's new, dynamic faces. My ankle throbbed, but I hoped that I could loosen it on the court once the blood started flowing. Wrapping my ankle like a mummy beforehand, I played a couple of minutes but couldn't move without a limp.

Arnie pulled me aside.

Your gait, he told me. It's off.

I spent the rest of the game receiving treatment, wondering why my ankle was not progressing the way it should.

Back in Detroit, I underwent an MRI with Dr. Benjamin Paolucci. He told me that I had a bone bruise. I had never previously heard the term. To me, it sounded like it was just a little boo-boo. That's what was causing all this pain? *Hurt or injured?* Later, much later, I learned that

MRIs were mostly suited for providing answers on soft tissue injuries like sprains and not issues that deal with bones.

I bypassed the final couple games of the regular season in preparation for the postseason. We had finished as the seventh seed, drawing the Miami Heat. Every step felt like a knife stab to my ankle throughout the opener. I was not myself, not even close, and we dropped the game. I hoped that a couple days off would allow the pain to subside a little. The medical staff gave me a Medrol dose pack that was supposed to help with inflammation. I accepted the postcard worth of pills with the instructions to take six the next day and taper them off until I took the last one on the final day. I started the cycle and woke up the next morning by rolling my ankle from one side to the other. My foot felt the best it had since February. I tested it out on a stationary bike under Arnie's supervision, and he agreed and even allowed me to participate in a short tune-up practice before Tuesday's game.

Now I didn't even think about my ankle. Miami stood in my crosshairs. If we could swipe a game here, momentum would be on our side. My ankle held up at the start of the game. I was in my zone and drained a couple mid-range jumpers, including one over Alonzo Mourning, who drew me on a mismatch.

Pop.

I had broken my nose and my toe. I had been elbowed, pushed, and shoved. I had absorbed charges from Karl Malone and Shawn Kemp. I had fallen down on the court and rallied to rise more times than I could count.

This was something different. Something deep inside my left ankle gave. Chip, unbeknownst to me, ascertained that my gait was off and my grimace was on. He yelled for Dr. Paolucci to order that I be subbed out. Rather than listen to him, Dr. Paolucci instead offered Chip an explainer on how athletes sometimes manifested pain in their own head. I finally signaled for my own substitute. Every step jolted me with a shock of pain that radiated from my ankle and up my leg. I kicked a chair out of frustration with my one good leg, probably not the best idea, but I needed an outlet.

Later, after the narrow loss, we flew aboard Roundball One, the McDonnell Douglas DC-9 that Mr. Bill Davidson had purchased for our team flights. Arnie sat one seat over and looked just as puzzled as me. The team expected me to undergo another MRI once we landed.

Have you had an X-ray?

No.

Arnie was shocked.

Make sure you get an X-ray.

We touched down at nearly three in the morning. Mike Abdenour and I arrived at the imaging center about an hour later. The only worker was a poor stiff who drew the midnight shift. He was a technician, not a radiologist, which meant he could take the image but couldn't offer details on what the results entailed. The MRI out of the way, I remembered to inquire about an X-ray. The technician walked, I limped, over to an adjacent building. He flipped the lights on and performed the X-ray on my foot. It didn't take a doctor for a diagnosis when he retrieved the images moments later.

Holy shit, Mike yelled. Don't move!

He pointed to my tibia, the shinbone that connected my ankle and knee. The imaging looked like someone had taken a machete and sliced off the interior bone of the ankle that protruded out. It was broken. The entire time, I had been walking without assistance. A few hours earlier, I had been on the court, curling around screens. Looking back, I don't think Dr. Paolucci had kept Arnie completely in the loop regarding my health. To me, Dr. Paolucci had been upset over the strong relationship Arnie had with Mr. Davidson. The joke, with probably some truth in it, was that Mr. Davidson had already written Arnie into his will. Still, a synergy should exist between the athletic trainer, strength coach, team doctor, and head coach. I would have never asked for an X-ray without Arnie's adamant recommendation. I now know this because I've consulted with countless doctors, but the X-ray should have been performed after the game against Philadelphia. Often, a bone bruise precedes a fracture. At some point, I likely had a hairline fracture that continued receiving more and more stress until the bone had completely displaced.

Mike found me a wheelchair and guided me to my car. I followed him to our training facility, where he brought me some crutches.

I looked up, noticing the sun starting to light the day. And I once thought the day at Duke that started with a loss and ended with a broken nose had been the longest of my life. Strangely, though, I felt a weight lifted. I had felt something wrong in my body for a while. I finally knew the origin. This, I figured, was something easily solvable.

15

THAT optimism lasted for all of a couple minutes. Chip Engelland re-layed the argument he had with Dr. Benjamin Paolucci a couple days after the X-ray. I seethed. A doctor questioning my injury was not the one I wanted operating on me.

Sound familiar?

Miami swept us out of the playoffs, another season that started with high hopes deflating in the winter cold before dying in the spring. I visited Dr. John Bergfeld of the Cleveland Clinic the day after the season ended. Dr. Bergfeld came highly recommended, and he said he could make my ankle right. By that point, I didn't even want a Pistons representative in the room with me during the procedure. The anes-thesia slowly coursed through my body. I woke up to find five screws, a plate, and a nasty zipper scar zigging and zagging up my ankle. Dr. Bergfeld told me the surgery had been a success and I was on the path to recovery.

Arnie Kander accompanied me back to Cleveland for monthly checkups. All the X-rays and CT scans reflected signs of progress, but I was still stuck in a cast for the next couple of months.

One day, I bumped into Tom Wilson at the airport. He relayed the news that Joe Dumars had assumed control of the front office and all personnel decisions. I had seen about as much of Joe his first season of retirement as I saw of him off the court when we were teammates, which is to say, not a lot. I didn't know if Tom had offered the disclosure as a courtesy heads-up or if he believed Joe and I had a relationship from his playing days that would help lead me back to Detroit.

I didn't anticipate arriving at free agency on an injured leg. I was open to potentially leaving the Pistons, a thought that hadn't really crept into my consciousness before the injury. Magic, Jordan, Isiah. They had all won their championships with the organizations that drafted them. I wanted that same route for my career. But now I was wearing-a-Carolina-hat irate, upset that they had not pinpointed my injury earlier, and dismayed at the overall direction of the franchise. We were on the ascent at one juncture, poised for a breakthrough. That summer I could only see signs of regression within the organization. We were not getting better. The franchise couldn't even settle on a coach.

Lon Babby kept me up to date on what he heard from other organizations, murmurs that intensified as July arrived. Tim Duncan, also his client, was one of the crown jewels of the free agent class. Lon didn't provide me insights into Tim's mindset. I doubt he offered Tim tidbits on my thinking. Tim and I had a mutual respect for the craft of basketball. We were not super close, although we were both aware that we were free agents who shared an agent and possessed the collective ability to disrupt the NBA's power structure.

Out of the blue, Joe called. He told me to have fun talking to teams, that I deserved the opportunity, that he and the Pistons would be ready when I was prepared to talk. I hung up confused. He had made anything but a hard sales pitch. The conversation conjured memories of how Detroit had fumbled Allan Houston's free agency.

July 1 arrived, bringing with it the start of free agency. I decided to hear out the Orlando Magic first. They were an organization again on the upswing with a young coach in Doc Rivers, reimagining themselves after the Shaquille O'Neal and Penny Hardaway pairing had reached a premature ending.

The NBA had previously allowed teams to pick up free agent targets on their own planes. When Detroit recruited Bison Dele, I had hitched a ride with him back to Los Angeles on Mr. Bill Davidson's plane to visit Tamia. Such a luxury was now labeled an unfair advantage between the league's haves and have-nots.

I needed some additional time to maneuver through the terminals of Detroit Metro Airport on crutches for the flight to Florida, so our alarm clock woke Tamia and me up early in the morning.

We were about to leave for the airport when Alvin Gentry showed up on our doorstep. The Spurs had recently hired him as an assistant. He dropped off a booklet about San Antonio on behalf of the organization, almost as if to ensure San Antonio had the distinction of being my first interaction with a team during free agency. Gregg Popovich was a respected figure, and they were championship ready, especially if Tim stayed put. But the franchise didn't possess much financial flexibility. It was a scenario to debate later, although later wouldn't include Alvin. He accepted the Clippers head coaching gig a few weeks later. One of his only duties as a Spurs assistant that summer involved waking up at the crack of dawn to deliver the booklet.

We landed in Florida, spotting Tim and his girlfriend, Amy. We were catching up when Bob Vander Weide, the son-in-law of the Magic's owner, Richard DeVos, and the team's chief executive officer, picked us up. We first stopped at the RDV Sportsplex, Orlando's sparkling, state-of-the-art practice facility. I smiled as we entered, clocking that all the team's employees wore T-shirts of Tim and me in Magic jerseys. The

Magic's general manager, John Gabriel, guided the tour of the mammoth, 365,000-square-foot facility that held several basketball courts, ice-skating rinks, pools, and even hair salons and restaurants. Unprompted, he insisted there would be room for Chip Engelland on their coaching staff if I ultimately chose Orlando. He knew we had been working together and had noted the progress.

Next, Vander Weide took us to his impressive house tucked deep inside a ritzy, gated golf community. Doc and the real Doc, Julius Erving himself, an executive vice president for the team, took over the presentation. We discussed a bit of basketball before someone suggested checking out the golf course. We hopped in a couple of carts, took a couple of turns, and came across Tiger Woods readying to tee off. I had to give it up to them. Their timing was as immaculate as Bob's house, too much to be a coincidence, but cool nonetheless. Tiger looked up and waved before pounding a golf ball into smithereens, far enough to where it disappeared from my line of vision before dropping a couple feet in front of the pin. The drive impressed even me, anything but a golf devotee. That night, Tamia told me that she had never seen so many grown men in awe of another grown man.

Now it's sacrilegious imagining Tim Duncan in anything but a Spurs jersey. Back then, he offered the impression that he was more on board with joining Orlando than I was at that moment. He had been in San Antonio for only a couple years and had already captured a championship. Tim was a family person. His father had been ill, and to my memory he wanted to live in Florida, a short flight away from his childhood home in St. Croix. We were all at dinner inside a private room at the Contemporary hotel's California Grill. Everyone was relaxing, joking, and laughing, when Amy, soon to become Tim's spouse, asked Doc Rivers if girlfriends and wives could travel on the team plane.

I don't allow that, Doc replied. They're business trips, and you don't bring family members on business trips.

Amy's entire mood shifted, but I didn't really think much of it until later when Tamia and I were back in our hotel room.

He ain't coming, Tamia said.

What do you mean?

Did you see her reaction?

Yeah, but that doesn't mean anything. He seems all in to me.

All in all, we enjoyed the trip. The franchise teetered on the brink of contention and could get there with an injection of talent. Rumors, though, were already circulating that I had committed to Orlando, even though I remained far from reaching a decision. I still had visits remaining with Chicago, New Jersey, New York, San Antonio, and Miami. A sportswriter from *The Detroit News* stunned Tamia and me by sitting across the aisle from us on the return flight to Michigan. I jokingly told him to prepare for three hours of no comment between takeoff and landing. Back in Detroit, the airport allowed Tamia and me to exit the plane right on the tarmac and step into a waiting car to avoid the media throng.

Once home, I called Lon. Hobbling through a series of airports and shuffling through practice facilities had lost its appeal after having done it once in Orlando. We asked that the remaining teams visit us in Michigan. The other organizations likely regarded the Magic as possessing an unfair recruiting advantage because I met with them at their place, but they acquiesced to the request.

We offered the remaining teams two-hour windows at my offices on the corner of Square Lake Road and Telegraph Road in Bloomfield Hills. The Knicks contingent filled the first slot. Their traveling party included their coach, Jeff Van Gundy; Madison Square Garden's CEO, Dave Checketts; General Manager Scott Layden; and Vice President Steve Mills. A diverse set of actors accompanied them, including Star Jones, Chazz Palminteri, and Peter Boyle. They took seats at a conference table with me, Tamia, and Lon. The actors spent the first few minutes extolling the virtues and benefits of living in New York City.

Then someone popped in a videotape. Faces of famous New Yorkers and Knicks fans—Spike Lee, Jerry Seinfeld, Brooke Shields—took turns on-screen asking me to come play in New York. Honestly, I thought it was pretty dope.

If you're impressed by Disney World, wait until you see Broadway, Checketts said.

Leon Robinson appeared on-screen after Shields. I couldn't help but see his face and think back to my Duke days. He had a large role in *The Five Heartbeats*, a movie we had watched as a team during a rare break on the climb to the first championship.

Come on, man, he said. You got to come to New York. I know you're in Detroit, but the women here in New York. Oh, my God.

I glanced at Tamia, who rolled her eyes. I had no idea why the Knicks didn't do their homework, realize I was married, and slice that comment out.

The montage ended. Van Gundy's eyes lit up while discussing his team, the idea of pairing me with Latrell Sprewell, and me teaming with Allan Houston again. I only knew of Van Gundy from afar and respected his coaching abilities. The media portrayed him as a guy with perpetual bags under his eyes, almost as though the city constantly drained his energy. In the room, he was passionate, oozing charisma and personality. The Knicks were fresh off a recent finals loss to San Antonio. They didn't possess cap space and threw out the idea of trading Patrick Ewing to facilitate a deal. I had grown up admiring Patrick and respected him as a person and basketball player. To me, he was intertwined with the Garden, the city, its lights.

I didn't want anything to do with quickening Patrick's exit from New York. Still, they left me with a scenario to contemplate, even if it would take some warming up for Tamia if that was my ultimate decision.

The Nets were next. They had just suffered through a tough season but showed promise with a new leadership team in Rod Thorn, the executive who had drafted Michael Jordan to the Bulls, and Byron Scott, a young coach and a former player with the Showtime Lakers. I mostly accepted the meeting because of Michael Jackson. The player who had first sparked my love for the game had played a few NBA seasons before accepting management positions at the U.S. Olympic Committee and Turner Sports. He was now the president of Yankees–Nets, the regional sports network that broadcast those teams. Our meeting was casual, friendly, though I doubted either side expected a deal to come to fruition.

We broke before visiting with Popovich and the Spurs. He was insightful and encouraging. They still didn't have any financial flexibility. The Spurs offered a short deal with the promise of a more lucrative one soon. It was a risk that I just couldn't take, especially when I was already on crutches.

I encountered the opposite scenario during my conversation with the Bulls. Jerry Reinsdorf, their owner, attended with his general manager, Jerry Krause, and Tim Floyd, their new coach. Reinsdorf and I had a relationship. My mom had performed some consulting work for his baseball team, the Chicago White Sox. The Bulls were still trying to reshape themselves after Jordan's retirement and had plenty of money to spend. The organization arrived with their own video. Oprah Winfrey came to life on-screen, pitching Tamia and me on the wonderfulness of the Windy City. It was appealing. But Chicago did not present much of a better situation than the one in Detroit that I was already considering leaving.

The Heat arrived last. Pat Riley carried a covered-up poster board.

I'm a dreamer, Riley began.

He exuded confidence, leadership. I could see how he had steered the Lakers to those championships. I sat back, allowing his words to sink in.

I want to think big. You clearly want to play with Tim Duncan, and you want to play with Tim in Florida.

He dramatically yanked the cover off the poster board to reveal photos of me, Tim Hardaway, Alonzo Mourning, Jamal Mashburn, and Tim Duncan, all in Heat uniforms.

How about that starting five? Let's allow ourselves to dream, because we can.

Chills ran up and down my spine. That squad would be unstoppable. One thing: How in the world was he going to pull off this coup with all of the cap restraints?

Riley dreamed with his eyes open. Of course, that squad didn't manifest itself. I went another direction, as did Tim. But it did not surprise me when he persuaded LeBron James and Chris Bosh to join him in Miami a decade later, somehow finagling their salaries to fit with Dwyane Wade in forming a squad destined to add to his many championship rings.

My mind cycled through all the possible paths with the different organizations, the virtues of staying in Detroit, of leaving, the question of how I wanted my career to evolve over the next three, five, ten years.

I was exhausted. I called Tim to see how he was faring with his deliberations. By that point, we had taken to talking almost daily to pair our destinations. I thought he had been willing to commit to Orlando during our visit. I sensed his mind changing during subsequent conversations, his enthusiasm over potentially playing in Orlando diminished with each call. Popovich and David Robinson had obviously been in his ear.

Can you come to San Antonio for a visit? he asked at one point.

I had just met with San Antonio and didn't want to hobble to board another flight and solicit a deal for far below market value.

I asked him to reconsider Orlando. The organization had hosted Tracy McGrady shortly after we had left Florida. He was a kid who had really prospered during the second half of the previous season, coming into his own. In Toronto, Vince Carter's athleticism earned headlines and highlights. I had left impressed with McGrady's dogged defense more than anything else when we played them. Gabriel was confident he could find a way to sign all three of us.

Tim said that he'd think on it. We all know what happened there. He made the right decision for himself in creating a dynasty in San Antonio.

I took a couple days to weigh my options. Orlando kept jumping to the forefront of my consciousness. They had finished the season break-even without a player most would regard as a franchise cornerstone. They were a lunch pail group, guys like Darrell Armstrong, Bo Outlaw, Ben Wallace, John Amaechi. They played hard, determined, rugged.

Orlando, I decided, was the best fit for me and what I hoped to accomplish for the rest of my playing career.

Meanwhile, as I debated the offers, I had not heard anything from the Pistons since that awkward initial call with Joe. It was only fair to offer Detroit one last opportunity to influence my decision. I called Joe, telling him about all my meetings with the franchises and that I had chosen Orlando. He listened without asking if the Pistons could counter. I could now fully appreciate what Allan went through when he left.

I'm giving you a courtesy call, I said. I'm going to make my announcement Monday and write a letter to the city of Detroit.

Joe asked if I could wait a couple of days. No problem.

We hung up. The news of me leaving was everywhere within a couple of hours. I understood the Pistons needed to protect their brand, although I felt somewhat dismayed and even more confident in my decision. Six seasons with a franchise was nothing to throw away. I had envisioned retiring in Detroit when the franchise drafted me, but our relationship had run its course.

Seeking some quiet and a change of scenery, Tamia and I escaped to her family's house in Windsor. They had recently moved deeper into the suburbs and away from Ambassador Bridge. I was convinced no one could find me there. I was unplugged, playing with Tamia's younger brothers, when the doorbell sounded.

Grant, there's a man here for you.

For me? How?

I grabbed my crutches and meandered to the front door to find Bernie Smilovitz, a sportscaster with one of the Detroit news stations. Bernie and I went back. I grew up watching him when he worked in Washington, D.C., and I had performed live hits with him a couple times every month pregame at the Palace while I was with the Pistons.

Bernie? How did you find us? No one other than my in-laws knows we're here.

He smiled. A cameraman loomed behind him. A journalist, he said, never gives up his sources. So, can we do this?

He made it all the way out there. I had to give him that. I told him, his camera, and everybody watching that I was set to join the Orlando Magic. I was a little stunned to hear the words come from my mouth. Stating the decision publicly made it nearly official. A wave of relief and excitement washed over me. The decision had weighed heavily. In Orlando, I was certain we would be competing annually for championships. The Eastern Conference was again wide open. Chicago was finished. The Pacers and Knicks were aging. I was not even upset that Tim chose San Antonio once Tracy committed to Orlando a few days later. He was a star in the making. We would be a dynamic pair.

First things first. I needed to get this ankle right. Everything, I was told, was progressing as it should be.

16

IN early August, Tamia and I flew down to Orlando for the news conference to officially announce my signing. I had dropped in to see Dr. John
Bergfeld for a checkup a week before leaving. He confirmed that my
ankle was healing, enough so that I could ditch the crutches and walking
boot, and that he would forward my medical information to the Magic.
At that point, I had no inkling of the difficult stretch ahead. My only
frame of reference was the toe I had broken at Duke. That rehabilitation
didn't involve a recovery plan. I had to just wait for the toe to heal. A broken ankle, I would soon learn in agonizing detail, was much different
from a fractured toe.

I rushed to dress at our hotel for the conference when I realized that
I had packed only my right dress shoe. I guess I had gotten used to just
needing one with my left foot in a cast the past couple of months.

Where was Christian Ast when you needed him?

Hurriedly, I phoned John Gabriel and left a message. I know this
sounds weird, but, uh, is anyone around who has a size 15 dress shoe that
I can borrow?

He called back a little later. I think Dr. J can help you out.

I was relieved. A car picked us up, stopping at a secured parking lot inside RDV Sportsplex. Someone rushed a pair of Dr. J's shoes to the car. I had just started walking a few days earlier, and now I was literally walking in the shoes of a legend.

We exited the car and I quickly learned why people in Orlando did not wear dark three-piece suits like the one I had on. I was already sweating in spots I didn't know I had just like at our wedding. Well, I was, after all, on the verge of finalizing another long-term commitment. We were whisked inside, onto a practice court, where Tracy McGrady and I met with the media. I had agreed to terms with Orlando, prepared to leave a Brinks truckload worth of money on the table. Call me privileged or possibly out of my mind. I thought accepting less would help Orlando's flexibility, and I didn't feel much generosity in assisting my previous franchise through a sign and trade. Gabriel, though, insisted that a trade would aid Orlando's ability to retain the frontcourt tandem of Bo Outlaw and John Amaechi. I had landed a larger salary through the trade, and the Pistons acquired Ben Wallace, a tenacious rebounder I had hoped to team with, and Chucky Atkins.

Sometimes, I told the reporters, to embrace what's next, you have to let go of the past. The good and the bad that's happened, it's time to move on. I'm looking forward to establishing new relationships and accomplishing new things with this organization.

I was ready to form those bonds immediately. Huddling with the training staff after the news conference, I was told they would start working with me after Labor Day. Tamia and I lingered in Florida for a couple days to gain a feel for Orlando and scouted houses, landing on a gorgeous spec home overlooking a lake. The home wouldn't be ready until November. We agreed to wait. This was a move for the long haul, and we could hold out for the place of our dreams.

Back in Michigan, Mike Cragg asked to stop by for a visit. Mike had been the sports information director when I attended Duke, advancing to work on the administrative side and head fundraising efforts. We met at a Bloomfield Hills restaurant whose claim to fame was that it was the last place anyone had seen Jimmy Hoffa alive and breathing.

At lunch, Mike mapped out a plan to create an endowment fund for athletic scholarships independent of the basketball program. I was all in, seeing it as a means to give back to the program, and told Mike that he could rely on my support to help build the fund.

Over the next few days, my attention turned toward working on goals that would pave my way back onto the court. But I didn't have a template on what, if anything, I should be working on to regain my ankle's strength. I decided to call Arnie Kander for guidance. We had done some light rehabilitation before free agency, while my foot was still in the boot. He was kind enough to work with me a couple of times after I signed with Orlando, instructing me to slowly walk in a figure eight and ascend a flight of stairs. Finally, he conceded that he would be putting his job at risk by continuing to see me. I didn't want to put him in a difficult position. Alone, my rehabilitation the month before I returned to Orlando devolved into walking as much and as far as tolerable.

With Labor Day approaching, I needed to find short-term housing in Orlando while our house was being finished. I figured my days would revolve around training and rehabbing, and so I settled on the Arbors, an apartment complex kitty-corner from the practice facility. The apartment was bare bones and consisted of two bedrooms, a leather couch, and a love seat. I had better digs as a Duke upperclassman. But it would do. I was ready to grind. I had just signed a contract for nearly a hundred million dollars and felt like Rocky Balboa as I lugged my spare belongings from my car up the three flights of stairs on a tender ankle.

Exhausted, I ambled over to secure the door, only to find the lock was broken. I wasted a couple of minutes trying to fix it and then just slid the love seat in front of the door to block it. That way, I figured, the sofa would make a noise if someone tried barging in at night. Dragging the sofa became a nightly ritual. And whenever I arrived back home, knowing the door had been unlocked, before opening the door I'd ball my fists and ready myself for a fight. Once in, I'd inspect closets, look under the bed, and peek behind the shower curtain to make sure no one had been inside while I was gone. I still have no idea why I didn't just call the management office to report the broken lock like a rational person. I might have been nervous hurtling toward a season with a new franchise while still on the mend, or I just didn't want to seem like a perpetual complainer.

Tamia visited after a couple weeks of that cycle.

This door won't lock, she said.

Oh, yeah, just slide the love seat in front of it, I explained as though it were the most reasonable act in the world.

I can't believe you're staying here. You have to go up some stairs. Anyone can see. When I came in, I felt like everybody was watching me, and then I had to go around this dark corner. I can only imagine being here at night. I'm not staying here.

That was my last night at the complex. We booked a hotel. Thank you, Tamia, for showing enough sense for the both of us.

———

Guys ran up and down the court, getting after it, when I arrived at the practice facility that first day. The athletic trainer, Ted Arzonico, asked how I preferred my ankle taped. I hadn't so much as dribbled a basketball since that playoff game in Miami, let alone run or undergone any strength training. I entered prepared to follow the guidance of the team's medical experts for the next steps of my recovery. Ted had no reservations about throwing me out there, and I was under the impression that he had reviewed my medical history and progress. Plus, I lived to hoop. Give me the green light, tell me that I'm fit to play, and I am game. The entire roster was here nearly a month before the mandatory reporting date, an encouraging sign. Immediately, on the court, I saw that I had underappreciated Tracy's ability. I had thought of him as a young player with a high ceiling. Up close, he dominated both sides of the ball. Mike Miller, our rookie, possessed impressive length and shooting range. Our interior players were diligent, hard workers. It all provided confirmation that the team would be formidable.

Quickly though, I sensed that my body wasn't right. The previous season, I had been healthy for a game against Orlando. I had done whatever I wanted while Monty Williams guarded me. He was my teammate now and gave me the business in our pickup games. I stayed out there, pushing myself through three scrimmages. I had arrived in Orlando with a large contract and larger expectations. I wanted to deliver on the promises I made and the future I envisioned for myself. Inside, I would always be the person who yearned to please. Participating in practices, open runs, and drills depicted traits of leadership.

That night, the adrenaline from being on the court again dissipated. My ankle felt as though someone had poured lava on it. A cycle of fitful starts and stops commenced, a routine that, in retrospect, made about as much sense as me dragging the love seat to block the door. I'd practice one day before needing two or three days off just to be able to train again. I iced my ankle every hour on the hour. Chip, after a couple of weeks, flew down to Florida. He was supposed to join the coaching staff, yet no one within the organization had extended themselves to him. Chip watched practice, off to the side, while the coaches convened in bird's-eye offices overlooking the practice courts. One day, we sat in the bleachers after my teammates had cleared out from the gym.

You're not right, he said. What are they having you do from a rehab standpoint?

What do you mean?

You have no balance, no strength. I mean, I can see the atrophy in your left calf.

First, I wanted to ensure everything was straight with Chip and his employment. He had proven pivotal in unlocking different facets of my game and deserved peace of mind that he had a job waiting for him here. I called Lon Babby and asked him to inquire about Chip's role within the franchise. They were the ones, after all, who had proposed bringing him on board. Gabriel told Lon that Doc Rivers had had a change of heart, that he didn't believe in shooting coaches. I was crestfallen, although there was not much I could do. Doc eventually came around and said that if a deal had been made, the organization would honor it. He allowed Chip into the facilities and at games, but that was about it. Chip and I agreed that he should solicit other offers. The team's public relations head, Joel Glass, secured Chip passes for the next couple of seasons that allowed him to arrive early for games and scout how visiting teams worked out their players. He gained valuable insight, using the time to improve and propel himself to his position today as one of the game's elite assistant coaches for Gregg Popovich in San Antonio, credited with overhauling Kawhi Leonard's offensive arsenal, among many other contributions.

With training camp on the horizon, my ankle wasn't capable of holding up to a rugged schedule of games. Tamia was set to drop her sophomore album, *A Nu Day*, and swooped in and out of town for promotional work. She was a rock, capable of finding solutions to any Rubik's cube of a problem. At that point, though, I was not sure if she could relate to my struggles. How could she? I'd confide in her about my ankle, telling her I was in pain and that it wasn't healing correctly. She'd soothingly recite passages of Scripture to me. *For God has not given us a spirit of fear, but of power and of love and of a sound mind.* The words were consoling but not completely applicable. My hindrances were physical, not mental. My dad was my next confidant. He told me that the lasting pain was the result of scar tissue forming, that it was routine when returning from a significant injury. Lord knows he was an expert in dealing with battle scars from his playing days. Tamia and my dad both probably (and rightfully) assumed that as a professional athlete with a lucrative contract I was receiving top-notch medical care. Still, the doubt and pain lingered. I turned to Lon. He related a story about his daughter once having an irrational fear of traveling up escalators as a middle schooler. I hung up the phone slightly perturbed and disturbed. The one downside I found in Lon's representation was that, being his first sports client, I was the de facto guinea pig. He had never previously steered anyone through an injury. He assumed that everything would resolve itself. He never made that mistake again after witnessing the totality of my ordeal.

Those were three of the closest people in my life with three different reactions, yet all somewhat questioning whether I felt what I definitely felt.

In hindsight, they likely all trusted that the training staff had been taking care of me and following protocols. But there were no directions to follow. My rehabilitation with Ted consisted of a few repetitions with a resistance band—ten to the right, ten to the left, ten up and down—before practicing. That, combined with my own ritual of downing Advil and icing my ankle, wasn't a plan put together by anyone with a medical degree of value.

Our team boarded a bus, snaking up north for training camp in Jacksonville. I was twenty-eight years old, entering what should have been the prime of my playing days, yearning to earn every cent of this contract and then some. Doc was a player's coach, once a point guard in the league. He was a disciple of Pat Riley, who was probably still out there somewhere making Alonzo Mourning run laps. A season earlier, Doc tried dictating the tempo for the season by holding a fitness test, taken straight from Riley's playbook, at the toll of midnight on the first day of camp. The ploy worked for that Magic team in forging an identity that was about heart and hustle. At the University of North Florida, Doc again insisted on the test, five series of seventeen sprints the width of the court. Somehow, someway I finished in the required time, even though it now felt like someone was twisting a knife into my ankle on top of the scalding lava. I limped through one or two preseason games over the next couple of weeks, unable to play the bulk of them. My leg should have set up residency in Antarctica. I soaked it as soon as I left the facility, from early afternoon until I was ready to call it a day at night.

An athlete's mindset is a mix of bluster and bravado, a constant effort to silence skepticism, narrow in on the present, and attack the challenge ahead. *Stay in the present.* Opening night, I was out there, hand over heart, as Tamia harmoniously sang the national anthem in front of a sold-out crowd at TD Waterhouse Centre. I was so hyped for my first game in Orlando that I won the jump ball for opening possession against Jahidi White of the Washington Wizards. My timing was off, but I was mostly comfortable throughout thirty-three minutes of play in a straightforward win, the first, in my mind, of many to come.

I thought Teddy was going to punch me, Doc told reporters after the game. He kept yelling, *he's limping,* and I was trying to ignore him because I was trying to see if Grant could play through it.

We flew to Miami, of all places, after the game for a back-to-back against the Heat. That was the city that informed me of the severity of my ankle injury, prompting me to finally seek an X-ray. I couldn't sleep. The buzz over the first game with a new franchise had left. My ankle let me feel all of the 1,980 seconds I had played. I knew the sensation of typical soreness after a game. This wasn't it. The next day, I took the court during warm-ups but didn't have enough mobility to play against the Heat. Philadelphia came to Orlando a couple days later, and I hobbled around for thirty-six minutes in a loss. I had regressed to where I was a couple months earlier. Every time I played required two or three days of recovery just to return to the court again.

Dr. Joe Billings, the Magic's doctor, asked me to undergo a CT scan following the Philadelphia loss, the first set of imaging I had done since my Orlando arrival. The team decided to shut me down for a month to see how my ankle reacted to rest. Dr. Billings directed me to Florida Hospital Rehab, a clinic connected to the training facility, and I started a rehabilitation program for the first time since my ankle surgery.

While I was at the clinic, my ankle improved with balance and proprioception exercises. The focused program forced my muscles, tendons, and joints to reintroduce themselves as a functioning unit. More exercises were added over the weeks. I worked on my cutting and explosiveness. Slowly, my ankle felt like it had rounded a corner. The team, through Tracy's dynamic play, kept winning in my absence. I participated in a couple of practices and received an all clear to play, joining the team on a West Coast trip in mid-December. Just like with Monty, I had played against a rookie, Lamar Odom, the previous season and dominated the matchup. This time, in Los Angeles against the Clippers, I felt like I was standing in cement. I couldn't stay in front of the guy. Next, we played in Seattle, where the ankle pain ratcheted in intensity and I had to pull myself out of the contest.

I had pushed myself for a month. All that time, the ankle pain lay hidden in the background, waiting to resurface. I limped to the bench, deflated by the knowledge that I wouldn't be on the court again for a long time.

Dr. Billings performed the imaging for another CT scan a couple days later, explaining that they revealed a nonunion fracture.

Another completely foreign diagnosis. What's a nonunion?

Well, let's say that you're holding your ring finger and your pinkie together and that's one bone, Dr. Billings said. They break apart, and the goal of surgery is to fuse them back together. A plate and screws unite the bones as they heal. In this case, your bones are repaired, only they healed as two separate bones instead of together.

Again, I felt slightly relieved. I had been hindered since Labor Day. We were nearing Christmas, and I had finally received confirmation that, yes, something was wrong and, no, I was not just imagining the extreme discomfort.

The revelation initiated a series of conversations, discussions that really should have taken place over the summer. Dr. Bergfeld was dumbfounded that I had been playing for months. The timeline he had forwarded to the organization outlined a targeted, gradual rehabilitation before returning to basketball-related activities sometime in mid-December. I had been oblivious to that schedule, playing, struggling, and limping to stay on the court when I had not received proper medical guidance, let alone clearance. Through the phone calls, I learned that Dr. James Barnett, who had been Orlando's team doctor, had died with his wife in a tragic plane crash in early September. Dr. Billings had replaced him, heading a medical staff in mourning and transition. I didn't recall ever meeting Dr. Barnett. I'm not sure if my recovery plan had been forwarded, lost, or disregarded, because I had arrived as a marquee free agent with a large contract and the pressure to produce. I still honestly don't know what happened.

I do know that I didn't follow any types of protocols. I wish I had the foresight to take more initiative. At that point, though, I was trying to follow the direction of my new franchise.

My first season in Orlando had lasted all of four games. Occasionally, my mind drifted back to my college days, when I did everything possible to play in the NCAA tournament. I accepted the setbacks and prepared myself to return to the court even better than before.

First, I had to find the right surgeon to operate on the nonunion, and as I found out over the years, they are incredibly difficult to fix. Doc encouraged me to seek the best care I could find. If you have to leave Orlando, do it, he advised. If you have to go to Timbuktu to find the best doctor, do it.

My dad advocated for the Duke staff to handle the procedure. You know Dr. James Nunley and Dr. Frank Bassett, he suggested. You know the environment. You're comfortable with them, and they'll just want you to get healthy.

Penny Hardaway's ordeal with the Magic's medical team also loomed in the back of my mind. He had experienced lingering knee pain while still with the franchise, enough that he left the team for months at one point and rehabilitated in Houston. I never solicited Penny for insight on his experience, and I probably should have.

From my perspective, Dr. Bergfeld had performed successfully on my ankle. My issues started after the surgery when the lines of communication became crossed and I found myself without a rehabilitation program. I wanted to avoid a similar outcome. I wanted everyone—doctors, trainers, team executives, coaches, me—to be aligned. I followed the recommendation of the Orlando Magic's medical staff and met with Dr. Mark Myerson, the president of the American Orthopedic Foot and Ankle Society. I consulted with Dr. Myerson inside his Baltimore office, its walls adorned with pictures of athletes across all of sports. He had a sterling reputation, and he greeted me with a warm smile and expressed complete confidence about healing the nonunion. He laid out a timetable for my complete recovery. I left convinced. My dad made another late plea on Duke's behalf a couple days later. In time, I learned that he had been on a conference call with Dr. Myerson, Dr. Bassett, Dr. Nunley, and Dr. Bergfeld. The medical community works best when it prioritizes the sharing and exchanging of information for the patient's benefit. The goal of the call had been to discuss my medical history, introducing a new doctor to ones who had previously worked on me. On the call, Dr. Myerson had shown dismissiveness toward the other professionals. But my dad wanted me to be comfortable in whatever direction I chose and didn't disclose the interaction with me at the time.

Dr. Myerson performed the hour-and-a-half operation at Baltimore's Union Memorial Hospital a couple days into 2001. He removed the plate and five screws from the first surgery, grafted a piece of bone from my hip to my ankle, and fastened three new screws to promote healing. The previous April, I had not wanted any Pistons employees present for my surgery. This time, Dr. Billings assisted Dr. Myerson. The Magic's GM, John Gabriel, also was in the room.

Waking up, I felt an intense urge to scratch myself. I started scratching all over, except for the place where I really needed the relief, my ankle. Dr. Myerson was pleased with the surgery, telling reporters that the original fracture did not heal because of a lack of blood flow around my medial malleolus bone. The prognosis was for a full recovery, he said, adding, I am very pleased with the procedure.

His assuredness left me elated, relieved that I was on my way after one lousy, lost season. In Orlando, Gabriel proposed that I hire a physical therapist to assist my recovery and provided another set of recommendations. I interviewed a few candidates, landing on Vinnie Hudson, a teacher at the University of Central Florida who had worked with other professional atheletes. Earlier, I had systematically and scientifically broken down my offensive game. I no longer wanted to leave anything to chance and would apply the same methodology toward my rehabilitation.

Vinnie and I established our base at LGE Sports Science Institute in Lake Nona. I had read an article about the facility, started by a group of performance-enhancing specialists at the cutting edge of sports and technology. The center counted Pete Sampras and Jim Courier among their clients.

I watched as Orlando finished the season 43-39, a tick better than the previous year, and dropped a first-round playoff series to Milwaukee. In my absence, Tracy had blossomed into a star. I couldn't wait to see how we paired on the court.

That June, around the time of the NBA Finals, I visited Dr. Myerson's office for a scheduled checkup. He had removed the cast a few weeks earlier.

You're 85 percent healed, he declared after looking over the latest set of images. When you get back, you need to start working out on the court.

The advice surprised me; it went counter to my expectations of gradually building up to training again. Recovering, I had learned, should involve periods of rest to allow for healing followed by slowly adding stress to the surgically repaired joint. The cast, for example, had allowed for healing, while walking with a boot provided a bit of stress on my ankle.

With Chip, I had diagrammed a return, engineering building blocks of progression toward physical and mental milestones. We began our work away from the team. They had seen me the prior season, and, though limited, I could still play in bursts as the player they envisioned upon my signing. I wanted to present the organization and fans that player again. Chip and I located a quiet gym inside an apartment complex on the fringes of Orlando, implementing five stages of my return. I reacclimated to the court in the first step, gripping a basketball's leather, dribbling it on the hardwood, performing pivot exercises, and lobbing up some stationary shots. I performed the same drills with some added pace in the second phase. I gained some confidence, trusting my body a bit, and fully exerted myself as we entered the next leg.

Contact, Chip and I discussed, was inevitable once I started playing again. We talked about the potential for trepidation, the apprehension of navigating tight spaces with a twice-surgically-repaired ankle. Chip recruited an area college player to challenge my shots and play defense in the fourth stage. We switched roles and I reacted off him, sliding from side to side, cutting off his angles.

As summer gave way to fall, I prepared for the final phase of practicing and running up and down the court with my teammates. You're well on your way, Chip said, to again being an All-Star player. When that day happens, I'll celebrate by wearing a Hawaiian shirt to the game.

The search to mend my ankle hampered my ability to bond with my Orlando teammates. Monty Williams was a notable exception. His family lived just a couple of houses down from us. He had grown up in nearby Prince George's County and had played college ball at Notre Dame. Over the years, I had developed the impression that I had somehow rubbed Monty the wrong way in the past. As teammates, he divulged that he had caught interviews of me as a teenager where I unconsciously separated myself from my dad's sports legacy. At the time, I had just wanted to carve my own identity. But Monty thought I should have been proud of my dad and his heritage—which I always was, even if my words did not always reflect that admiration.

Monty had two precious girls—a toddler, Lael, and a baby, Faith—with his amazing wife, Ingrid. Tamia and I spent a lot of our downtime at their home. It was not often we genuinely enjoyed being in the company of another couple. They were immaculate models for the family we hoped to one day have. Watching Monty love and dote over his young family was inspiring. I sometimes went over to his house while Monty traveled with the team. Really, Tamia and I would go to visit the girls. Lael was the most precocious child we had ever met—charismatic, smart, and bursting with energy. Tamia and I admired her so much that years later we named our second daughter in her honor. We had been at their house, in fact, watching their daughters frolic around the living room with *SportsCenter* playing in the background, when news that I had kicked off the Duke Basketball Legacy Fund with a one-million-dollar commitment came across the screen. I had forgotten to tell Tamia, learning an early, invaluable marriage lesson that it would be best to keep her in the loop regarding financial obligations of that magnitude.

Monty and Ingrid, through our interactions with their girls, could probably surmise that we planned to start a family soon.

We were not completely sure how to navigate parenthood while simultaneously steering separate, ambitious careers. That I was completely clueless about babies or parenthood barely registered. I later learned that no one is truly prepared to start a family, and most of parenthood is about love and instinct.

That summer, Tamia excitedly told me that she was expecting. We found out that we'd be parents of a daughter. I pushed my recovery to the background. Tamia was probably upset over how much I fussed over her. I constantly worried whether she ate or rested enough.

Away from the team, I attended all of the doctor checkups. Our daughter's pending arrival provided a burst of hopeful anticipation during a difficult time. The contract I had signed came with expectations. No one had said anything negative in front of me. But I sensed a growing communal fatigue. The local media turned hypercritical, unaware of the full extent of my ankle injury.

I suppressed the negative thoughts by focusing on the next goal, the next milestone to cross.

———

In September, Dr. Myerson told me that I was ready to go. Later, I noted that he had not declared me healed. I entered the final phase of my recovery, transitioning to playing pickup ball.

The Magic had acquired a couple of well-known figures over the summer. Horace Grant was already a beloved figure in Orlando from his first stint with the organization. Patrick Ewing might have been on his last legs, but he was still Patrick Ewing.

I did not dominate the pickup games, but I contributed, cultivating confidence and finding a rhythm. Doc planned to position me at point guard. I endured two-a-days through training camp and the preseason with no hiccups or setbacks. Our squad looked like an early contender. Tracy continued his ascent. Mike Miller was fresh off being named rookie of the year. I felt optimistic and eager to prove myself.

My season ended before December.

The ankle pain again turned excruciating just before Thanksgiving 2001. I underwent another series of imaging with Dr. Myerson, whom I had communicated with frequently. Sometimes, I would feel bad because he'd drop whatever he had going on to answer my call. But that was the type of relationship I wanted to cultivate with a physician, one who wouldn't leave me with any unanswered questions or lingering concerns. On one visit, Dr. Myerson declared that I needed another surgery, this time to inject plasma into the ankle to promote healing.

Endure this now, I told myself after the procedure and through another half a year of rehabilitation. I'll be able to make it all up on the back end of my career.

Maybe, by that point, I should have been skeptical of hospitals. I still viewed them as healing stations, a crucial stop on the path to recovery. I had set foot in so many, tolerated so many checkups and procedures, that the athlete in me had never questioned what could go wrong inside a hospital. That changed late in the evening of January 22, when Tamia informed me that it was time for her to go to the hospital. Our daughter was on her way. I grabbed my crutches and headed to the car. My mind raced during the ride to Arnold Palmer Hospital for Children, pondering every doomsday scenario. The hospital had suddenly become the scariest destination in the world.

I parked in front. Attendants scrambled to bring Tamia inside, where nurses hurried to make sure she was as comfortable as possible. I witnessed a miracle unfold before me, the birth of that beautiful baby girl now crying on Tamia's chest. Myla Grace Hill. My love for her was immediate and immense, more powerful than anything I had ever felt before.

We were discharged the next day, received at a full house where our parents met and fussed over their new granddaughter. They lingered a few days, ensuring that Myla's and Tamia's needs were met. It dawned on me once they left that now Tamia and I were really in it. There was no turning back. I couldn't even recall the last time I had held an infant this young, if ever. I didn't even know if Tamia's parenting knowledge was much greater than mine. Tamia gave Myla her first bath at home as I held a camcorder off to the side. She dried Myla, wrapping her in a swaddle before picking her up in a warm embrace. Myla started heaving and I immediately panicked, fearful that my baby was choking.

Calm down, Tamia said. She's just spitting up.

That showed how clueless I was those early days and just how natural of a caretaker Tamia turned out to be. She proudly spent nearly every moment of those first few weeks nurturing and bonding with Myla. I felt a little guilty as the days passed. I was desperate to form a similar bond. My immobility prevented me from changing diapers or rising in the middle of the night with Myla. I was cautious of even holding her much her first couple of months. I could spend hours, though, simply observing her, waiting for the smallest of her gestures, awed that I played a small role in the creation of someone so beautiful.

That summer of 2002, Dr. Myerson held my latest ankle scan in front of me.

You're healed after all this time, he declared. I didn't say it the year before, I'm saying it now, you're 100 percent healed.

My ankle soon told me otherwise. I encountered the same roadblocks as the previous season, successfully completing training camp, upbeat over another dawning season, only for the pain and irritation to settle in November like clockwork. I booked another visit with Dr. Myerson, who told me I was being limited by tendonitis in the tendon that connected my calf muscle to the bones inside my foot. I took that anatomy class at Duke. I was aware of where that muscle was, how it worked. I questioned whether the pain originated from the posterior tibial tendon, but Dr. Myerson remained adamant.

I was determined to play, to save what I could of that season for me and my team. Dr. Billings, our team physician, prescribed me a Medrol dose pack to mask the pain. I had taken the steroid a couple years earlier in Miami, where it had provided temporary relief. I started the cycle and again felt an immediate and temporary alleviation. I played nimbly that Christmas Day, when we hosted Detroit for a nationally televised game, enough that I guarded their point guard, Chauncey Billups, the entire length of the court. I could also almost pinpoint the moment the medicine wore off when a knifing sensation started minutes into our next game against the Memphis Grizzlies.

I flew home, undergoing another round of CT scans and MRIs.

My nickname should be Radiation Man because I've taken so many scans, I joked with the media. If I take one more, I'll be glowing.

I missed several games, trying to find the source of the ever-present pain. We traveled to Washington for a nationally televised game in mid-January. I knew that my season was over, and I shouldn't have attempted to give it a go. But the game represented the last opportunity I would ever have to play against Michael Jordan, who had returned to play for the Washington Wizards and planned to retire again at the end of the season. The pain was at a point where I could walk, and that night I tried to play. Jordan was older, only flashing his prior self in nostalgic glimpses. I defended him and he torched me that first quarter, recycling the same play again and again by running through a double screen and curling at the right elbow before burying a jumper. I recognized the play happening before it even unfolded, yet I was still helpless to stop him. Physically, I couldn't stay with him. I didn't know if my ego had gained the best of me in wanting to play against him that final time or if I just wanted to play in a game so close to home. Now I just knew that I didn't belong on the court. The first quarter ended. I fought back tears as I walked past our bench, down a hallway in the MCI Center, and into the visitors' locker room, another season ended before I really had the opportunity to get going.

Over the next few days, I quieted my mind by spending more time with Myla. Finally, I was able to nurture our bond. I had been so limited and Tamia was so present that Myla had started to feel solely like Tamia's child her first year of life. Now I often packed Myla into her stroller, taking her for leisurely walks in the late afternoon. I would continue searching for every option and opinion to restart my playing career. Regardless, I reminded myself on a walk one sunny day, basketball carries an expiration date. I looked into Myla's endless eyes.

This precious girl is what's real, I thought. She's here for life.

My dad again encouraged me to fly to Duke and brainstorm with Dr. Nunley and Dr. Bassett. But I felt invested in Dr. Myerson. He had operated on me twice, expressing confidence at every step along this laborious process. We sent Dr. Myerson the results of my most recent imaging and arranged a conference call with my dad, John Gabriel, Lon Babby, and Vinnie Hudson.

Your old fracture is fine, he said. It looks like there might be a new one. But I've done everything that can be done.

What should I do?

Well, you should consider retiring.

Dr. Myerson essentially washed his hands of me. He had always been patient with my inquiries. Now he seemed to regard me as a nuisance. I had spent months trying to play on my ankle since my most recent procedure, tolerating as much pain as I could. Retiring couldn't have been the best possible medical advice. I was thirty years old. I was offended by the suggestion.

We're now going to start taking control of this, I declared to Vinnie. We're going to do what we need to do to get better.

———

My expanding art collection provided some inspiration. My dad had encouraged me to start my own, those art gallery visits as a child paying dividends he never could have imagined. An appreciation coursed through our bloodline. His mother, Elizabeth Hill, had encouraged him to develop an appreciation for the arts at an early age.

I didn't think of myself as overly creative. I did enjoy the meaningful expressions of heritage and culture that art can depict, like the Romare Bearden that routinely caught my eye in Mr. Cliff Alexander's office. My own collection began clumsily. At Duke, I had purchased a print of a painting by Ernie Barnes called *Chaos in Cameron* that celebrated the 1986 Final Four team. At the time, I had hoped it would spark conversations with women.

Thankfully, my motives turned more meaningful. I was drawn especially to African American pieces and leaned on my dad for his opinion as I started my collection in earnest. I had been fascinated with the Harlem Renaissance, a time, the 1920s and 1930s, when Blacks fleeing the terror of the Jim Crow South were arriving at a new, more subtle terror of discrimination in northern cities. Still, African Americans persevered and showcased pride and innovation in fashioning a creative hub and displaying their gifts for the world.

I sought pieces that reminded me of my cultural inheritance, that transported me to my childhood days, sitting in the lap of my grandfather Henry Hill as he smoked from a cigar pipe and wove stories about picking cotton until thick calluses covered his hands. Or when we visited my great-grandmother in New Orleans and she reminisced of a childhood spent feeding horses sugar on an Arkansas farm.

Art was open to interpretation, a snapshot of the artist's vision at that point in time. We could view the same piece and be inspired differently. Appreciating the ingenuity of someone's imagination provided a lens to remember those who plotted the roads for us to follow.

My collection eventually expanded to include titans of the art world, including Bearden, Elizabeth Catlett, John Coleman, and Hughie Lee-Smith.

I was always refreshed when admiring them, appreciative and inspired by all that African Americans have endured and the beauty crafted from an often-painful history.

———

You should come to Duke, Dr. Bassett said. We can figure out what's going on.

He had reviewed scans of my ankle. His voice expressed calm confidence absent any cockiness. Dr. Bassett had fixed me once when I had sought outside opinions. I found myself turning to him again.

I caught a flight a couple days later and basked on a familiar campus with faces I recognized in Dr. Bassett, Dr. Nunley, and Dr. Claude Moorman.

They quickly diagnosed the chronic issue that had cut these years out of my basketball career and caused me to question myself. Scans revealed that my left leg was extremely bowed, curving outward from the knee.

I don't know how you've played one game like this, Dr. Bassett explained. It's like having a car where the tire treading wears off with time.

You can change the tire and it'll be fine for a while, but it is going to eventually wear down again. Fix the alignment and it'll provide a longer shelf life.

My ankle was the tire. My leg was the car.

Standing in front of a mirror in Dr. Bassett's office, I noticed for the first time that my left leg protruded out more than my right. The doctors suggested that realigning the knee in the future may be beneficial. They outfitted me in a walking boot to see if the stabilization would further healing while we sought a more permanent fix. In the meantime, they encouraged me to seek additional opinions. Dr. Myerson, my primary physician, who had once been so accommodating, refused to take my calls. To this day, I'm not sure why or how he missed properly diagnosing my injury.

I took Vinnie Hudson's suggestion to consult with Dr. William Hamilton in New York City. Dr. Hamilton's operating days were behind him, but he was still regarded as one of the country's premier foot and ankle doctors. I spotted Mikhail Baryshnikov, the famed Russian American ballet dancer, walking out of his office just before my appointment. It could only be a good omen if Baryshnikov trusted Dr. Hamilton with his legs. Dr. Hamilton was a classic old-school practitioner, in his seventies with an open shirt and an ascot. He inspected my gait pattern and studied my imaging. He presented a similar diagnosis as the Duke doctors without having ever talked to them, describing how my foot striking the ground at an awkward angle caused repeated stress. If I changed how my foot landed, I'd improve my mechanics up the chain from my foot, ankle, knee, hip, lower back, all the way up to the shoulders.

Dr. Hamilton consulted with the Duke physicians over the phone and confirmed their leanings.

I have one question for you, Dr. Hamilton declared. Do you want to continue playing basketball?

When I'm healthy, I'm competitive, I responded.

Here is what you're going to do, he said. You have an affinity for Duke University. You've got a great doctor down at Duke by the name of Jim Nunley. And Jim Nunley is going to do a procedure on you called a Dwyer procedure, an osteotomy that breaks a wedge of bone from the calcaneus to realign the foot.

I underwent my fourth surgery on my ankle in the spring of 2003 at Duke Medical Center. Dr. Nunley alleviated the pressure by removing a piece of bone from my heel.

How was it? I asked Dr. Nunley as the anesthesia started to wear off.

It went well, he said, adding that he had encountered some issues closing off the incision.

Every time you have a surgery, that area of the bone calcifies, he clarified. As you cut skin open, repair it, cut it open, repair it, it loses its elasticity. Particularly in your ankle, where there's not great blood flow.

I thought of all the twists that had occurred during those three lost seasons of playing without a proper rehabilitation plan, the death of Dr. James Barnett, enduring enough surgeries to nearly fill the fingers of a fist, and my misplaced faith in Dr. Myerson, who had treated the symptom instead of addressing the issue. I had signed with a fan base that voted against paying Shaquille O'Neal in his prime, and I had every intention of living up to the contract. I wondered why I couldn't have received a proper diagnosis earlier and why my body had to be susceptible to a misalignment in the first place.

Those thoughts were wiped aside. I pulled myself back to the moment.

The worst was finally, firmly behind me.

I had no clue that the most frightening episode of all was about to come.

17

I returned home a couple days after the latest, last surgery and was plopped on our couch, my leg elevated and buried beneath layers of blankets. My teeth chattered. My body shivered. Sweat rained down my face.

I heard Tamia walk through our front door.

I don't feel right.

Don't be so dramatic.

Do you mind grabbing a thermometer? I sheepishly stammered.

I felt bad asking. I had lovingly, and only occasionally, taken to referring to Tamia as Nurse Betty, the character from that Renée Zellweger movie. Her responsibilities increased every time I went under the knife. The surgeries weighed as much on her as me. She had preemptively declared that she couldn't endure another procedure two procedures ago. I required assistance accomplishing the smallest of tasks I had once taken for granted, such as reheating a plate of food. She helped in those mundane areas and tolerated the tiny urinal that sat near our bed, so I didn't have to hobble to the bathroom to relieve myself at night. The reliance on her drained both of us. Sometimes, I felt as helpless as a child. She found one of Myla's infant thermometers to take my temperature.

She grimaced. Okay, she said. This is crazy. It says your temperature is 104.2.

We were first-time parents. Every room in our house probably held a thermometer or two. She quickly grabbed another one.

Now it says 104.1. This can't be right.

She checked with all the thermometers that she could locate. Each depicted a fever above 104 degrees. The shakes took hold of me, and I had to piece together most of what followed over the next few days from other people's accounts. My arms started convulsing, flapping wildly, and my speech deteriorated to nonsensical gibberish.

The team was on a road trip. Hurriedly, Tamia called Vinnie Hudson, who had visited us at the house the previous day. She passed the phone to me, and I responded to Vinnie with what he later described as childlike babbling.

He advised Tamia to escort me to the hospital as fast as possible; he would phone Dr. Joe Billings to meet us there.

One shaky foot after the other, blankets still draped over me, I made my way from the family room through the kitchen and into the backseat of the car, propping my left foot on the center console.

Tamia clutched the wheel, giving me a quick, panicked glance. My entire body writhed uncontrollably. She navigated the car down roads slickened by an afternoon thunderstorm as I tried retaking my temperature with unsteady hands. The car screeched in front of the emergency room at Florida Hospital in downtown Orlando. Tamia dashed inside. Medics followed her back out with a wheelchair a few seconds later and helped me out of the car.

We barely made it through the hospital's front door when I heard Tamia's voice.

Turn him around. Get him back in the car.

She held her phone with one hand. Her other hand directed the attendants back to her car, still stationed at the valet. We were at the wrong hospital. Dr. Billings was at another Florida hospital, in nearby Winter Park.

She was adamant. So was the medical staff.

He needs to see a doctor right now.

Tamia insisted that I be seen by my physician, and they saw the futility in trying to convince her otherwise.

They placed me back into the car. We arrived at the right hospital a few minutes later. Dr. Billings and a contingent of medical officials waited out front and eased me straight onto a gurney.

Someone, a doctor I'm guessing, pelted questions as we raced inside the facility and through a corridor.

What's your name?

What year is it?

Who do you play for?

Can you count backward from one hundred?

I strained to answer the first question when we arrived inside a hospital room. People scurried everywhere. Two attendants on each side of me struggled with strapping my arms and chest down to control my spasming body. I gasped for breath; it felt like someone had just dropped a heavy dumbbell onto my chest. They frantically tried removing the cast from my ankle.

A clear thought rose up in my mind.

This was it.

I was dying. I thought about Tamia, and missing Myla growing up. My eyes closed.

———

The room was calm when I opened them. I heard the methodical hum of working machinery, the steady drip of intravenous therapy.

Tamia hugged me, alerting the medical staff that I had awakened. I looked down. The cast was gone. My leg, from my knee down, revealed several shades of purples, blacks, and reds. A staph infection had ravaged my body through the stubborn incision that refused to properly close. My body was in sepsis, struggling to fight the infection trying to make its way to vital organs like my lungs and heart. I spent the next few days in the intensive care unit in a thick fog. A nurse bathed me. A bedpan rested at the side of the bed. Ironically, I was under enough heavy medications to not feel pain for the first time since the surgery at Duke.

The cloud lifted, enough that I could start appreciating escaping a near-death experience. The fever broke, and scans showed that no blood clots had formed. Doctors outfitted me with a peripherally inserted central catheter line to deliver medication through my arm into my chest and discharged me from the hospital. I returned daily over the next several days to sit in a hyperbaric oxygen chamber to help fight the infection and induce healing.

I was home recovering when Dr. James Nunley called, concerned. He asked me to take a picture of the infection and send it to him. Now, this was 2003. Cell phone cameras were still a few years off. Tamia somehow figured out how to capture the image, upload it onto a computer, and email the file to Dr. Nunley, a process that took hours.

Dr. Nunley and Dr. Scott Levin, certified in both orthopedic and plastic surgery at Duke, phoned the next day.

We need you to come to Duke immediately.

I anticipated a quick visit, believing that they just wanted to ensure that the infection had been corralled. I packed a change of clothes and caught a charter flight with my dad, who had come to visit us after the scare.

You have a hole in your foot, Dr. Levin told me after inspecting my ankle.

What? I thought I had been progressing, that the worst was behind us.

You're going to need a free flap to properly close the wound.

He explained how a free flap was a more difficult undertaking than a skin graft; it involved detaching a piece of healthy skin from the body and attaching it to my ankle.

We'd normally take the skin from your butt or your lower back and use the tissue from there, he said. But taking it from a lower extremity may add more hurdles to playing basketball again. I'd like to take it from behind your left arm, between your triceps and biceps.

The last thing I remember before the free flap, or microvascular tissue transfer, was the look from Dr. Levin. I'd recognize a game face anywhere. In the extremely delicate procedure, he used an operating microscope to remove healthy tissue from my left arm, where the blood vessels were only about a millimeter wide, and passed them through sutures so small they could fit through a human hair.

He transported the vessels into my ankle that contained the osteomyelitis with the goal of clearing the infection, resurfacing the wound, and preserving the bone. Later, Dr. Levin explained to me how this was an all-or-nothing procedure and that patients often lose the afflicted limb to amputation when the tissue transfer is not successful.

I came to while hearing the familiar voices of Jim Nantz and Billy Packer. The 2003 NCAA championship game between Syracuse and Kansas played somewhere in the background. I had played in the game less than a decade earlier, although it now seemed like eons.

I was still slightly dopey following the six-hour surgery. My mom, who thought of everything, passed me my eyeglasses. The room came into focus. My leg was elevated, my ankle sore, my left arm immobilized and raised. My biceps felt warm. Actually, my entire body burned. I desperately needed to itch everywhere. My mom scratched my shoulders. That was how I found out I was allergic to the Percocet that I had been administered.

Thankfully, Dr. Nunley declared the surgery a success otherwise. My parents stayed close over the next few days. Tamia remained a constant, doting presence. We laughed that she was spending too much time lounging with me when she complained one day of a slight numbness in her extremities.

John Gabriel visited a few days after the surgery. His facial expression crossed the point of concern once he viewed my ankle. Neither of us could have envisioned this scenario when he had recruited me to Orlando. It looked like I had a miniature football attached to my ankle. His look revealed equal parts disbelief and fear. I was sure that he had left the hospital believing that I'd never set foot on an NBA court again.

He'd be right, in my opinion.

That's the reason I almost laughed when Coach K dropped by to see me a couple days later. He was fresh off another Sweet 16 appearance, vowing to lead the team deeper into next season's tournament.

You're going to get back out there on the court, he said, projecting the same confidence he had when I was a freshman and he declared we would be national champions.

I had learned not to doubt him after that meeting. But I couldn't fool myself. Time in hospital rooms provided endless opportunities for thinking. I had trained myself to look past any roadblock. I spent years bartering with my mind that if I did this diet or trained this way or endured this one last surgery, I'd be able to recoup for lost time on the back end of my career. I could console myself with the fact that I had been dealing with a bone issue, not a joint or a ligament injury. I understood cartilage: once you started losing that connective tissue, it was just a matter of time before your playing days ended. I had passionately believed that I'd be on track once my bone healed.

This time was different. Coach K told us to focus on the present. My present was here, recovering, and I was grateful to be alive in it. The NBA couldn't be further from my mind. Goals changed. Priorities evolved. Myla needed a father. Tamia needed a husband. I vowed that this would be my last ankle surgery. I was in this hospital room, which needed to be kept miserably hot to ensure that the flap took to my skin, because of basketball. I just had a fifth invasive procedure on my ankle because of basketball. I nearly lost my life because I had tried so many times to get back to basketball.

What more could I possibly do to return to the thing I loved if that love was no longer reciprocated?

I had flown to Durham with one change of clothing. I stayed for six weeks, the first week at the hospital. Doctors fitted me with another peripherally inserted central catheter line before I relocated to the Washington Duke Inn & Golf Club, where the staff kept tabs on my recovery. The line injected vancomycin, one of the world's strongest antibiotics, straight into my bloodstream every eight hours for a month. They called the medicine one of the last lines of defense for a reason.

That spring, Orlando faced Detroit in the playoffs' first round. The Pistons were revitalized, the Eastern Conference's top seed. Tracy McGrady performed magnificently in capturing the league's scoring title and leading Orlando all season. He sizzled in the playoffs, guiding the Magic to a three-to-one series edge against Detroit and to the precipice of a sizable upset.

It feels good to get into the second round, Tracy prematurely declared.

Detroit rallied to win the series.

Meanwhile, I was recovering at the hotel, my attention not on the Magic as I'd prefer but on carefully wrapping garbage bags around my ankle and arm, trying to make sure the areas did not become moistened in the shower.

In May, I was finally cleared to return home. The flap was an ever-present reminder of the entire ordeal as I transitioned over the weeks from the cast to crutches to being able to walk again. The scorching Florida summer prevented the option of wearing pants most days. I covered the flap with a brace, even while at home, slightly ashamed over what I viewed as a disfigurement. My foot resembled a brick with toes, but eventually it started feeling slightly better. I found out through reading a *USA Today* article that the Magic were seeking an injury player exemption that would provide salary cap relief if I was declared sidelined for the entire approaching season. Gabriel called, asking that I fly to New York, where an independent doctor would make the determination. To my knowledge, the organization had not discussed my status with the doctors who would actually know my prognosis, mainly Dr. Nunley and Dr. Levin. Returning wasn't at the forefront of my consciousness, but I still called and asked Dr. Nunley for his opinion out of curiosity.

Dr. Nunley didn't hesitate. He told me and the independent doctor that I would be able to return if I made that decision.

I gazed out the window, marveling at all the different colors of blue the ocean could hold as our plane descended onto the Caribbean. Tamia and I had decided to take a trip to celebrate our four-year wedding anniversary and leave the ordeal of the past few years behind us. We scooped up Myla and headed off for the paradise of Turks and Caicos for a vacation on the island's secluded northern tip.

The trip furnished everything we sought. We were as light as the breezy air, losing hours, spending days lounging in the warmth of the sun and the calmness of the water. We got ready to head home, refreshed and renourished.

At the airport, Tamia tried filling out our immigration forms.

I'm having trouble holding the pen, she told me. Can you finish these? No problem.

Once home, Tamia mentioned that her elbows and fingers tingled, as though she had somehow struck her funny bone in an awkward fashion. She still possessed a thick medical book from her pregnancy, one that explained what type of doctor should be sought depending on a variety of symptoms. She pulled it out, thumbed through it, and booked an appointment with a neurologist.

She stayed in the hospital for a week as doctors performed various tests to unearth the cause of her illness. I was a wreck.

We had just celebrated putting my injury saga behind us. I was walking without pain. The flap had taken to my ankle.

None of that mattered now. My wife was suffering. I thought back to when she had told me of the numbness she felt while at Duke. Was that the first indicator? The odd sensations, Tamia said, had spiraled throughout her hands and feet. She often felt fatigued.

Finally, a doctor informed us that every other possibility had been ruled out. He diagnosed Tamia with multiple sclerosis.

We were both stunned. I didn't know much about the debilitating disease, in which the immune system devours the protective covering of the nerves. The little I did know ramped up my anxiety. The only people I had previously heard afflicted with the disease were the actors Richard Pryor and Annette Funicello. The disorder invaded their bodies, robbing them of their mobility and functionality. I tried projecting strength for Tamia's sake. Inwardly, I was as frightened as I had ever been. All the grief I ever felt for myself evaporated. I had assumed the injury liabilities involved with playing basketball. I could maintain a quality of life even if I could no longer play. I was frightened that the doctor had just handed Tamia a death sentence. She was the last person deserving of this. She had not put herself at any risk. She took care of herself by eating and sleeping right.

The joke among Magic players was that if you were injured in Orlando, the first place you should head to was the airport rather than the hospital. Florida doctors had saved me during the staph infection, but a little truth existed in every joke. I could count plenty of instances involving Magic players complaining of misdiagnoses.

We booked another flight to Durham. A Duke neurologist confirmed Tamia's diagnosis.

The specifics of Tamia challenging and confronting the disease are hers to divulge one day, if she so chooses.

I will write that we had exchanged vows of in sickness and in health. We meant them.

By then, Tamia had already released the first few singles for her third album, eventually titled *More*. The album, in my unbiased opinion, was incredible, the culmination of her growth and talent as a vocalist, and had been slated for an August release. The illness blunted the momentum, delaying the drop.

We had leaped into marriage early in adulthood, perhaps slightly naive about the hurdles that all couples confront and unprepared for the unique challenges we would face. It was easy for someone to conjure a life of luxury by marrying a professional athlete if they viewed only the accompanying trappings of success. Our marriage had long ago revealed Tamia's resiliency.

My routines were timed to the minute from the moment I rose on game days. My mind wouldn't be in the right place if I deviated from one aspect of my schedule. Tamia, from the moment she paid for our first date, possessed her own sense of self-worth and identity. She amazed me before her performances—how she could be at ease, chilling and joking, while sitting in a chair as a stylist finished her makeup. Minutes later, she would flip a switch, delivering laser-like focus in providing an ovation-worthy concert before thousands of people.

We got our strength from each other.

She accepted the diagnosis, determined to attack the disease. Routines changed. Every step was not easy; we learned that each body responded differently to multiple sclerosis. I recouped lost time with my family as we adapted to our new reality. I enrolled in a commercial real estate course, figuring that I may as well be productive with my time if I was pivoting from basketball. But Tamia, as always, stayed on beat. She continued as the same devoted mother and amazing wife. She wrapped the album and performed with Beyoncé, Alicia Keys, and Missy Elliott in one of the largest tours of the year.

She persevered with her professional career while dealing with multiple sclerosis.

Her strength was inspiring.

———

Shaquille O'Neal invited us to a charity boxing event one night that August, the main card featuring himself against Antonio Tarver. We were not overly close at the time, although Shaq was a neighbor. Tamia and I took our seats at one of the dinner tables that enclosed the boxing ring. Shaq greeted us and asked to inspect my ankle. I lifted up the brace. He frowned like a gawker who could not look away from a bad car accident.

Why would you even think about trying to play again? he asked.

The NBA season was approaching. Shaq would be back in Los Angeles with the Lakers soon.

Well, if you ever want to use my gym, let me know.

I called him the next day and took him up on the offer. Shaq offered me his garage door opener. I started slipping out of my house when everyone was asleep, making the short walk over to Shaq's. His home was probably all you imagine it to be. The garage door opened to a showroom containing several Mercedes, Rolls-Royces, and motorcycles. Framed jerseys of Hall of Fame football and basketball players lined both sides of a hallway leading to the gym's door. A large television loomed above pictures and trophies commemorating his career on the wall closest to the entrance. I often turned on the television, lobbing free throws, while consuming a game—usually one featuring Shaq's Lakers in a prime-time matchup. The gym's ceiling was low. Perhaps, I thought, that was the reason why his free throws were so flat.

The feeling of being inside a gym without an agenda proved rejuvenating. I had lost years struggling to come back to the game, and in the process I had lost the vision of why I had pushed so badly in the first place. Inside Shaq's gym, I was out of view of any coach or trainer. The solitude returned me to those days of childhood when I would brush through the woods behind my house, making my way to the elementary school playground. It had just been me and the basket when I would imagine draining that last bucket. That was my core relationship with the sport, one that predated the NBA, endorsements, commercials, and even those special years at Duke.

It all began by finding a passion and purpose through this beautiful game.

As the routine continued, Jason Rivera, an assistant equipment manager with the Magic, partnered with me to rebound the shots. Jason's assistance allowed me to focus on the games between free-throw attempts. I had always watched basketball, dating to when we first set up that old basement Betamax, studying the sport, but also often losing myself as a mesmerized fan. In college, Tony Lang and I used to watch games of Vegas getting up and down the court, blasting teams out of the arena. In Detroit, I'd often grab a bite to eat after my own game and hurry home to catch the West Coast games on television. Basketball becomes pure harmony when all five members of a team move in rhythm as though somehow connected. I had misplaced the joy of just enjoying the innate synchronicity of the sport, an affection regained as I shot set shots while appreciating Kobe Bryant attack a defense, Steve Nash split a double-team, or Tim Duncan coolly bounce a shot off the backboard and into the rim.

I'm forever indebted to Shaq for allowing me access to his gym, even if he's probably not the best guy to owe a favor to. I shudder at the day he'll come to collect, but it is what it is.

———

Meanwhile, I had synced my fall and winter medical checkups to Duke basketball games. I never really had the chance to soak in the atmosphere at Cameron as a spectator and found myself enjoying the environment.

My ankle's consistent progress encouraged Dr. Nancy Major, a musculoskeletal radiologist at Duke.

The CT scans revealed additional healing with each visit. We agreed that part of the recovery owed to me resting instead of undergoing a rigorous rehabilitation. The flap, she explained, was circulating healthy blood into my ankle.

After a few of those reassuring follow-ups, Vinnie and I agreed to start training again. We didn't have a goal in mind other than gauging how my body responded to targeted stress. Vinnie encouraged swimming as much as possible, and I spent so much time in the pool that I joked I was on the verge of developing flippers. We incorporated other cardio workouts and exercises aimed at strengthening my entire body. Soon, we increased the workload by expanding to on-court drills during the early months of 2004, progressing from free throws to spot shooting and jump shots.

I often attended Magic home games, watching from the back of the arena with the film guys. My status with the team remained up in the air during a brutal season for the franchise. The organization fired Doc Rivers during a long losing streak. John Gabriel followed him out the door a short while later. The organization replaced him with John Weisbrod, the

Magic's chief operating officer, who possessed a hockey background. Weisbrod imagined fashioning a basketball team in a hockey image by gathering no-nonsense players. From my perspective, he picked a war of words with Tracy, baiting him into a response. Over the summer, Weisbrod would jettison Tracy in a blockbuster trade, denying us the opportunity to ever formulate the partnership we had imagined sitting on the podium a few years earlier, me filled with optimism and dressed in Dr. J's dress shoes.

The organization spiraled toward the lottery's bottom. The season almost over, I had cleared every medical hurdle. I was all in on returning a final time. I didn't know what, if anything, I could make with the time left in my career. But I had confidence I had more to offer, that retiring then, at the age of thirty-one, would be like waking up early from a dream.

I debated playing a few games at the end of the 2003–2004 season to provide momentum heading into the next year. The organization nixed the plan for, in my opinion, two reasons: they wanted the best odds at the first overall pick, which meant stacking as many losses as possible, and an insurance company had paid most if not all of my salary throughout my injured years.

Those years you were hurt, we made money, Weisbrod confirmed to me at one point.

18

A N amped audience filled TD Waterhouse Centre. From inside the tunnel, I awaited my introduction, hearing the crescendos of cheers. I did not want to disappoint the crowd; it had been awhile since I had been this anxious to step on a basketball court.

But no basketball would be played that day. The start of a fresh season was still a couple months off. I was ready to offer my endorsement to the Democratic ticket of John Kerry and John Edwards in the approaching election against President George W. Bush and Vice President Dick Cheney.

As Bruce Springsteen's music blasted from speakers, Tamia offered some sage advice. Use the five *B*s: Be brief, brother, be brief.

Moments later, I stood with Kerry and Edwards, extending each my Orlando Magic jersey as a keepsake. I had purchased them earlier that day from the team store, acknowledging to myself the irony that Richard DeVos, the owner of the Magic, and his family, were major Republican Party donors.

It's been a long four years for me with my ankle injury, I told the crowd. But it's been an even longer four years for our country.

Kerry, a decorated Vietnam veteran and Massachusetts senator, criticized Bush's handling of the Iraq War and his health-care policies. Florida would, as usual, serve as a crucial swing state in the presidential
election. The race reflected division, although a tame version when compared with today's climate of extreme polarity. Over those next few
weeks, Tamia and I appeared at fundraising events for Kerry and Edwards, lending our voice and support to the ticket and party that most
closely aligned with our ideology.

Political involvement was somewhat rare among athletes my age. As
a group, we were far from the days when Muhammad Ali, Bill Russell,
John Carlos, and Tommie Smith shed light on inequities.

Growing up, I had witnessed the civic participation of my parents.
They had attended fundraisers, knocked on doors, and advised local and
state officials on issues large and small. I viewed my own activism as the
natural progression from watching their involvement, those enlightening
conversations that fed my worldview and led to my own desire to see a
more equal and just society.

My personal success was the wildest dreams and hopes of my ancestors springing to life, the aspiration that each generation could travel a
little bit further than the previous one. But no person of color, no matter
how famous or rich, can escape the constant splinters of daily life that
chipped away at one's humanity and cut like razors.

Most law enforcement officers perform heroically at an oftentimes
dangerous occupation. I still instinctively become nervous if I spot police while driving, a reflex born of lifelong experiences. Police routinely
pulled me over in high school, even when I maneuvered slowly out of fear
of striking a deer in the night's darkness.

Looks like your taillight is broken or your headlight is out, they
would say—even if they were not—but while I'm here, let me run your
information.

My parents had given me the talk. In those interactions with law enforcement, I remained quiet and respectful, even though I knew I had done nothing wrong.

People of color often sustained routine indignities like those, minor until they were not.

Back in 1993, I had accepted an offer to be a counselor for Michael Jordan's youth camp at Elmhurst College in Illinois. My broken toe might have been in a boot, but I figured I could still learn a lesson or two by watching Jordan work with the kids. Jordan arrived at his camp in a different car every day, changing them like the rest of us changed clothes. He'd stay for about five minutes during the day, returning at night to play pickup with the counselors once the campers had departed for their dorms. Fresh off our national championship, I was often the next most recognizable figure throughout the day. I signed autographs until my hand cramped and smiled for pictures until my cheeks hurt.

The night before the camp ended, some counselors suggested heading over to a club owned by one of Jordan's Chicago Bulls teammates, Cliff Levingston. We stayed only a few minutes, making sure to leave early in an effort to be ready for the final day. We didn't make it far. As soon as our car turned right off Lake Shore Drive, a dozen cop cars and a paddy wagon appeared, boxing us in. A light soon blinded me. A voice amplified by a megaphone commanded us to put our hands up. I reflexively raised mine, hitting the roof of the car. From the front seat, I twisted and turned my arms, easing my hands out the window as slowly as possible.

An officer opened the door, training a rifle at my face. Heart pumping, I followed his clipped directions, planting my face into the sidewalk, the boot on my ankle twisting at a painful angle as the officer handcuffed my wrists behind me.

Earlier, I had been the center of attention, signing autographs and taking pictures. Hours later, I was again the center of attention, a gun aimed at me, hands shackled for no apparent reason.

We're counselors at Michael Jordan's camp, I pleaded. We're just going back to campus.

The officers ran our IDs.

Mistaken identity, one said. You guys fit the description of some people who were firing out of their car.

They disappeared as suddenly as they had arrived, leaving us to collect our psyches and bodies off the ground.

Moments like those captured the ephemeral essence of celebrity and the constant, inherent dangers of being Black. For me, they also captured the necessity for civic involvement.

Kerry and Edwards, of course, went on to lose the election. I remained undeterred. I enjoyed being involved and only engaged more in subsequent election cycles.

Players of my era, and maybe even Jordan too, are sometimes retroactively criticized too harshly for a lack of political engagement. Systemic racism and inequalities have existed as long as this country has. We were at the mercy, back then, of the news that filtered out from prominent media outlets. I would have no way of knowing of an injustice that happened in, say, nearby Toledo, Ohio, when I lived in Michigan, unless the media reported the story and I just happened to pick up the paper or catch the evening news that day.

Today, I'm proud that athletes across all of sports are politically active in mobilizing voting initiatives, calling out inequalities, and holding those in power accountable. The advent of social media has facilitated greater involvement. Athletes are conscious of themselves as brands, way more than I was when the term seemed so foreign back in the day. They've grown up comfortable speaking to audiences, whether they are the superstar of their respective sport or an adolescent with a handful of social media followers.

The more people involved, the better.

———

Throughout the summer and fall of 2004, a series of hurricanes pummeled the Gulf Coast. The timing was less than ideal for a team mini-camp in Vegas designed as a meet and greet for the Magic's many new faces. Tamia stood stunned as I guiltily prepared to leave just before Labor Day weekend, not so much upset over my own departure as over the fact that the organization still insisted on the camp, the men of the households leaving with another hurricane forecast, while the debris from the previous one remained strewn in our neighborhood.

The Magic were essentially a new team. Johnny Davis, an assistant to Doc Rivers, had replaced him as head coach. Steve Francis, Cuttino Mobley, and Kelvin Cato, former members of the Houston Rockets, were dividends of the Tracy McGrady trade. Our poor record the previous season netted the team Dwight Howard, the top selection from an Atlanta high school, and Jameer Nelson, a young point guard, in the draft. They joined recent acquisitions like Tony Battie, Hedo Türkoğlu, and DeShawn Stevenson. Aside from me, Pat Garrity—my partner for hours of pool workouts as we both worked our way back from surgeries—was the only holdover from a season earlier. In Vegas, we scrimmaged in the morning and early afternoons, using the rest of the day to gather at the pool or grab dinner. Dwight was a mostly sheepish, quiet kid. Much of the rest of the team, though, enjoyed being boisterous and loud. I didn't recall ever laughing as much around a group of guys.

On the court, I knew I was nowhere close to where I wanted to be. If the game of basketball is about rhythm, I was years off the beat. Steve, fresh off an All-Star season, awed. Cuttino, a crafty southpaw, showed he could score. Dwight displayed raw athleticism. Initially, I struggled keeping pace. My concerns, thankfully, orbited around playing the game and not whether I could physically perform. My ankle held up in Vegas, as it did, weeks later, throughout training camp in Jacksonville. I slowly discovered my limitations, designing ways to counter them, bridging the gap between the player I had been and the one I had become. My midrange jumper developed into my bread and butter.

We opened the season by hosting the Milwaukee Bucks in early November, my first game since I had walked to the locker room in fear and heartbreak after trying to play one last time against Michael Jordan almost two years prior. I had passed every test to that point. This is it, I thought to myself during the national anthem. Against Milwaukee I curled around screens with urgency, knowing a bit of separation would be the difference between a clean look and a blocked shot. I popped up for jumpers when the defender stood on his heels. I picked spots to leak out early on fast breaks. Steve won the game on a late layup, and I finished with twenty points in thirty-three minutes.

We were off to a decent start when Utah arrived shortly before Thanksgiving. A couple seasons earlier, the Jazz had started a rookie named Andrei Kirilenko on me. My instinct then was to attack any young player who guarded me. Instead, Kirilenko rejected my shot on successive possessions. I took the sendbacks as another sign that I had fallen, unaware that Kirilenko wasn't just any rookie but had played professionally in Russia, where he developed a reputation as a hard-nosed defender. This time, I locked in for our matchup, eager to prove that he couldn't get the best of me so easily. I got going early, along with Steve, through mid-range jumpers, leaners, and drives into the lane. I ended the evening with a win and thirty-two points, my most since joining the Magic.

Soon thereafter we landed in Indiana for a night off before playing the Pacers. Indiana was talented and versatile. The organization hadn't missed a beat in transitioning from the days of Rik Smits, Mark Jackson, and Derrick McKey to Ron Artest, Stephen Jackson, and Jermaine O'Neal with Reggie Miller as the primary holdover.

Our night off, the Pacers played a nationally televised game against the Pistons in Auburn Hills. I ordered room service, eager to catch the game and get a good night's rest, comforted knowing that the Pacers would be weary after playing the defending champions and flying home. To my surprise, the Pacers walloped the Pistons. Near the end of the lop-sided contest, Artest unnecessarily fouled Ben Wallace, sparking a flare-up between the teams. A spectator lobbed a drink at Artest, who ran into the stands, igniting an all-out brawl.

So much for a quiet evening. Stunned, I watched the replays of my old arena transform into a giant barroom fight with chairs and punches thrown.

The next day, we didn't know if Indiana had made it home or if they would even have enough available players to field a team. Artest, Jackson, and O'Neal started serving what would be lengthy suspensions. The NBA decided to proceed hours before tip-off. The six Pacers who played, perhaps still amped off the previous night's adrenaline, performed com-petitively, and it required some effort for us to claw out an emotional win.

Over the subsequent weeks and months, debates erupted over the NBA's future viability. Pundits discussed whether the league had turned too Black and too urban to pacify corporate partnerships and middle-American fans. David Stern instituted a dress code for players and in-stalled the league's one-and-done rule that prevented high school players from entering the NBA.

We have all wanted to run into the stands at some point in our ca-reers. I had been held back before by coaches. The bile occasionally spewed at us from anonymous faces could be a lot. In my opinion, it was unfair assigning blame for the fiasco on the league's influx of youth. The league was much younger than when I had entered, it was true. I didn't have to look far to appreciate that trend. The organization had placed Dwight's locker next to mine, hoping that a veteran player could offer him some guidance. I tried. Earlier in the season, I had noticed Dwight stationing himself too close to the basket. He'd catch the ball and make a decent move, only to be pinned in below the rim with nowhere to go. I suggested that he provide himself some room by posting up higher in the paint. He looked at me as though I were senile.

He had a lot to learn, and he would over the years. Most high school kids panned out. Many, including Tracy, Kobe Bryant, and Kevin Garnett, developed into our league's stars. I doubt a few college games would have helped them develop more quickly.

———

I settled into a comfortable groove after extracting some revenge against Kirilenko and Utah. That game, more than any other to that point in the season, equipped me with the confidence that I could still do this.

Reflecting on that time, I'm not surprised that it took some games to regain my form. I recall being initially harsh on myself, rushing to prove that I could still compete.

What comes back now, more than any singular moment of my return, is that the overcoming of hurdles gradually faded from my consciousness, the routine becoming routine once again.

I'm glad I can't recall when the basketball no longer felt so foreign in my hands.

I take comfort in not being able to cite the first time I played in back-to-back games.

I'm happy that I can't remember when I no longer needed that extra millisecond to think about the potential costs of a sharp turn or a drive to the rim.

I'm not entirely sure how I made it through those lost years. I guess sports conditioned me to believe that there was always a chance. If I walked away from the game I loved, I wanted to know that I had done so after exhausting every opportunity, every avenue at my disposal.

During my journey back, I sought out stories of inspiration and overcoming obstacles. If you had one, I consumed it, from Seabiscuit to Lance Armstrong (although we know how his story ultimately turned out). I watched all the Rocky movies. I read a library's worth of self-help books on the powers of healing, both physically and emotionally. I turned to the Bible; Scriptures of faith and belief sustained me. I thought about my family and ancestors and all that they had endured.

Really, I flooded myself with positivity, or as much as possible. In doing so, I stopped myself from diving too deeply into my feelings, which isn't necessarily healthy. I constantly trained my focus on the next surgery, recovery, and rehab until I had finally arrived back on the court.

Our team had talent, but all that laughter in Vegas might have been a decent indicator that this roster wasn't going to be the NBA's most driven team. We were up and down throughout the season. I put up good numbers, along with Steve, and when the initial All-Star Game fan voting was revealed, I realized I had a shot at returning to the game.

Maybe the outcome partly reflected the results of a popularity contest. A lot of fans had expressed that they were happy to see me on the court again. Most people, I felt, could relate to being broken and putting yourself back together again, one step at a time. I even received cheers in Philadelphia, of all places.

Five years earlier, I had told myself that I'd make sure to pack an extra pair of contact lenses for my next All-Star Game. Little did I know it would take so long. When the league announced that I would be part of the Eastern Conference's starting five at the game in Denver, I cherished the feeling. I had never taken the All-Star Game for granted, but all the accompanying obligations off the court had at one point felt like a bit of a burden. This time, I was elated to experience every single aspect of the weekend festivities.

Before the game, officials yanked me and LeBron James from the layup line for a joint television interview. I offered my perspective as a veteran back for the first time in years. LeBron, in his first All-Star Game, provided his observations as a newcomer. I wondered in that moment if the experience was as overwhelming for him as my first All-Star weekend had been for me. LeBron wasn't alone in making his debut. I had played in my previous All-Star Game with players from a fading era: Gary Payton, John Stockton, David Robinson. Now newbies like LeBron, Dwyane Wade, Gilbert Arenas, Manu Ginóbili, and Amar'e Stoudemire dominated the rosters from both conferences.

I was an elder statesman. Players excitedly told me that they had worn my shoes growing up.

One of the game's many beautiful aspects is that it continued to be as engaging and dynamic as ever as these young players became the new faces of the league, just like when those of my time—Kobe, Kevin Garnett, Penny Hardaway, Allen Iverson, and others—supplanted the generation of Jordan, Magic, and Bird.

Being there, soaking in this moment, turned more surreal when I listened to Tamia deliver a soulful rendition of the Canadian national anthem to thundering applause. Both of us had made it, having fought hard through adversity. I thought of the many times I wondered not just whether I could resume my career but whether my leg would permit me to live a life free from disability.

I took my place on the court and flashed a quick smile at Chip Engelland, sitting next to Tamia at mid-court, wearing a colorful Hawaiian shirt in the freezing cold of a Denver winter.

19

AN opportunity arose to rejoin the Detroit Pistons.

The thought tantalized me. My path hadn't crossed much with that of my teammate turned boss, Joe Dumars, since I left for Orlando. He had helped engineer Detroit's championship team in 2004, a core that had vied annually for the Eastern Conference crown as I focused on navigating a successful return to the court. I never experienced another issue with my ankle, but a sports hernia had limited me much of my 2005–2006 season.

Joe and I reconnected in the spring of 2007 as I neared another free agency. I was determined to finish the season healthy and to walk off the court in my Magic jersey, pouring everything into the stretch run, pushing us into the playoffs, where Detroit stood as our opponent. The Palace was electric during the series; the arena invoked in me waves of nostalgia. By that point, we had exhausted ourselves. Detroit quickly took the series, and Joe invited me to give him a call at the start of free agency.

As the playoffs continued, I accepted an invitation from ESPN to serve as a studio analyst for the later rounds alongside Michael Wilbon,

Jon Barry, and Dan Patrick. I had never imagined myself in television, especially as an active player, but figured it wouldn't hurt to get some reps in. The Spurs and Cavaliers, led by LeBron James, met in the finals. The network asked me to fly out for the games, and at a Cleveland hotel I ran into Jack McCallum, a veteran *Sports Illustrated* journalist. Jack had covered my entire professional career, and after we exchanged pleasantries, he offered a copy of his latest book, *Seven Seconds or Less*, a curtain-pulling reveal of a season with the Phoenix Suns. As an opponent, the Suns perpetually left me confused. They hurried up and down the court, their players shooting the ball as though it were on fire. They played little defense, yet often won.

I accepted the book, eager to learn some of the method behind the madness. I devoured most of it during downtime between the games, gaining a deeper appreciation for the team's principles and personalities. Their coach, Mike D'Antoni, advised his team to shoot early and often. Their point guard, Steve Nash, was flanked by pogo jumpers like Amar'e Stoudemire and Shawn Marion. They outscored opponents by attempting three-pointers and scoring on fast breaks. The coaching staff, it seemed, was both cohesive and loose, devoted to developing alternative paths to winning in the NBA. The environment Jack portrayed read like one players could prosper in.

I set the book aside once I was home and began thinking through my priorities with free agency approaching. Any change would be a drastic one. Not just for me but for our growing family. Tamia was expecting our second child, a daughter we would name Lael Rose. I was excited and anxious to be a dad of two girls. My love for Myla was infinite, and her precocious personality had blossomed. Was a parent's love for his children a supply that's finite? Would my love for our new daughter steal from my existing devotion to Myla? I would take a bullet for Myla. How could one person take two? Tamia advised me not to worry, that we would learn instinctively how to love them individually and collectively. She'd be right, of course, but the concerns still nagged me as we planned for Lael's arrival and I debated scenarios.

If I had been a betting man, I would have wagered that we would have stayed in Orlando. We had just purchased a new home in the area with eyes on remodeling it over the next few months. We had come to view Orlando as home, the place where we had welcomed our first daughter, even though the basketball portion had been arduous. Bob Vander Weide, Orlando's chief executive officer, had floated the idea of me retiring and joining the front office a couple times during those injury-stricken seasons. I had regarded the overtures as signs not of disrespect but of pragmatism. The organization might not have enjoyed my rigidity, but I needed to see the commitment through and prove to myself that I could battle through the adversity.

That summer, the franchise endured another embarrassing kerfuffle by hiring a college coach, Billy Donovan, to replace Brian Hill. Donovan apparently had second thoughts and requested to be released from the contract a week later. The organization landed on Stan Van Gundy, Jeff's brother, who had previously served as Miami's coach. I met with Van Gundy a week before free agency, and he pitched an enticing offensive overhaul; he said he hoped to utilize me in pick-and-rolls in facilitating Dwight Howard's movement to the rim.

But when free agency arrived, days passed without me or Lon hearing anything from Orlando's front office. I took the hint that the organization was ready to move on, as was I, bringing closure to a strenuous, difficult journey. The roster once constructed around me and Tracy McGrady no longer existed. Orlando planned to build around the young core of Dwight, Hedo Türkoğlu, and Jameer Nelson.

Let's make it right, Joe told me over the phone. We can pay you. Mr. Bill Davidson is still here and wants you back.

The more I contemplated returning to Detroit, the more I realized that I couldn't chase my past. A reunion would have provided a nice career bookend. But I wanted to preserve my memories of playing at a high level in that jersey.

A couple of franchises extended sizable offers. I kept returning to Phoenix. The organization had not really been on my radar before reading Jack's book. They were on the brink of contention, having recently lost a gut punch of a postseason series to San Antonio, and had hired Steve Kerr as general manager. Steve and I had always gotten along, and I was sure he had the steady demeanor necessary for the role.

I soon found myself on the phone listening to Coach D'Antoni's pitch.

You looked great this past season, D'Antoni said. You come here, I'm going to play you a lot. Thirty, forty minutes. Look, we don't go hard in practice, and we have a great training staff. Besides, it's more physical and taxing to play in the Eastern Conference, where you're beating each other up. We play with so much speed that no one can even put their body on us.

The vouching for the training staff was refreshing. I had read that their staff, led by Aaron Nelson, was cutting edge in the fields of recovery and injury prevention. They had helped resuscitate the career of Antonio McDyess following his devastating knee injury.

Phoenix reflected a franchise with championship potential, an innovative coach, and a pioneering training staff. I accepted a two-year deal with the Suns, leaving more lucrative offers on the table.

The next couple of weeks were a scramble. Tamia was due soon. Myla and I boarded a plane out west with instructions to find a house and tour elementary schools. Tamia probably didn't fully trust my judgment on either, so my mom accompanied us.

While we were in town, the Suns asked me to drop by for a physical. Aaron and Dr. Mike Clark, Aaron's mentor whose work revolutionized injury prevention and recovery enhancement, spent close to two hours meticulously measuring the range of motion in different parts of my body.

It was a bittersweet experience. They requested that I squat while raising my hands above my head.

I couldn't.

Part of me was happy that I had signed the contract before this visit. The short trip also reminded me of how much I had endured and the cost I was still paying. Afterward, as Lon Babby and I shared a car back to the hotel, I fought back tears. I felt like I was finally on the verge of receiving the detailed medical attention from a franchise that I had long sought. I knew after that short initial visit that my time in Phoenix would be well spent.

We located a school for Myla and a house in nearby Paradise Valley. Lael arrived on August 9. The next week, Tamia and I pulled up at the home she had never visited, our two young girls in tow.

It was a somewhat chaotic beginning to a rejuvenating adventure.

———

The pledge of playing until my lungs emptied came tied to a caveat.

If you pass up three-pointers, I'm gonna sit you, D'Antoni warned. When you get the ball, let it fly.

Today's NBA is a D'Antoni fever dream with centers chucking it up just past the half-court line. Back then, D'Antoni pressed ahead of the entire league, and his declaration countered nearly everything I had ever learned about systematically probing a defense for the best look. I had the system mostly down, I thought, by the time our season opened in Seattle against the SuperSonics. I shot every three I could from wherever I was, finishing one for seven on those attempts. Thankfully, I improved with reps, walking the line between knowing my spots and range and not being a shy shooter.

The team's core had been together for a few seasons, and I found myself quickly assuming a leadership role as a veteran. Steve was soft-spoken but an incredible leader. Amar'e was otherworldly talented, yet young.

The franchise proved itself to be everything I had imagined it to be. We held a slim lead atop the deep Western Conference as the All-Star break approached. A championship run appeared in our grasp.

D'Antoni phoned one day on a three-way call with Steve.

I'll get fired if you guys mention anything, but we have a chance to get Shaq from Miami, he said, the words excitedly tumbling out in his West Virginia drawl.

Steve and I expressed skepticism. We were all about running up and down. Shaquille was up there in age, more pound and plod. But D'Antoni believed Shaq could be pivotal in helping us escape the conference by adding a throwback interior threat. Such a move would help us keep pace with the Lakers, who had just landed Pau Gasol from Memphis. We'd be trading Shawn, a dynamic player on both ends of the court, who had grown disgruntled over his contract.

I ended the call with Coach D'Antoni and Steve and dialed Shaq. He had won a championship since joining Miami, but the relationship seemed to have soured. He was aware the franchise was soliciting deals and amenable to a move. Lately, he had been out with a hip injury. With him, I knew there was a difference between hurt and hurt-hurt.

I'm good, he said. Get me out of here.

D'Antoni was happy to hear the briefing. He advised me to relay Shaq's declaration to Robert Sarver, Phoenix's majority owner. Robert usually stopped by our locker room, and I motioned him over near the trainer's table after a game, watching his eyes grow bigger over the possibility of bringing Shaq to Phoenix.

Steve Kerr caught the end of the conversation and offered to walk with me to my car.

He had worked one of Shaq's playoff series a season earlier as a television analyst.

I just don't know if Shaquille can move anymore, he said.

He showed hesitancy over such a seismic trade. Steve had been in enough locker rooms to know that any minuscule move could drastically change a roster's chemistry. And trading for Shaq would be no small-sized addition. But D'Antoni and Robert were aligned. They had been tauntingly close to a championship and sought an edge. They were all in.

The trade occurred two days later.

Now, Shaq is my guy. We had become closer since he had let me use his gym. But he couldn't maintain our offensive pace. He reminded me of when Christian Laettner had sometimes fouled to make sure he caught up and touched the ball. Occasionally, Shaq fouled an opponent just to catch his breath. In the locker room, though, he remained in his prime. In March, we added Gordan Giriček, a decent swingman from Croatia and one of my old Orlando teammates. On offense, Gordan made the mistake of often looking Shaq off instead of feeding him in the post.

Strike one.

One day, Gordan walked the aisle on our team flight, while Shaq watched *Blue Chips*, the movie that he, Penny Hardaway, and a few others had starred in more than a decade earlier.

Shaq, you watching when you were really good, Gordan said with a laugh in his thick accent. Now you garbage.

Strike two.

Less than a week later, we were fighting for playoff position, prepping for a pivotal game against Dallas. Coach D'Antoni delivered his pregame speech. Afterward, I followed my routine by using the restroom. I didn't know what strike three was, but I reentered the locker room to find Gordan passed out on the floor, the training staff attempting to wake him up.

Shaq, the culprit, stood off to the side.

He shrugged.

I had to put him in a sleeper hold, he said. I got tired of him.

Acclimating took a few games, but we figured out a way to meld Shaq into our game plan, instilling sets designed for him to touch the ball. We were the Western Conference's fifth seed in the playoffs, and finished just two games behind the top-seeded Lakers, a testament to the conference's competitiveness. We opposed the Spurs in the opening round. That first game, Tim Duncan connected on his lone three-pointer of the entire season, sending the game into a second overtime, where Manu Ginóbili clinched the win on a late layup. San Antonio successfully employed the Hack-a-Shaq, deliberately sending Shaq to the free-throw line through-out the series. I'm not sure if we ever recovered from the opening heart-breaker, and San Antonio defeated us in five.

Surprisingly, Coach D'Antoni left the organization after the loss. I'm still not really sure what happened behind the scenes that caused his sud-den departure.

That fall, Tamia and I were invited by Michelle Obama to attend her speech at a convention center in downtown Phoenix. The presidential election was only a couple months away, and Michelle's husband, Sena-tor Barack Obama, was running a historic campaign as the Democratic nominee.

I had introduced Senator Obama a year earlier at a campaign fund-raiser in Potomac, Maryland. Back then, I just knew of him as a fresh-faced figure on the national political scene. At the time, everyone believed that another family connection, Hillary Clinton, would run away with the Democratic presidential nomination. Beforehand, I thought it'd be fun to practice my opener before Myla's preschool class. I don't think I had ever witnessed kids so bored and would not soon forget the look of utter embarrassment on Myla's cherubic face once I had finished. Thankfully, the actual introduction fared better. Senator Obama proceeded to captivate the audience with his unifying vision in outlining his agenda and sharing his goals.

His campaign had only gained momentum since as Senator Obama went on to beat Hillary in the Democratic primary, rising to become favored in the national race against Senator John McCain and in line to become our country's first Black president. Now Michelle was stumping for him in Arizona, a conservative state and McCain's home base. I thought it might have been a fruitless overture, but Michelle proved that she commanded an audience just as large as her husband. She was every bit as magnetic as Senator Obama. She thanked Tamia and me for attending, telling the crowd that my mom had helped mentor her for years. The connection, she said, started through Elizabeth Alexander, the daughter of my mom's business partner, Mr. Cliff Alexander, who had been something of a big sister to me growing up. Elizabeth and Michelle were friends from their days in Ivy League schools, and Elizabeth connected Michelle with my mom, soliciting her advice on how to navigate corporate board work in Chicago.

Senator Obama, of course, advanced to win the presidency and then gain reelection. Over the years, Tamia and I developed a rapport with the Obamas, also the parents of two daughters. I would introduce President Obama at various events or campaign on his behalf. I'd play basketball with him and participated in the first lady's Let's Move! campaign, accompanying her to the 2012 Olympics in London as part of the president's official delegation.

But in Arizona, the disclosure of her relationship with my mom was, at the time, news to us.

We called my mom from the car and relayed Michelle's story.

Yep, my mom said. That's all true.

You never told us.

There was never any reason to.

She never stops surprising me.

———

D'Antoni's exit led to some turnover. However, we rebounded from not qualifying for the playoffs in 2008–2009 to playing in the Western Conference Finals a season later under the leadership of Alvin Gentry, my onetime coach in Detroit. By that point, Alvin was more seasoned, having spent time around the league and under D'Antoni. He incorporated the bulk of D'Antoni's offense. The ball usually found Steve's hands during our possessions. I could still score on my footwork, probing angles for an advantage. The best feeling was beating my defender down the court, taking pride when his coach yelled at him for not getting back faster. Steve was a daring passer, unafraid to thread the needle. I secured more uncontested layups and dunks than ever before.

Alvin also placed a bit more emphasis on defense. By design, we were never mistaken for defensive juggernauts. Over the years, though, we had boasted quality individual defenders in players like Shawn, Raja Bell, and Boris Diaw. As those guys departed, I became our primary wing defender. For most of my career, my offense had been my best defense. Now, at thirty-seven, I was chasing scorers in the prime of their careers, guys like LeBron, Kobe Bryant, Carmelo Anthony, Chris Paul, and Dirk Nowitzki, without the luxury of being able to go back at them on offense.

Playing at a constant breakneck speed required staying in shape and exploring the nascent science behind sports recovery. Steve, who came into the NBA a couple years after I did, became a kindred spirit in that pursuit. We discussed how ageless triathletes competed at a rigorous professional level without the use of trainers or the resources at our disposal. We had no excuses. Steve and I vowed to hold each other accountable in not allowing our age to be a reason for an athletic decline. We were among the earliest converts to use recovery compression boots, now a staple for every NBA team. I initiated conversations with athletes from all sports who authored lengthy athletic careers—people like Jerry Rice, Dara Torres, Laird Hamilton, and Darrell Green—picking their minds about stiff-arming Father Time as long as possible. The common thread was that none viewed their age as a hindrance late in their professional lives. I became more disciplined about my sleep and stricter about my diet and frequented acupuncturists and chiropractors. Phoenix's training staff also played a crucial role. They represented the evolution of the work Arnie Kander had performed back in my Piston days. They looked at the body from a global perspective instead of regionally. If a player had a sore hamstring, they examined the entire kinetic chain, figuring that any body part could be the root cause.

My body responded. I played in eighty-two regular-season games in 2008–2009, a first for my career.

I came to relish the nightly defensive challenges, constructing strategies with the same energy I once poured into maximizing my offensive repertoire. Elite scorers typically outmaneuvered strong defenders. My goal was to limit a Carmelo or LeBron as much as possible. For example, Carmelo preferred bullying his defender, facing up, and doing his damage on the baseline. I tried working him to the middle of the court, staying at his feet, placing myself between him and the basket. Or I knew that LeBron and a full head of steam was an equation for winding up as a spectator on a poster. I located LeBron the second we took a shot on offense, forgoing crashing the boards. In the half-court, he tended to drive to the rim when he attacked right and to pull up for a jumper when going left. I tried funneling him left, content to live with the results of him attempting contested jumpers.

Kobe, and to a lesser extent Portland's Brandon Roy, were the two players who could make a defender go bald. They were assassins on the court who left no evidence to excavate. It was fruitless trying to unearth Kobe's tendencies. He didn't have any. He was skilled in every facet, eternally on the attack, adept at driving right or left, turning over either shoulder, shooting from long distance or mid-range. The tougher the shot, the more he enjoyed taking and often sinking it.

He had seen everything, so I mixed strategies with him, trying to be as random on defense as he was on offense. Sometimes, I played him physically. At other moments, I offered him space. Sometimes, I forced him left. Sometimes right. Occasionally, I might even have purposefully smacked him on a shot attempt so that he anticipated contact his next shot. My hope was that he didn't get comfortable or gain a rhythm.

The only thing worse than Kobe scoring was when his teammates became involved. In 2010, I stuck on Kobe as his primary defender in the Western Conference Finals. But the Lakers were too deep, with players like Pau, Andrew Bynum, and Lamar Odom. We dropped the series in six games.

———

I didn't think much of it when Jalen Rose shot me a text message out of the blue in the spring of 2011.

It's all good. All love. Much respect.

Maybe it was meant for somebody else. We had more of a mutual respect than a deep kinship, despite competing against each other since we were kids. He had retired from the game a few years earlier, and I was still chasing a championship. We had spoken a few months earlier when he asked me to participate in an ESPN documentary about our college years. I arranged to be interviewed during a road game in Miami, but the production crew had tried switching to a time that conflicted with our morning shootaround. That was the last I had heard about the documentary.

The logic behind Jalen's text became evident a few days later when ESPN promoted the *30 for 30* documentary about the Fab Five.

I hated Duke and I hated everything Duke stood for, Jalen said in a teaser the network recycled over and over. Schools like Duke didn't recruit players like me. I felt like they only recruited Black players that were Uncle Toms.

I took offense at such a blanket, erroneous allegation. No person wanted to be called an Uncle Tom, one of the most offensive terms to call someone who is Black. Beyond that, it just wasn't accurate. We had hosted and recruited Chris Webber, the Fab Five's most popular player. I had seen Coach K recruit countless guys who chose another university over Duke. I knew Jalen had some issues with his father being a former NBA player and absent in his life, and maybe there was some lingering jealousy over my dad's impact in mine. But I didn't owe any apologies for my dad being present.

Still, I reserved judgment and watched the documentary. The grainy footage lured me back to that transformative juncture in my life. It was interesting hearing their thoughts and reflections from that time, while I was on my own intersecting journey.

To me, Jalen's words didn't immediately demand a response. I planned to just keep it moving. Soon after, though, I caught Jalen and Jimmy King on another television interview concerning the documentary. They didn't shy away from the previous comments or distance themselves with any type of qualifier by saying that that was how they had viewed Duke players from the prism of their teenage years. They laughed and cracked jokes. It felt like Jalen was playing both sides, trying to be cool with me in private, projecting himself as edgy in the public sphere.

I was in the middle of a season. My competitive juices flowed. I called Tamia and mulled it over with her. We decided to wait and watch. I was confident a journalist or analyst would deliver a column or a voice-over that would bring some levelheadedness to counter Jalen's rhetoric, to remind us that all Blacks come from distinctive experiences and circumstances out of which is woven our rich cultural tapestry. There was no authoritative list of markers that magically authenticated one's Blackness.

Crickets.

No one promoted the conversation that I believed should be taking place.

I'm a hip-hop head. You come at me, I respond thoughtfully like any cutting response record.

We were in New Orleans after playing Houston the previous night with downtime before our game that evening. I skipped my pregame nap and started writing:

To hint that those who grew up in a household with a mother and father are somehow less Black than those who did not is beyond ridiculous . . . I caution my fabulous five friends to avoid stereotyping me and others they do not know in much the same way so many people stereotyped them back then for their appearance and swagger.

The New York Times published the op-ed, and the article created some buzz. I wanted to spark dialogue, although most just splintered into camps like a couple decades earlier. Jalen called and apologized. I was not one to hold grudges. We quashed it within a week, and in a weird way the whole ordeal brought us closer as friends than we had ever been.

———

In Phoenix, we didn't reach our ultimate goal of a championship, but those seasons proved invaluable for my psyche. I didn't anticipate how much I actually needed Phoenix's habitat when I originally signed back in the summer of 2007. Tamia and I enjoyed a community of friends in the parents of Myla's classmates. The organization fostered an environment centered on friends and family, something I learned during my first training camp at the University of Arizona's McKale Center. The night after our opening practice, I received a phone call from Aaron Nelson inviting me out to a bar with more than half the team for some conversation and a cold one. The thought of drinking at camp seemed foreign to me until then. As a team, we were often together on the road grabbing dinner or catching a movie. Family members occasionally traveled with the team, and it would be nothing for Robert Sarver to join us for a game of cards. A lounge for family members was near our locker room. My dad would be stunned when he visited and witnessed players spending halftime with their kids before finishing the game.

I never required the commercials or the signature shoes. I earned that recognition and accepted them. Don't get me wrong: the accolades were all nice. But they were the seasoning sprinkled on top of the meal.

More than anything, I needed to know the passion I poured into the game could again, after all these years, be reciprocated. I needed to be part of an organization where I could be healthy and add value to a franchise.

Phoenix, thankfully, provided that palate cleanser.

20

PLAYING professional basketball demanded a sort of cognitive disso-
nance. I poured everything I had into becoming the best basketball player
possible from the time the game took hold of me. Yet, all along, I knew
that my life's purpose was not limited to the game. Being in the NBA was
the culmination of a dream, and in some sense the prolonging of adolescence. The activity that rewarded me, offered validation, and, in some
respects, defined me through my teenage years to nearly middle age would
one day no longer be viable.

In the beginning of my playing career, I worried what, if anything,
would await me at the end of it.

The end of one journey was here.

My body told me before my mind accepted the reality. My goal was
to play and be competitive in a young man's game until I was forty, fulfilling the pledge to recoup some of those frustrating lost moments.

The Suns flipped their roster, opting for a rebuild in the summer of
2012. Steve Nash moved a little farther out west, joining the Lakers, and
tried recruiting me to the purple and gold. I wound up in Los Angeles as

well, only in the adjacent locker room at Staples Center, signing with the Clippers. They were an organization transitioning out of being the perpetual doormat they had been throughout most of my career. They were young, exciting, anchored by a dynamic pick-and-roll combination in Chris Paul and Blake Griffin and veteran bench players like Chauncey Billups, Willie Green, and Jamal Crawford.

Our first preseason game, against Denver in Vegas, the team celebrated my fortieth birthday with dinner at the nightclub Tao. I swear, my body knew that I had hit the goal and went off like it was set to a timer. My right knee had already been limiting me for a couple days, the same joint that had bothered me since the summer of 2011, when I had inadvertently damaged some cartilage in it while working out. A doctor told me then that had I been younger, he would have advised an invasive microfracture surgery. He cleaned it out then, and I underwent another surgery on the knee later that season, which should have been enough of a signal that I was on borrowed time. Instead, I flew out to Düsseldorf, Germany, for a consultation with Dr. Peter Wehling, a molecular orthopedist whom Kobe Bryant and some other athletes had started to vouch for. I settled on his Regenokine procedure, a process that basically involved manipulating my blood to increase the potency before injecting it back into my knee.

Now that same knee was acting creaky again. Our next couple of preseason games were in China. I tried battling through the exhibitions before doctors shut me down, saying that I needed at least a couple months to recover. I returned in January, casually flicking the ball in during our nightly pregame layup lines as guys like Blake and De-Andre Jordan transformed them into dunk contests. The team showed talent, yet the main pieces were a little young to break through, and we lost a first-round playoff series to the Memphis Grizzlies. I logged twenty minutes in the last game after sitting the entire series, not thinking that it'd be my final time on the court, just trying to find a way to limit Tayshaun Prince before moving on to a next matchup that never arrived.

We flew back to Los Angeles the next day, and I drove to the apartment where I stayed throughout the season, while Tamia and the girls remained in Arizona.

Well, how does it feel? Tamia asked over the phone. You're retired.

My circadian rhythm was accustomed to two annual extremes. There was an adjustment in entering the season, going from enjoying moments with my family to suddenly having our lives dictated by the NBA calendar. The end of the season, especially for a playoff team, proved equally jarring. We went from spending every day—practices, games, dinners, plane rides—with one another to going our separate ways, often spread out throughout the country or the world. In that fleeting moment when Tamia asked, my first thought was that I could possibly give this thing a go for another year. I hadn't accumulated much stress on my body during the season and had ended it healthy. This team, I told Tamia, may just need a coach like Doc Rivers, someone who commanded respect and could get them over that next hurdle—not knowing that Doc would become the organization's coach in a few weeks.

As the days passed, I underwent a physical on my knee, packed up the apartment, and moved back home. I became more comfortable accepting that my playing days had ended. TNT invited me to join the *Inside the NBA* crew during the Eastern Conference Finals between Miami and Indiana. Surely, they anticipated me just chipping in some analysis and lobbing a few jokes at Shaquille O'Neal's expense.

I made my decision to retire public before the sixth game of the series. The moment was not heavy or emotional. I experienced a stillness. The latter stages of my career had been a constant fight, a worthwhile tension of struggling against the established perceptions of an aging player and working to compete against younger players. Everything had required more preparation, attention, and energy than it had before. I had spent nearly two decades in this league, experiencing a wide spectrum of highs and lows. There was serenity in calling it a career.

———

We moved back to Florida. I co-founded and became a general partner of Penta Mezzanine. My group essentially raised money to provide growth capital for lower- and middle-market companies. In a nutshell, mezzanine financing revolves around providing debt. Private equity shops often utilize it instead of banks to raise money and maintain control.

My involvement in the fund stemmed from being inspired in different ways by a couple of books. One was by Reginald Lewis and Blair Walker titled *Why Should White Guys Have All the Fun?* The book centered on Lewis's path in becoming the first African American to build a billion-dollar company, TLC Beatrice International Holdings Inc. He had grown up in Baltimore, and his half brother, Jean Fugett, had once been a teammate of my dad's on Washington's football team. Reading how a Black man had amassed such a fortune was motivating. Another book, *Barbarians at the Gate*, was the behind-the-scenes account of the takeover of RJR Nabisco, whose sale was at the time one of the largest and most acrimonious purchases ever of a company. Henry Kravis, a participant in it and a pioneer of the leveraged buyout, happened to be the parent of a Dukie. The pursuit of the company, all the moving parts, and the structure of private equity firms was eye-opening. Those books made me aware of the potential rewards of a career in finance and business.

I thought I could lend my celebrity and my experience to the fund. I had begun investing and learning about real estate while hurt in Orlando and had amassed a strong portfolio of income-generating properties that I operated through my family office. To source deals and talk to investors, I relied on my communication abilities. Just like in recruiting, I didn't just sell a track record or investment thesis; I was true to myself in telling my story and being authentic. We established a robust pipeline. Naively perhaps, I felt that I could quickly learn the business. As on a basketball court, I soon appreciated that everyone has a role to play.

With the talented Kristen Ledlow, I also co-hosted the relaunch of *NBA Inside Stuff,* the influential basketball highlight show once guided by the likes of Ahmad Rashād, Willow Bay, and Summer Sanders that targeted younger viewers on Saturday mornings. I had entered television with an open mind, although I expressed initial hesitation over whether it would provide much post-career fulfillment. Studio work came more naturally. I had acclimated to the pace throughout the repetitions ESPN and Turner had afforded me during my playing career. *Inside Stuff,* though, was mostly scripted. I obsessed over whether I was delivering lines with the right inflection. In December 2013, I ran into, of all people, Ahmad, Willow, and her husband, the chair of Disney, Robert Iger, at, of all settings, a Christmas party at the White House. I relayed my inner doubts to Ahmad and Willow, telling them that I felt like an untested actor miscast in the sequel of a successful original. They reassured me and suggested that I be myself in making the script my own. Their stamp of approval, along with Kristen's talent and professionalism, helped me find steady footing with the show.

Looking back, I wish I would've offered myself some time to decompress after my playing career, to exit the hamster wheel and take a moment to exhale.

But I was hardwired to advance to the next goal, tackle that new hurdle, climb that farther mountain, hoping that the attributes necessary for success in sports could be channeled into other pursuits. Every athlete experiences somewhat of an identity crisis when their career ends.

I thought retirement was a rocking chair and some lemonade, Tamia told me one day.

I had tried positioning myself for this pivot throughout my career, possibly out of paranoia, although I had always been curious about the innate characteristics that made people successful. I appreciated the circles my parents moved in, the people they could call for counsel, the corporate connections they had forged as alumni of Yale and Wellesley. To my benefit, people throughout my playing days had answered their phones and fielded my questions. I picked the minds of business leaders, gleaning insight into their work. Sometimes, on the road, I'd reach out to Sterly Wilder, my academic coordinator at Duke, and ask her for the numbers of prominent alumni, inviting them to coffee or lunch. I explored the road maps provided by former athletes. Roger Staubach discussed transitioning into real estate with me. Junior Bridgeman, a former NBA player, relayed how he started investing in restaurant franchises. I visited with Dave Bing, the onetime Pistons legend who built Bing Steel from the ground up and later became Detroit's mayor.

I didn't need to unearth a ground-shifting revelation each and every meeting. Shortly after joining the Pistons, I had read about a promising Pacific Northwest software company and learned that one of their high-ranking executives hailed from Michigan. I sat for coffee with Steve Ballmer when we next played the SuperSonics in Seattle. Nothing came from that particular meeting, but I found enduring significance from cultivating relationships and building bonds that outlasted my playing career.

In my season in Los Angeles, I had started grabbing breakfast with Bruce Karsh. Bruce co-founded Oaktree Capital Management in 1995, becoming the global asset management firm's co-chairman and chief information officer and a limited partner with the Golden State Warriors. Importantly for me, Bruce was also a Dukie. We started meeting regularly at the Four Seasons, talking life, discussing investments, debating basketball and whatever else came to our minds.

Meanwhile, the Clippers, in that moment, were experiencing success like never before, poised to rival the revered Lakers for the city's affection and attention. Eric Miller, the son-in-law of the team's owner, Donald Sterling, started dropping by our Playa Vista practice facility, and one day we struck up a conversation. Eric informed me that the family's main business was real estate and that they might soon explore selling the franchise for estate planning purposes.

At our next breakfast, I relayed the nugget to Bruce, telling him that there may be a play to one day purchase the Clippers. At that point, I was still playing, and the thought was more of a whimsical idea than any firm plan in gestation.

My dad had long aspired to purchase and run a sports franchise, to use his intellect for change and impact. He had convened several partners who tried returning the NFL to Baltimore in 1987; however, the group disbanded before the league finally brought the Ravens to the city nearly a decade later. He tried purchasing the Baltimore Orioles before the owner, Eli Jacobs, sold to a group of Baltimore investors led by Peter Angelos. He formed a group with Roland Betts, his classmate at Yale and Delta Kappa Epsilon fraternity brother, and they had neared a deal for the Washington Bullets, Capitals, and the Capital Centre, but Abe Pollin decided at the last moment to retain ownership. Another potential deal to land the New England Patriots collapsed when the asking price soared.

His dream of guiding a franchise provided the impetus for me to one day explore the possibility myself. The Jerry Jones book I had read left me fascinated by the gumption it took for him to leverage every penny in his pocket to buy the Dallas Cowboys and transform them into America's team. I didn't possess the wisdom to know how or when it would happen, just the conviction that one day I'd like to be able to own a team. Mark Williams, long ago the student manager at Duke, had since advanced to a life in finance. Sometimes, we'd discuss whatever elaborate deals were happening in the sports and corporate worlds. I'd listen as he detailed the dynamics and economics behind a stadium deal or new arena, letting my imagination wander following those conversations, pondering how I'd operate my own franchise.

I had enjoyed building relationships with all the team owners I played for, except, coincidently, Donald Sterling. He approached the team only a couple of times my lone Clippers season. In Detroit, Mr. Bill Davidson had seldom flaunted his wealth, yet entertained my questions concerning business and money while we batted tennis balls back and forth on his clay court. I was making more money than I ever thought possible, I would think at the time, and he was the one paying me, my teammates, and every employee in this organization.

In Orlando, I held different political ideologies from the DeVos family, and Richard DeVos did not visit the team often. But he had made sure to address the team every once in a while, stressing the importance of saving our earnings.

In Phoenix, I cultivated a different relationship with Robert Sarver. He was the boss, but he was also about the same age as me and often passed as one of the guys.

Around the same time Bruce and I started discussing the possibility of purchasing the Clippers, David Stern announced his retirement as NBA commissioner, with Adam Silver, his deputy, expected to succeed him. We scheduled a meeting with Adam, another Dukie, hoping to see if an opportunity to land the Clippers existed.

In February 2014, Silver assumed office as I busied myself with the mezzanine fund and my television work and awaited our meeting.

Then chaos erupted.

The gossip site *TMZ* released an audio recording of Donald Sterling telling a female companion to avoid being publicly seen with Black people and to not bring any to Clipper games. The backlash was rightfully swift. My former teammates debated boycotting a playoff game against the Warriors. The crisis was a challenging introduction for Silver to his new role, and he acted decisively in banning Sterling from the league and mandating a sale of the team.

The prospects of discreetly acquiring the franchise or gaining right of first refusal vanished. The swift sequence of events caused Bruce and me to leap into hyperdrive, quickly formulating a plan to buy the franchise. In our pursuit, Bruce asked Tony Ressler to join us. Tony, a private equity tycoon who co-founded Apollo Global Management and Ares Management, agreed, and the three of us met in Los Angeles to gather information and crunch numbers, now anticipating an open bidding process for the Clippers with several heavy hitters involved.

That Sunday, I caught a plane back home and continually checked for any updates on the Clippers. Late at night, an article drew my attention. Shelly Sterling, Donald's estranged wife charged with selling the team, had met with Steve Ballmer at Nobu Malibu. I immediately called someone in the know. They got back to me, saying that we could also meet with Shelly, but it would have to take place the next day, on Memorial Day. I scrambled to secure a flight reservation, and before I knew it, I was back at Tony's Malibu house, eating hamburgers, strategizing about how we'd interact with Shelly. Bruce wasn't able to make the meeting. Tony, I quickly found, was an easy guy to be around. He was married to Jami Gertz, one of the nicest people on the planet and an actress who starred in *Twister*, the movie that Tamia and I had watched on our very first date. Tony and I had a lot of the same core values and principles, an important aligning, in my opinion, to figure out before entering a business endeavor. Someone could be the smartest person in the world, but there was little point in entering a partnership if they were a drag to be around.

We made the short drive over to Shelly's house. When we arrived, we were asked to wait near the front door. Her previous meeting was running a little late. The windows were open. Not only could we see Shelly sitting with Patrick Soon-Shiong, one of the minority owners of the Lakers, but we heard their entire conversation. The situation became even more awkward when I could no longer hold it in after waiting nearly half an hour and meekly walked through the middle of their ongoing meeting, apologizing as I headed to the restroom.

When we were invited in, I played up the one thing I had going for me that no one else did.

I know what it's like to put on a Clipper jersey, I told her, figuring that if we were even with another group, that bond could possibly be the tiebreaker.

Once a Clipper always a Clipper.

I told Shelly the potential I saw in the franchise, that I had felt it while wearing the jersey.

If they sold to us, Shelly asked, would she be able to retain her seats and ability to enter Staples Center through the loading dock?

That seemed reasonable enough to me.

Shelly invited us out to Nobu after the meeting. Our table was in the middle of the packed restaurant, not the most discreet setting. Shelly seemed interested in our conversation, though, and we felt confident as Tony drove me back to my hotel.

The next morning, I boarded a flight for New York for our long-scheduled meeting with Adam. Information flew everywhere. I knew that we were a group already familiar to the NBA and that we would come in with a solid bid. But I started wondering if the combination of the public interest in the sale, the Clippers being recognized as an ascending franchise, and the location of the team in a mega market like Los Angeles could cause the bids to soar astronomically.

Ultimately, that's what happened. On a Thursday, we submitted a bid to purchase the Clippers for $1.2 billion, a figure that would have shattered the price for any previous sale of an NBA team. The next day, Steve Ballmer bid $2 billion, an offer that Shelly accepted.

There was money and then there was Microsoft money. I'd have been more disappointed had the offers been closer to each other. All in all, it had been an exhilarating week. I had been involved in plenty of transactions, but never one of that magnitude with those types of business titans. We might not have won, but I viewed the experience as a beneficial lesson for the future.

Over the next few months, Tony and I kept in touch, discussing potential franchises that might be sold soon. I was in no rush to seriously explore anything, possibly fatigued and even humbled from the rollercoaster ride of trying to secure the Clippers, when the Atlanta Hawks found themselves facing another racially charged gaffe. An outlet had published a years-old email written by the team's principal owner, Bruce Levenson, expressing misdirected concern that African American spectators were driving away white suburban fans from Hawks games. Levenson, one of Donald Sterling's biggest critics, apologized, resigned, and announced his intention to sell his controlling interest in the franchise and the operating rights to Philips Arena.

One day, Junior Bridgeman reached out, excited about the possibility of purchasing the Hawks. I shared my fear of being a serial bridesmaid.

But teams rarely hit the market. Plenty of people and groups with the assets desperately want one. And they are often sound investments that only increase in value. Junior convinced me that as former players and successful businessmen, we'd be an asset to any group. Richard Chaifetz, a Chicagoan who launched ComPsych Corporation, soon joined our pursuit.

To that point, Tony had given me the impression that he'd only be interested in securing a team located near his West Coast base. I gave him a call while we assembled a bid for the Hawks, hoping to understand the specifics of how he and Bruce came to their valuation of the Clippers. Tony, somewhere off in Europe, told me to forward him the key facts and figures.

He called back less than ten minutes later.

This is what it's worth, he said, and this is what I would pay.

Eventually, we made a strong offer, but not enough to make it out of the opening round of bids in February.

———

Craig Barry, the executive vice president and chief content officer for Turner, asked me one night if I had a second after wrapping up a segment on NBA TV's *Gametime*. He guided me into a room with Albert Vertino, Tara August, and a few other high-ranking executives. Albert, or Scooter, as everyone called him, had grown up with me on the basketball court; we had played AAU ball together. I kept growing, while he went into television producing.

Craig cut straight to the point.

We'd like you to call the Final Four on television with Jim Nantz and Bill Raftery for CBS, he said.

I was not anticipating the offer at all. I didn't think that I was ready and would surely look like an amateur beside those two broadcasting legends.

I quickly said yes.

It was one of those opportunities that you accepted in the moment and figured out the rest later.

Maybe I should have seen the overture in the making. I had worked the previous NCAA tournament as a studio analyst, an exhilarating if dizzying experience. Through the years, I had tried paying attention to college basketball as much as possible through a hectic schedule, keeping one eye, of course, always trained on Duke. I joined a studio group with Matt Winer, my doppelgänger Steve Smith, and Seth Davis, an acquaintance from Duke. The support staff provided us with packets of information detailing the teams in the tournament; however, the sheer number of universities made it impossible to research the rosters in depth.

I would land on a nugget to share, hoping that Steve or Seth had not already used it by the time the camera panned to me as we worked at a pace so fast that I never knew whether we were being broadcast on CBS, TNT, or truTV. Thankfully, Seth knew all the teams inside and out and enjoyed hearing himself talk, which usually allowed me enough time to deliver a coherent bit of analysis before we dove into the next matchup. For the Final Four, we aired on-site from Dallas at the mammoth AT&T Stadium. The city and circumstances brought memories flooding back of the Final Four I attended as a child with my dad in Dallas, back when Duke really caught my attention. I felt connected to the tournament and all its unique magic and unbridled possibilities for the first time in years.

Calling games had held less appeal. In my mind, I was only then finding traction co-hosting *Inside Stuff.* The idea of being at an arena, trying to add commentary for two hours, intimidated me. Tara had cajoled me into calling a few NBA games, saying that if I didn't like it, she wouldn't ask again and we could move on. I reluctantly agreed, calling San Antonio against Dallas on the opening night of the 2014–2015 NBA season, followed by a couple other early-season games. I had not considered that the outings, in effect, had been an audition.

Comfort on air, I was finding, as with many things, was about getting my repetitions. A tinge of self-consciousness existed with every word that left my mouth. Had I said too much? Not enough? Was I interesting? Scooter, in particular, helped break down the essence of an analyst's role, advising that the viewer had just witnessed the play. My job was to pull the curtain back in explaining how a player got open for his shot or why the defense rotated the way it did. I was still learning to get my voice to pierce through crowd noise and music when Craig summoned me.

Just like nothing would have completely prepared me for playing in the Final Four, nothing would have primed me for calling one. Leading up to the weekend, I called the Big Ten Conference tournament and the early-round tournament games. It had been a mad scramble trying to gather enough information on all the players, coaches, and programs. Sometimes, I used time-outs to flip through reams of information before we came back live. The process reinforced what I already knew, that this was an experience to be cherished, that there was a responsibility in telling everyone's story respectfully and to call a game that featured a program's first trip to the tournament with as much care, enthusiasm, and knowledge as I would a Duke game.

Calling games was a craft, just like playing basketball, and I pulled from the experience of Jim, Bill, and our talented sideline reporter, Tracy Wolfson, all selfless veterans who wanted to see this rookie succeed. The entire CBS production was steeped with tradition. Our producer, Mark Wolff, and director, Bob Fishman, were the same pair who worked that very first Final Four on CBS in 1982, the one that I watched from my basement, one of the many signs of generational harmony between the network and the tournament.

We were a team, just like the ones I had played on throughout most of my life. In a similar way, camaraderie and togetherness off the court translated during our game time. We spent an exorbitant amount of time with one another from the Big Ten tourney on, watching teams, calling games, interviewing coaches and players, going to dinner. I hadn't had many deep interactions with Jim since walking off that court in Charlotte after the championship loss to Arkansas when he told me I had a bright future. From afar, I had always admired his tact in calling games, his consistent preparedness, and his deep reservoir of knowledge. Jim advised me to not hesitate to interrupt him if I needed to inject a piece of analysis. An iconic figure offering me that type of runway was both gracious and calming.

Quickly, calling games had evolved into the aspect of broadcasting that I enjoyed most, almost a placebo for the burst of adrenaline from playing—just without the risk of getting hurt, save for an overzealous player diving out of bounds for a loose ball. On game days, the routines were nearly identical, from the breakfast meeting and nap to dressing and making my way to the arena, entering through a loading dock, and arriving for pregame huddles with my team inside a locker room. From courtside, I watched the players maneuver through their layup lines before we stood for the national anthem. The same nervous, budding energy coursed inside me, the buildup to when the players walked out on the court and the referee lobbed the ball in the air.

Early on, Mark Wolff advised me to try to get lost in the game. Originally, I had not understood the words. Soon, I found myself completely absorbed in the action, enough so that the thousands of screaming fans were reduced to dull background noise and I felt like we were just three people who could be anywhere, watching, reacting, analyzing a basketball game.

That year, the Final Four comprised blue blood programs: Michigan State, Wisconsin, Kentucky, and, fittingly, Duke. That the games were in Indianapolis, where I was with a bunch of fresh-faced, starry-eyed kids who stunned a behemoth Vegas team a quarter century earlier was not lost on me.

I had worked Duke games throughout the tournament, so some of the disbelief at, say, sitting across from the benches and seeing my former teammate and close friend Jeff Capel on the sidelines as an assistant coach had worn off by the Final Four. My job was to be as objective as possible in announcing the game down the middle. Yet there's always going to be that connection to the brotherhood when I'm calling a Duke game. I guarded against just watching my coach, being in awe that he was not just plying his trade after all these years but still on top, still imagining the untapped possibilities every spring.

Strands of that teacher-and-pupil dynamic still existed between Coach K and me. He had always been that authority figure, someone I could turn to for advice. Over the years, our relationship evolved into more of a true friendship than anything else. His pace might have slowed, and his hair might have thinned some. His steely eyes still held the same intensity they always had. He still sauntered onto the court looking like he was ready for an all-out brawl.

But he was no longer the underdog coach, striving for his first championship. He had become a national icon.

Change is one of life's guarantees. We have all witnessed the collapse of once-giant businesses and institutions that were too stagnant to evolve. Coach K changed with the times. He received criticism for the number of one-and-done players who stopped at Duke for a turnstile stay on their way to the NBA. But the notion of a player with NBA potential spending four years at a university became fantastical. The risk of injury was too great, with too much money at stake. I did believe something tangible got lost in the constant turnover, that Coach tried to compress into a few short months what he previously did over the course of four years, and players were missing out on forging some of the bonds that would forever unite them with Duke and Durham. Coach's success in modernizing the program was evident. I sometimes wondered how he did it. He was best at forming relationships, a coach who, back then, took different approaches each season in adapting to the various personalities. I did know that he was constantly learning, taking what he could from great players he had coached—whether it was Johnny Dawkins, Christian Laettner, other players in his program, or LeBron James and Kobe Bryant during his stint with the USA Basketball Men's National Team. Those interactions, I believe, kept him fresh, continually moving forward.

That weekend, I took silent satisfaction while calling a game where Duke picked apart Michigan State. Afterward, the CBS production team convened in the basement of an Indianapolis landmark restaurant, St. Elmo Steak House, to celebrate Jim's twenty-fifth Final Four; his first had also been my first as a player. My parents joined us, along with Mark Williams, who had made the drive from Chicago.

Jim grabbed the microphone, quickly offering another example of why he was the best in the business. His beautiful monologue touched nearly everyone in the room. When I say everybody, I mean everybody. He talked about his daughter, his agent, a buddy from school. He thanked Tracy, Bill, and me. He weaved in a story about seeing my parents on a train one day.

Spotting Mark, whom I didn't believe he had ever spoken to or met prior to that day, he said, This is my buddy Mark. He went to Duke as well. Mark was the manager of the '92 basketball team.

Hold up. I looked at Mark.

Did you tell him that?

No.

I knew this well—the long wait during the day until the sun finally dipped on the evening of the championship game. As announcers, we went from scrambling around that weekend, caravanning to practices, games, and appearances, enjoying the pomp and pageantry of the Final Four, to counting down the hours until Duke and Wisconsin finally tipped off that Monday evening. During the downtime, Jesse Itzler phoned. Jesse was a friend from back in the day, an entrepreneur and successful 1990s rapper who had joined one of the groups that had advanced in the bidding process of securing the Hawks.

Neither of the two final groups can get to the finish line, he told me.

I stored the information for later, hopping into the van that took us to the arena.

The game teetered back and forth. Two Duke freshmen, Tyus Jones and Jahlil Okafor, led Duke down the stretch, outpacing Wisconsin's more seasoned players. It hit me with about a minute left that we were going to win this. It didn't come across on the broadcast—at least I hoped not—but my analyst hat was off. I was proud of my school, my program, my coach.

Back at the hotel, Dukies all over burst out in jubilation. I surveyed the smiling faces of players from different seasons and teams, relishing the afterglow of a fifth championship. It was a moment of pure elation, another reminder of the Final Four's magnetism. In that moment, I thought back on my own relationship with the Final Four.

I was the curious child videotaping the games at home, studying and dreaming.

I was the passionate teenager lucky enough to experience the games in person, rooting for and watching my team win and the next season witnessing that same program lose in one of the greatest upsets of all time. I was able to really soak in the environment that next year without a team to cheer for and homed in on Duke.

I played with two championship teams and lost one other in a heartbreaker.

Now I was an observer, a steward for the tournament with the best seat in the house, watching my school again celebrate climbing the steepest of hurdles. My long journey had brought me to the exact same place where it all began.

I was home.

———

I waited a couple days before reaching back out to Tony, informing him of Jesse's disclosure. I was hesitant to earn a strike three in trying to buy a franchise and wary of confronting the same roadblocks placed in front of my dad in his pursuit. But I saw an opening. I was in Atlanta once a week, taping *Inside Stuff* and appearing on NBA TV. The more time I spent in the city, the more it reminded me of D.C. back in the day, brimming with diversity, a place where young, ambitious people of all colors could find a home and make an impact. The city would back a successful basketball franchise. I told Tony we had a genuine opportunity to form a connection with the franchise, the fan base, and the city. Over several days, our conversations gained momentum. We invited Jesse and his wife, Sara Blakely, the founder of Spanx, as well as the businessmen Steven Price and Rick Schnall, to join our efforts.

After we spent a few hectic weeks putting everything together, the NBA accepted our bid at the identical number Tony had estimated back when Junior and I were exploring an offer and I had asked him to quickly glance over the deck. We endured a comprehensive excavation of our backgrounds, equal parts comforting and nerve-racking, before the approval process was completed. We celebrated with a late June dinner on the eve of the NBA draft, the partners and their family members toasting to a new venture.

Tony and I assumed our seats for a press conference the following day. I scanned the crowd, smiling when I saw Mayor Andrew Young in attendance. Mayor Young was an early leader of the civil rights movement, a confidant of Dr. Martin Luther King Jr.'s who became the successful mayor of Atlanta, saying once that he was glad to be mayor of a city where the mayor had once thrown him in jail. He had grown up in New Orleans before embarking on a life that would inspire people throughout the country. His mother, Daisy, taught school, and his father, Andrew Jackson Young Sr., worked as a dentist. There weren't too many Black families involved in dentistry in the Crescent City back then. Vivian McDonald, my grandmother, was a lifelong friend of Daisy's, and I fondly recall eating gumbo as a kid at their home on visits to New Orleans.

I could see in his eyes that the day made him proud. Michael Jordan and, before him, Robert Johnson were the only two Black people to have ever owned the majority of an NBA franchise. I was forty-two years old, two years removed from playing, and now vice-chairman and co-owner of the Hawks.

Quickly, I settled into a role of doing whatever was needed in providing strategic direction, empowering our employees, and striving for an environment of success. When I played in Orlando and Richard DeVos visited the team, he'd tell us that his main role was to be the organization's biggest cheerleader. Those words stayed in the back of my mind as I learned the gears that drove our organization, how the departments interconnected.

My game night became decidedly different from when I played. Now I thought about the cleanliness of our arena, what type of music was being played, whether people looked entertained. I wondered how the players on the court could focus on their tasks when so much transpired away from the court, reminding myself that somehow I had managed to do so year after year.

Some retired basketball players, my peers who became analysts, enjoyed that they could become absorbed in a game, dissect it, and leave without the final result keeping them up at night. They no longer had to live and die with the results like when they played.

With the Hawks, I still had skin in the game. I wouldn't have anticipated that I would obsess as much over wins and losses now as when I had played the game myself. That roller-coaster ride between jubilation and misery remains a constant.

But it is a feeling I have found familiar comfort in.

———

One mark in the evolution of the game is that NBA teams now feature staffs entirely devoted to sports medicine. Most owners consider players assets and want to ensure their investments pay off. When I had arrived in Orlando, I felt some pressure to get on the court and immediately show the franchise returns on the commitment they had made. The pendulum eventually swung the other way. Franchises sought long-term dividends. Recovery became a bigger emphasis. Teams studied the biometrics of players. Most now know when they go to sleep, when they wake up, how much protein they eat, and how hydrated they are on a given day. I thought of my dad and his career, when players numbed themselves with medication and played at all costs, and I thought back to the issues and challenges that I had experienced throughout my career. In some ways, it is definitely better to be a professional athlete in this day and age.

On the other hand, a season is supposed to be challenging and arduous. Making it through an eighty-two-game schedule and fighting through the playoffs presented a test of endurance. The joke was that *W* and *L* used to stand for "wins" and "losses." Now they stand for "workload." Athletes, in my opinion, are conditioned to perform on a regular schedule. I always felt funky when I was out a day or two and needed another day or two just to get to where I had been prior to the rest. If you're not in tip-top shape, you're more susceptible to getting hurt.

I sometimes questioned: Are we doing the right thing? Are we too cautious? Are we too conservative?

The data may support caution from a health standpoint. If anyone gets that, I do. That aspect is comforting and refreshing. But it is something I struggle with.

21

THE sun breaks through the morning clouds. Tamia sleeps next to me. I take a couple extra moments to rise, delaying the inevitable.

How much discomfort will my first steps bring today?

Some days, it is manageable, a constant, pestering nuisance, the feeling of a couple loose pebbles grinding inside a cramped shoe.

Other times, the throbbing ratchets up. Each stride feels like a timid probe on fiery coals. The ankle flap has evolved to resemble the patchwork of a crafty grandmother who ran out of cloth while knitting a sweater and finished with whatever leftover material she could find. Whether mild or intense, the agitation serves as a daily reminder of the toll my playing career has extracted.

My feet hit the floor. I roll my weight on the mended ankle from one side to the other, left to right, and back again.

Bearable. Worse than pebbles. Better than coals.

In the shower, I rotate the knob until scalding water gushes from the nozzle. Tamia will probably say something later. The water will still be hot when it is her turn. I assume that risk. The searing shower jump-starts the blood flow to my ankle. I kick it around a couple times.

I have spent most of my life running, jumping, starting, and stopping. Now I do not jump. I cannot run. I need to sit if I spend too much time outside, taking set shots with Myla and Lael. If I golf too much, I am laid up the following day. Joint replacement and possibly ankle fusion surgeries, I am told, are in my future. I am trying to delay that day for as long as possible. One can probably understand my reluctance to go under the knife again. On those days, I ask myself whether it was worth it to come back to the game. What was I chasing? What kept me going? Would I have kept going if I had known that I would be left with an arthritic, painful ankle? I believe so. I have a love affair with the game. My life still revolves around it. But more than anything, I loved playing it. It saddens me knowing that I will never play it again. I wish I loved golf as much as I loved basketball.

Inside the shower, my mind races. I had never given myself the opportunity to reset and reflect when I retired from playing. I maintained the mindset of an athlete, staying in perpetual motion, discarding setbacks, advancing to the next play. I had faced insecurities, doubts, fears, throughout my career. I hid them. The bull and the matador, the disregarding of fear for the sake of focus. Now that the game was over, all those emotions are here, demanding interest paid for attention overdue. Frustration, disappointment, strands of resentment, arrive in bursts. I had started on one path, keeping pace with the posters of my childhood, the Magics, the Jordans, the Birds. I didn't wholly appreciate or experience those moments, too narrow-minded about continuing toward catching my heroes. Then that path bifurcated. My mind turns to the team employees and medical professionals who abdicated their responsibilities, the infection that nearly killed me, the career that turned from its promise.

I own part of an NBA franchise, call college and pro games on television, started a mezzanine fund, have worked in real estate, and serve on several corporate boards. Down the road, I will assume stewardship as the managing director of the USA Basketball Men's National Team. I have always believed in hard work, believed that production provided purpose and a sense of accomplishment, whether it involved washing a car until it was spotless or closing on a significant deal. My parents remain role models, influential movers and shakers when most of their peers have long retired. But for the first time it is clear to me that I am traveling a hundred miles in part to compensate for my playing career that had detoured.

I arrive at now. I exit the shower somewhat unsettled.

Tamia awakens. Everything on my mind tumbles out.

I never could understand how you were able to just keep going, push through, and not let any of this affect you, she says.

Maybe it did.

Maybe I am confronting this now, in the spring of 2018, because a reckoning was arriving. I will know soon whether I will be inducted into the Naismith Memorial Basketball Hall of Fame. I convince myself that the distinction does not matter, that my crowning accomplishment was resuscitating my career in Phoenix.

Maybe it does matter.

Fittingly, I will find out around Final Four weekend, that site of so many transformative moments in my life.

———

Hugging and kissing the girls goodbye, I flew to Omaha, where Duke would meet Kansas with a Final Four berth on the line. Jim Nantz, Bill Raftery, Tracy Wolfson, and our production crew all gathered for dinner the eve of the game; the steak sizzled and the wine flowed.

I confided in them that a call from John Doleva, the Hall of Fame's president, informing me whether I had made the cut, could arrive at any moment.

I imagined the pockets of time that I would be free. We would be tied up with the game the next day. I planned to hop on a plane immediately after to join my family on a quick vacation before Final Four weekend.

What if he called while we were on air tomorrow?

The next day, as players warmed up, producers in my ear asked whether I had heard anything.

Not yet.

The excitement over the matchup electrified the air as I glanced over at Duke's sideline. It was another young, talented group. I had met most of the players a few times. Back in the day, Art Heyman occasionally visited my Duke teams. Art had piloted the Blue Devil teams that helped lay our basketball foundation. He earned the most outstanding player award at the 1963 Final Four, later becoming the first overall NBA draft pick. He'd weave tales about the time he dropped thirty against Virginia or when he punched North Carolina's Larry Brown during a game, igniting an all-out melee. The stories captivated us, although they seemed part of an ancient era.

The players who followed me at Duke called me G-Money when I returned to campus for pickup games as an NBA player. After a few years, I became Big Bro, then Uncle. Now I was the new Art, an artifact of a past generation the current players knew they were somehow tethered to. They were eternally respectful in calling me Mr. Hill. They showed natural curiosity about those championship seasons under a younger Coach K, those years when me, Christian Laettner, Bobby Hurley, Brian Davis, Thomas Hill, and Tony Lang stamped Duke atop college basketball's hierarchy.

Nearly a decade earlier, I had realized I wasn't as close with a lot of those guys as I wanted to be. People matured—most of us, at least—over the years and naturally drifted apart. After college, I had devoted my attention and energy toward my family, establishing myself in the

NBA, and persevering through injuries. Christian and I weren't even all that tight as teammates in Detroit. But that 1986 Duke team with guys like Johnny Dawkins, Tommy Amaker, and Jay Bilas remains inseparable to this day, and I wanted to reestablish the same unity with my group. I had just finished a fulfilling experience producing and narrating a documentary on the Duke track legend Al Buehler and engineered plans with Turner to create a documentary on our back-to-back championships. I hoped to celebrate those teams, introducing them to a new audience, while utilizing the documentary as a convenient conduit for us to all reconnect.

We executed the documentary, and to make a long story short, some guys declined to participate. If our 1992 starting five was the Jackson 5, everybody wanted to be Michael Jackson. Those personalities and egos meshed back then. Not so much as adults. I wanted to rekindle those relationships, and in the end some became even more strained. I remained close with some guys on the team and distant with others. The displeasing outcome reinforced that those memories were incredible lightning-in-a-bottle moments that could be clutched close and cherished but never replicated.

Coach was the thread that forever united us. I looked over to him. Yep, same look in his eyes, same swagger with every step that he would have until his final game. It should be a good one. Just like when I played, Duke and Kansas represented a collision of college basketball titans. The teams were trading baskets like body blows in the first half when my phone buzzed, revealing an unfamiliar caller.

I motioned to Jim and Bill, who had told me that they could go a couple possessions without me if the call arrived during the game. I removed my headset and rolled my chair back as my heart raced.

Hello?

A telemarketer launched into his script.

I couldn't help but laugh at the ironic timing. No, I didn't need any additional insurance. I hung up and took in the rest of a contested first half that ended with Duke clinging to a three-point lead.

I didn't want to be on edge during the second half like in the first. I decided to text John. He called.

Any chance you're gonna deliver the news today? My window is kind of small here. I can take it either way.

Sorry, Grant. I'm making the calls on Wednesday.

All good. I could at least become absorbed with the second half. Grayson Allen nearly clinched the game in regulation, but his attempt careened off the rim and Kansas squeezed an overtime win. I could only imagine what Coach would tell his sullen players inside the locker room. In the fall, I know that he would be rejuvenated, again armed with the unflinching conviction that his team could win a championship.

Soon, I was in the islands with Tamia, Myla, and Lael. The girls were on spring break, both growing up too fast, brimming with magnetic life and endless spunk.

A thick breeze off the ocean caused ripples in the pool's water. I propped my feet up to relax my ankle, pausing to enjoy these moments before flying to San Antonio for the Final Four.

My phone jumped. It was John.

Congratulations, he started.

The girls screamed. Tamia hugged me and started recording with her cell phone.

I hung up with John and called my dad, telling him the news, listening to the cries he tried muffling.

The enshrinement meant that those moments I didn't appreciate in real time had been recognized, that I had been the player I wanted to be even if I wasn't able to completely pursue the ultimate peak of my aspirations. I was not sure if I would ever be able to let go of the fact that my NBA career is a book with blank middle chapters. I took comfort knowing that that was all right. A lot of things broke my way. Some didn't. That's life. I could look myself in the mirror knowing that I overcame each struggle, break, surgery, and rehabilitation, with those replenishing seasons in the Phoenix sunset as confirmation.

The class announcement was made at the Final Four. I was honored to be grouped with players I respected, whom I competed with and against. They included Jason Kidd, who had been on the same journey with me since we were teenagers at Nike Camp; Steve Nash, my ageless Phoenix running mate; and Ray Allen, the skilled sharpshooter who played with Milwaukee, Seattle, Boston, and Miami.

The distinction did not feel tangible until months later when we gathered in Springfield, Massachusetts, an industrial city on the eastern bank of the Connecticut River, where James Naismith invented the game I love dearly. The girls would be watching television in our hotel room while I was locked in the bathroom, enshrinement speech in hand, reading it over and over again, surprised again at the nerves running through me and fretting over how I could possibly thank all the people who had lifted me in just seven minutes.

But before that, I was beckoned to mid-court at the Alamodome with the rest of the class during a break in the semifinal game between Michigan and Loyola University Chicago.

Quickly, after a cheer of recognition, I hurried back to my seat and slid my headset on. I was still on the call for a Final Four game where new legends would be formed, fresh memories carved, and a new champion crowned.

I wouldn't have had it any other way.

ACKNOWLEDGMENTS

I don't typically dwell on the past. Every trophy or award I collected during my playing career went straight into storage or was sent to my parent's house. I feared that seeing the memorabilia would be a reminder of past accomplishments and grant me permission to be complacent. I strived to stay in perpetual motion, challenging myself to never be satisfied.

A lengthy lead up exists before enshrinement into the Naismith Memorial Basketball Hall of Fame. The names of the finalists are released before the class is announced at the Final Four. The occasion forced me to reflect on my life and career. For the first time, I absorbed the totality of my highs and lows and realized that a story hopefully worth telling existed.

In some ways, the process of putting this book together proved therapeutic. I had never reflected on the sum of my decisions and choices, or tried to unravel and chart where I'm at now from where I began as a shy, introspective kid all those years ago. I revisited living in particular moments in time while preparing for and sharing discussions with Jonathan Abrams, who helped shape my thoughts and stories into these pages. The conversations allowed me to learn more about myself and how I view things differently now than as an adolescent.

I've already caught a couple eye rolls by saying this, but I truly believe that everyone should write a book or at least go through the exercise of reflecting and unspooling life lessons learned, pinpointing growth and failure, noting achievements and disappointments. I gained a deeper appreciation for the beauty and totality of life's peaks and valleys.

Plenty of talented people contributed to bringing this book into existence. David Larabell, David Koonin, and Matt Kramer at Creative Artists Agency saw promise in it when it was more of a seed in my mind than any firm idea. I'm thankful that Penguin Press believed that I had a story worthy of exploration. Scott Moyers displayed a sharp editorial eye and pushed me to dig deeper in places that needed further examination, and Natalie Coleman played a crucial role during the final stretch to bring the book home. Tommy Amaker, Kenny Blakeney, Chip Engelland, Vinnie Hudson, Billy King, Tony Lang, Quin Snyder, and Dr. Scott Levin all provided me with support throughout various junctures of my life and were kind enough to retrace those steps with me in conversations that enhanced and enriched my memories.

In reflecting upon my journey, I appreciate and value my family the most. We are a small, tight circle. The relationships we share are eternal and of deep meaning and substance. We share accountability, pride, support, values, and fulfillment.

My parents, Calvin and Janet, paved the way for me in life, providing me with examples of aspiration and purposefulness each and every day. You instilled in me a sense of discipline and decency, to be confident and show conviction in my decisions. To my mother-in-law, Barbara Peden, thank you for always being there for us.

My talented and beautiful wife, Tamia, is a constant source of strength and support. She has been at my side through every one of my journey's twists and turns and I am forever thankful for her constant companionship. The relationship we share with our daughters, Myla and Lael, is the most rewarding and fulfilling accomplishment that I have ever had or ever will have.

More than anything, I am just grateful.

And I think I may finally make some space for a display room in the house now.

PHOTO CREDITS

INDEX